D1207412

Blood and Fire

Blood and Fire

Godly Love in a Pentecostal Emerging Church

Margaret M. Poloma and
Ralph W. Hood, Jr.

NEW YORK UNIVERSITY PRESS

New York and London

NEW YORK UNIVERSITY PRESS
New York and London
www.nyupress.org

© 2008 by New York University
All rights reserved

Library of Congress Cataloging-in-Publication Data

Poloma, Margaret M.
Blood and fire : godly love in a Pentecostal emerging church /
Margaret M. Poloma and Ralph W. Hood.
p. cm.
Includes bibliographical references and index.
ISBN-13: 978-0-8147-6748-1 (cl : alk. paper)
ISBN-10: 0-8147-6748-6 (cl : alk. paper)
1. Christianity—21st century. 2. Emerging church movement.
3. Postmodernism—Religious aspects—Christianity.
4. Pentecostalism. 5. Love—Religious aspects—Christianity.
6. Church work with the poor. 7. Church work with the homeless.
I. Hood, Ralph W. II. Title.
BR121.3.P65   2008
277.3'083—dc22   2008018676

New York University Press books are printed on acid-free paper,
and their binding materials are chosen for strength and durability.
We strive to use environmentally responsible suppliers and materials
to the greatest extent possible in publishing our books.

Manufactured in the United States of America
c 10 9 8 7 6 5 4 3 2 1
p 10 9 8 7 6 5 4 3 2 1

Contents

Acknowledgments   vii

1   Godly Love and Post-Modern Christianity: An Introduction   1

2   The Man, the Myth, and the Vision   17

3   An Emerging Church Family and the Family Business   41

4   Charisma and Spiritual Transformation   64

5   Godly Love as Emotional Energy   94

6   The BnF Family and the Homeless Poor   117

7   Ideology and Tradition in Conflict   146

8   Smoke, Mirrors, and Holy Madness   172

9   Epilogue: A Social Scientific Assessment of Godly Love   198

Appendix A: Margaret Poloma's Reflections   217
     on a Research Journey

Appendix B: Methodological Appendix, with   223
     Survey Instrument (B-1) and Scale Construction (B-2)

Appendix C: Statistical Appendix, with Bivariate   239
     Matrix (C-1) and Multivariate Analysis (C-2)

References   245

Index   251

About the Authors   257

Acknowledgments

This project would not have been possible without the support of countless people both inside and outside Blood-n-Fire (BnF). Words of gratitude go first to David VanCronkhite, who cooperated with our research even in the midst of the tumultuous events that unfolded within a year after we began our study. He knew that we intended to do research and not an apologetic on the community. Whatever data we collected would necessarily be analyzed without an agenda. David welcomed us when we first proposed doing the research and encouraged us to continue when the tides turned in unexpected directions. He urged those at BnF to cooperate with us in virtually everything we asked to explore. As a schism within the ministry grew, David knew that some of the accounts we were hearing painted an unflattering portrait but that these stories needed to be heard together with those of loyal followers. He treated us with courtesy, respect, and even love as we sought to collect the array of narratives. Our work was full of serendipitous events; there were twists and turns that no one expected at the onset of the project. Most unexpected was the schism that occurred at BnF. As we explored various perspectives among those who sided with and opposed David, the schism extended to us. As researchers we could not take sides, and our refusal created tension between us and David that persists today. Our hearts are with those who left as much as they are with those who stayed, David VanCronkhite included.

We also wish to thank Cissy Watson, who trusted us with her account and the minutes from the board meetings, which included administrative details about the schism. Watson, together with former board member Woody White, encouraged us to give all we had to the project so that other boards might learn from the BnF story. We appreciate their assistance and support. Also, a special word of thanks to Vineyard pastor Johnny Crist, who helped to launch BnF in 1991, and David Kula, formerly of BnF Atlanta and Asheville, who graciously provided different perspectives on the appropriate role of an executive board in faith-based ministries.

Over one hundred unnamed respondents generously gave of their time as we conducted open-ended interviews, each lasting anywhere from twenty minutes to three hours. Many of the BnF members and a few homeless residents were interviewed more than once as events unfolded. We are also grateful to numerous unnamed homeless people who spent endless hours talking with Margaret, Ralph, and Ralph's research assistants, Christopher F. Silver and Zachary Smith. They shared with us in the Sanctuary where they had sought shelter, around the table of Sobre Le Mesa as they ate evening meals, and outside the buildings where those more marginal to the BnF community often socialized, telling their own stories of their lives at BnF. We also express our thanks to individuals who were enrolled in the Training Program; to the members of the Blood-n-Fire community, both past and present; to the leaders of Blood-n-Fire International; and to members of the Boards of Trustees over the years—to all who trusted us with your stories, we are grateful. Without you there would be no "data" to report. Of these respondents we would like to offer special thanks to Chris and Linda Franklin, Debbie and Eric Stagg, Scot and Meredith Thomas, LeAnn Pearson, Jill Royer, Steve Ruff, and Katina VanCronkhite. Through their willingness to dialogue with us over the years of the study, we have been able to provide a "thicker" description of the complex dynamics we observed at BnF. We also thank all past and present affiliates of BnF who have read an earlier draft of the manuscript and either formally or informally responded with their reactions and assessments. A special acknowledgment goes to Christopher F. Silver and Zachary Smith, who as research assistants conducted most of the in-depth interviews with the homeless and recovering addicts and provided a unique vantage point from which to offer their assessments.

We would also like to acknowledge the helpful comments provided by other manuscript readers who read the entire work, including Duane Crabbs, Mark Ford, Roger Heuser, Matthew Lee, Jeffrey Metzger, and Stephen Post. We are indebted to Rebecca Erickson for pointing us to interaction ritual theory as a sociological tool with which to analyze our data. Margaret also wishes to acknowledge John Zipp for his support and the sociology department of the University of Akron. A special debt is owed to Gray Temple, who was present at that first meeting the first author had with David in 1997 and who served as a sounding board through her years as a pilgrim and then an ethnographer of this faith-based ministry.

The original manuscript was greatly strengthened through the comments and ongoing suggestions made by NYU Press editor Jennifer

Hammer. We appreciate her interest in our project and the additional critique she obtained from three anonymous reviews. Although we were forced back to our computers before the manuscript could go to press, we gratefully acknowledge and appreciate the feedback.

Finally, but perhaps most importantly, we wish to acknowledge the Institute for Research on Unlimited Love under the direction of Stephen Post and the John Templeton Foundation (JTF) for the financial support for this groundbreaking project. The research narrative that follows has provided a theoretical and empirical foundation for a new three-year major collaborative project funded by JTF entitled "The Flame of Love: Scientific Research on the Experience and Expression of Godly Love in the Pentecostal Tradition." The goal of this endeavor by a team of theologians and social scientists is to establish an interdisciplinary field of study that takes God seriously as a perceived actor in human events as it explores human experiences of God's love and selfless service to others.

1

Godly Love and
Post-Modern Christianity
An Introduction

> No doubt there is much noise in evangelical Christianity. There
> are many false prophets (and false profits) out there, and all kinds
> of embarrassing things being done in the name of God. . . . Many
> of us are refusing to allow distorted images of our faith to de-
> fine us. There are those of us who, rather than simply reject pop
> evangelicalism, want to spread another kind of Christianity, a
> faith that has as much to say about this world as it does about the
> next. New prophets are rising up who try to change the future,
> not just predict it. There is a movement bubbling up that goes be-
> yond cynicism and celebrates a new way of living, a generation
> that stops complaining about the church it sees and becomes the
> church it dreams of. And this little revolution is irresistible. It is a
> contagious revolution that dances, laughs, and loves.
>
> —Claiborne 2006, 23–24

Beyond the kitsch of Christian television and the multifaceted
mega-churches that have captivated religion watchers is a post-modern
resistance movement with its headquarters on the Internet and many of
its congregants meeting in homes and urban warehouses. Its leaders are
calling the phenomenon the *emerging church,* and some, like Shane Claiborne, believe it is an "irresistible revolution" that will draw believers back
to the heart of the Christian Gospel. It is more than a theological critique
of modern Western Christianity. It is a religious movement that seeks to
deconstruct modern religion and to realign it with the dynamic process
that we call *godly love.*

Our initiation into this "irresistible revolution" did not begin with an academic concept or theory but rather with lived experience, details of which are presented in the appendix. One of the authors (Poloma) met Blood-n-Fire founder David VanCronkhite in the mid-1990s and became intrigued with his revolutionary vision, which was receiving national recognition in the evangelical neo-Pentecostal community. Although the phenomenon that would come to be known as the emerging church movement was yet to be labeled, BnF already exemplified its traits and principles.

VanCronkhite dates Blood-n-Fire (BnF) to 1991, when he and three others set out to downtown Atlanta from their suburban church to begin an outreach to the homeless. Within two years BnF was to become a visionary church of the poor heralding a revolution in which the marginalized would regain their pivotal place in Christianity. Beginning with a neo-monastic community in Atlanta that was to include people of all ages, races, and social strata, VanCronkhite proffered a vision for the Kingdom of God and its spread around the globe. At the time that we began our study in 2003, BnF was a thriving church in downtown Atlanta and boasted more than a dozen BnFs in other cities, both in the United States and abroad.

The Kingdom, according to VanCronkhite, would not come about through clever strategies or human power, but through the power of the Holy Spirit working through young people who had caught the vision that he was preaching. The story presented in this book offers a systematic study that explores the relationship between charismatic encounters with God, sacrificial giving of personal dreams and ambitions, and empowerment for service to the poor and broken. Personally knowing the love of God and experiencing its energizing power is at the heart of the vision and is central to what we are calling godly love.

Godly love, a theoretical concept derived from Pitirim Sorokin's classic work on love (1954/2002), represents an interface between the experience of divine love and human interaction. We utilize his theory, although we embed it within our modification of the contemporary microsociological theory of interaction rituals developed by Randall Collins (2004), which conceptualizes human interaction as a series of rituals. Used together, the scholarly work of Pitirim Sorokin, a mid-twentieth-century American sociologist of Russian descent, and Randall Collins, a contemporary American sociological theorist, provides a forum for presenting our observations on godly love at BnF. We are careful, however, to distinguish our own modified use of Sorokin's and Collins's theories from the viewpoints of the narrators of the many stories that form our ethnographic account of BnF.

Emerging Churches in a Post-modern World

Emerging churches have quietly developed within the past decade or so, primarily within the Evangelical charismatic subculture, to become one of several new congregational forms found at the close of the old millennium and the beginning of the twenty-first century (Thumma 2006; Livermore 2007). They represent a post-modern effort to return to a biblically based Christianity as a lived reality. Those involved in emerging churches commonly distance themselves from old labels, including the nomenclature that has been used to describe the various streams of American Pentecostalism (both classic and neo-Pentecostal variations) throughout the twentieth century. The roots of this growing movement, however, can be found deep within the Pentecostal worldview that seeks to bring heaven below to earth rather than to capitulate to the forces of modernity (see Wacker 2001; Poloma 1982, 1989, 2005). If modernity relativized and privatized religion, post-modernity challenges us to focus on religion as a form of life and not as a system of beliefs to be defended.

Thus the emerging church movement does not see itself as simply "another religion." As Eddie Gibbs and Ryan Bolger have noted:

> Modern culture created a secular realm and chased all spiritual things to the margins of society, first relegating them to church and religion and then to the individual's heart. . . . Emerging churches are communities that follow Jesus and the Kingdom into the far reaches of culture. Emerging churches destroy the Christendom idea that church is a place, a meeting, or a time. Church is a way of life, a rhythm, a community, a movement. Emerging Churches dismantle all ideas of church that interfere with the work of the kingdom. . . . For churches to resemble Jesus, they must include the stranger and not recognize two types of people. Modernity is a culture of exclusion. For emerging churches to look like Jesus, they must be countercultural through inclusion. Three "core practices" reflecting a post-modern posture that challenges the modern Christianity are intertwined in exemplar emerging-church congregations: identifying with Jesus' central message of the now-coming kingdom of God; breaking down the divisions between the sacred and the secular; and life lived within a community of believers for whom relationships are central. (Gibbs and Bolger 2005, 43)

Godly Love and Living the Law of Love

In this book, we define godly love as the dynamic interaction between human responses to the operation of perceived divine love and the impact this experience has on personal lives, relationships with others, and emergent communities. It is this social psychological process that is at the heart of the vision of emerging churches. Godly love begins with a relationship between God and the individual, but its empowering potential spreads to influence others and the community of faithful as it did with early apostles like Paul and Peter, saints of the poor like Francis of Assisi and Mother Teresa, founders of new religious movements like George Fox and John Wesley, and the millions of believers involved in the global Pentecostal movement.

Blood-n-Fire, the case study that provides the account of godly love in this book, is but one of countless congregations in the increasingly influential but loosely structured network of emerging churches. BnF is a religious community with an attendant faith-based ministry that sees God's love as the center of its vision for church, ministry, and mission. What BnF accepts as an experiential fact, the love of a biblical God for his creatures, we explore empirically, asserting that divine love is experienced as real and therefore can have real consequences. It is with the consequences as a benchmark that we seek to evaluate and assess godly love.

As with other emerging churches, BnF downplays doctrinal nuances of religion in favor of personal relationships: both an intimate love relationship with God and relationships with others inside and outside the church structure. Emerging churches like BnF are usually (but not always) independent entities eschewing denominational labels (Anderson 2006). They cannot be adequately defined by simply *what* they believe. The issue is rather *how* they believe. They strive to practice what leading spokesperson Brian McLaren (2004) has termed a "generous orthodoxy" that adheres to the essence of long-held Christian creeds ("vintage Christianity") while focusing on God's love and mercy rather than God's judgment. As with other congregations in this nebulous network, many of the teachings at BnF reflect a holistic approach that minimizes the sacred-secular divide. BnF worship extends beyond church walls, infuses daily life, and foreshadows the coming of the Kingdom of God.

Although the emerging church movement can be seen as a uniquely post-modern development whose beliefs are not argued for but rather simply embodied in the lived experience of their faith, similar dynamics can be found throughout the history of Christianity. Reflecting the wide gap commonly found between ideal culture and real culture, the great commandment to love God and love others as oneself remains a Christian goal to which many have aspired but few have attained. There are groups of people found throughout Christian history—ranging from the early church described in the book of Acts of the Apostles through countless reinventions, reformations, and revivals (including the plethora of new religious movements in twentieth- and twenty-first-century America)— that have created subcultures seeking to close the ideal-real gap. BnF is simply one experiment among countless others found in the history of Christianity. The advantage of BnF is that it is a *contemporary* "classical" effort to create a Christian community based on God's commandment to love thy neighbor as thyself.

Many emerging churches of the twenty-first century are spiritual de-scendants of the twentieth-century Azusa Street Revival (1906–9) that birthed Pentecostalism. Under the leadership of William Joseph Seymour, an African American and son of former slaves, an unusually diverse group of people (at least for a still–legally segregated America)—young and old, women and men, Americans and Europeans, Hispanics and Asians, blacks and whites—gathered to experience what they believed was the Spirit of God. From its humble Azusa Street beginnings, the Pentecostal movement—with its hallmark experiences of glossolalia or "speaking in tongues," healing, prophecy, and other signs and wonders—would spread throughout the globe (Robeck 2006).

Ever adapting as it emerged into a global Christian religious move-ment, now second in number only to Roman Catholicism with over five hundred million adherents, Pentecostalism represents a post-modern at-tempt to recapture the biblical worldview of mystery and miracle and to close the divide between the spiritual and the material (Wacker 2001). In this sense it is both *post-modern* as it moves beyond the limitations of modernity and *pre-modern* as it seeks to return to a pristine Christianity where the Spirit of God is palpable. The Pentecostal heritage is central to the story we tell in this work. Like other neo-Pentecostals and tradi-tional Pentecostals before them, BnF members sought to integrate the so-called natural and the supernatural with a spirituality that Steven Land described as "at once cognitive, affective and behavioral" (1993, 41), in which "affections are the heart of Pentecostal spirituality" (44). In pneu-matological theology, which focuses on the Holy Spirit or the third per-son of the Christian trinity, the Spirit of God is the "living flame of love" that "epitomizes the nearness of the power and presence of God . . . and celebrates the nimble, responsive, playful personal gift of God" (Pinnock 1996, 9). Many who came to BnF would find this theology made real as they prayed, played, and worked together in the BnF family, a community permeated with personal experiences of godly love that endeavored to share this reality with the homeless poor.

Our ethnographic four-year study provided ample time for complexities in the lived life of godly love at BnF to reveal themselves. We do not seek to privilege our own perceptions over those of others in the BnF community. Nor do we demand that the explanations provided by embedding our narratives with the theoretical views of Sorokin and Collins be accepted uncritically. We are careful to distinguish description from explanation. Our descriptions provide a cacophony of voices representing the complexity that is BnF, but as scholars we are guided by theoretical insights from social science and methodological rules. We must and do explore consequences when claims are made that are empirical and can be evaluated. For example, whether a soul is saved from hell is not a question we answer, but whether addicts abandon their habits is a question that can be empirically addressed.

Godly love as presented by systematic theologians and romantic philosophers can be easily idealized and criticized when the ideals fail to match reality. But reality is more often a kaleidoscope than a fixed specimen under a microscope; it can be multifaceted and sometimes ethereal (Anderson 1990). There is no single "reality" by which BnF can be said to succeed or fail. The account we present, therefore, is neither a theological treatise nor a philosophical critique of love, but rather a social scientific effort to capture descriptions and measures of reported ritual interactions of godly love. Although the effects of godly love are sometimes shrouded in shadows, the gray areas are illuminated by the use of many voices and narratives from the BnF community

Godly Love and Social Scientific Theory

Obviously the love we speak about is neither romance nor sexual intimacy. The love we explore in this book includes "the bonds of respect and acceptance that we sometimes refer to as filial relations and the selfless caring we refer to as altruism" (Wuthnow 2004, 256). In accord with Pitirim Sorokin (1954/2002), who for many is *the* sociological theorist of love, we also contend that love can include a supra-empirical component.

This component is integral to what we are calling godly love—love that is perceived to be of divine origin and with a human response that reflects, even if dimly, the compassion of God. Godly love is found at the center of Christian incarnational theology, which depicts Jesus of Nazareth as God taking on human flesh, who taught in word, by example, and through the power of the Holy Spirit that God is compassionate and unlimited love. Jesus reduced the many Hebraic laws and their prescriptions and pro-scriptions to one great commandment, namely, to love the Lord thy God with thy whole mind, heart, and soul and love your neighbor as yourself (see Matthew 22:38; Mark 12:31; John 13:34).

Christian Smith, in his discussion of "Why Christianity Works," un-equivocally states that for Christians, "The center and sustainer of all reality is a thoroughly loving God. God is Love." He proceeds further to describe this God:

> God showers gratuitous love on His children beyond measure or merit. God knows when a sparrow falls to the ground. But even more so, God intimately knows and cares about every unique human self. The Christian God does not love the idea of humankind. God loves actual individual people themselves, real persons just as they are. God does not only love people when they are nice and good, but even in their failings, ugliness, and willful wrongdoing. The Christian God's love is not conditional, contingent, quali-fied, or partial. It is total, self-giving, unmerited, absolute—overflowing from God's boundless goodness and tender loving-kindness. (2007, 171)

Christian Smith's depiction of a personal God who is a significant actor in the daily lives of many contemporary Christian believers reflects the lived religion of the BnF community. BnF regularly shared stories of divine encounters as members modeled and instructed others on how to see the divine signs and wonders around them. Yet due to the prescription of "methodological atheism" as the only lens through which to view social reality within the social scientific community, the very possibility of divine-human interaction has been at best overlooked and at worst denied by many scholars.

Unmasking a Theoretical Blinder

Modern social science has been dominated by this commitment to "meth-odological atheism," although it is increasingly recognized in post-modern thought as but one philosophical stance that is privileged no more than any other. At methodological atheism's base is an uncritical subscription to a social constructionism where nothing of experience is attributed to the object of experience. More balanced is the stance we take here, namely, that of methodological agnosticism. There is always the chance that those who claim to hear from God may actually be hearing from the divine (Bowker 1971). Human experiences reported by subjects as having come from God must be taken seriously, not simply as social constructions (which they partly are), but as actual ways in which God is experienced. In order to "take God seriously" we have sought to move beyond the methodological atheism that has permeated the social sciences toward a methodological agnosticism in which we use as real data the reported acts of God that informants assert they have experienced. Rather than deny their reality, we explore how a defined reality is maintained within a community of people who attempt to live it out (Popora 2006; Hood 2007). Our research on godly love thus seeks to explore the dynamic interaction between God and humans as reportedly experienced by the human subjects in this study—a dynamic we believe to be central for understanding religious behavior in Pentecostal and other biblically oriented communities and especially the new emerging church movement.

Pitirim Sorokin on the Ways and Power of Love

The concept of godly love is an example of what the renowned sociologist Pitirim Sorokin has called "love energy." According to Sorokin, "Love can be viewed as one of the highest energies known," and he contends that social scientists can study "the channeling, transmission, and distribution of this [nonphysical] energy" (1954/2002, 36). Sorokin observes that love energy is continually being produced through human interaction and that it can be stored within cultures as humanly produced catalysts of love (e.g., through religious and cultural norms, ideals, values, and rituals). Although his focus is on the love energy produced by human beings, Sorokin (1954/2002, 26) does acknowledge the "probable hypothesis" that "an inflow of love comes from an intangible, little-studied, possibly supraempirical source called 'God,' 'the Godhead,' 'the Soul of the Universe,' 'the Heavenly Father,' 'Truth,' and so on."

Sorokin has not only provided a theory of love that makes room for experiences of the divine, he has also developed a five-dimensional model for assessing love. Sorokin's first dimension of love is *intensity*. Low intensity love makes possible minor actions, such as giving a few pennies to the destitute or relinquishing a bus seat for another's comfort; at high intensity, much that is of value to the agent (time, energy, resources) is freely given. While Sorokin does not fully develop the different potential forms of intensity, his point remains clear. The range of intensity is not scalar—that is, research cannot indicate "how many times greater a given intensity is than another," but it is often possible to see "which intensity is really high and which low, and sometimes even to measure it" (1954/2002, 15–16).

Sorokin's second dimension of love is *extensity*: "The extensity of love ranges from the zero point of love of oneself only, up to the love of all mankind, all living creatures, and the whole universe. Between the minimal and maximal degrees lies a vast scale of extensities: love of one's own family, or a few friends, or love of the groups one belongs to—one's own clan, tribe, nationality, nation, religious, occupational, political, and other groups and associations" (1954/2002, 15). Sorokin's extensity resonates with the classic Western discussion of the "order of love." How does one balance love for family and friends (the nearest and dearest) with love for the very neediest of all humanity? As an example of extensity he offers St. Francis, who seemed to have a love of "the whole universe (and of God)" (1954/2002, 15).

Sorokin next added the dimension of *duration*, which "may range from the shortest possible moment to years or throughout the whole life of an individual or of a group" (1954/2002, 16). For example, the soldier who saves a comrade in a moment of heroism but may then revert to selfishness can be contrasted to the mother who cares for a sick child over many years. The duration of love can be longer or shorter depending in part on the type of love and the situation in which it is enacted.

The fourth dimension of love is *purity*. Here Sorokin wrote that pure love is characterized as affection for another that is free of egoistic motivation. By contrast, acting out of a desire for pleasure, personal advantage, or profit are signs of a love that is in some way "spoiled." According to Sorokin, pure love—that is, love that is truly disinterested and asks for no return—represents the highest form of emotion.

Finally, Sorokin discussed the *adequacy* of love. Inadequate love may be subjectively genuine, but it can have undesirable and adverse objective consequences. It is possible to pamper and spoil a child with love, in which case love has a consequence opposite of the love goal. Inadequate love is devoid of practical wisdom; adequate love achieves ennobling purposes and is, therefore, anything but blind or unwise. According to Sorokin, love can be judged inadequate in yet another way. It is possible that a person may have no loving intentions yet generate a consequence that is beneficial to others. For love to be judged adequate, loving intent and beneficial consequences must be in alignment.

Sorokin's five dimensions of love allow us to ask empirical questions about strength or weakness in different dimensions and how such differences vary with other dimensions. How intense, extensive, enduring, unselfish, and wise is any particular manifestation of love? These are questions that we will raise for the reader to assess throughout our narrative, and we offer them as a rubric through which godly love can be evaluated at BnF.

Randall Collins on Ritual Interaction Chains

Although Sorokin's brilliant work on love has lain fallow in the discipline that he helped to establish in the United States over seventy-five years ago, contemporary sociological theories have plowed ground into which Sorokin's seeds can be planted. One such theoretical development that is relevant to understanding the production and storage of love energy is interaction ritual theory, especially as explicated in the prominent work of sociologist Randall Collins (2004).

Collins derives his theory of interaction ritual from the works of the master social theorists Emile Durkheim, a pioneer in the sociology of religion, and Erving Goffman, a twentieth-century theorist who extended Durkheim's understanding of ritual as religious observance to common everyday interaction. Collins succinctly describes his work as an argument "for the continuity of a chief theoretical pathway from classic sociology to the present," suggesting the development of this pathway as follows:

> Durkheim launched sociology on a high theoretical level by providing an explanation for some of the most central questions: what produces social membership, moral beliefs, and the ideas with which people communicate and think. The key is that these are linked together by the same mechanism: ideas are symbols of group membership, and thus culture is generated by the moral—which is to say emotional—patterns of social interaction. . . . I interpret the theory through the eyes of Erving Goffman and the microsociological movement; that is to say, in the spirit of symbolic interaction, ethnomethodology, social constructionism, and sociology of emotions. (2004, xi)

We must, however, issue a cautionary note as we attempt to wed two discrepant theorists. Although Collins's theoretical discussion provides a key to discussing interaction rituals, including ones that we identify as godly love, unfortunately his microsociology shares the problem that we critiqued earlier as "methodological atheism." He identifies his view as being "inherently secular" (Collins 2004, 33) and seeks to provide a secular alternative to interpreting religious abstractions. In this sense his theory is inherently reductionist to religious experienced realities.

Collins has used his theory to discuss topics ranging from sexual interaction to tobacco rituals to the social production of individuality. Its main components of situational copresence, mutual focus of attention, and shared mood or affect are commonly found within the dynamic interaction of everyday situations as well as in the enactment of religious rituals. Of particular significance for this project is what Collins calls "emotional energy" (2004, 38), which is charged up by human participation in human ritual activity. "Ritual" for Collins goes beyond sacred rituals to include simple everyday behavior, and this model of ritual interaction is particularly appropriate for a better understanding of the interaction accounts presented in our story of BnF. Collins's theory, however, will need to be modified as we use his insight into interaction rituals to describe the significance of godly love.

According to Collins, ritual accounts are not one time events, but rather they are linked together and affect subsequent events through the storage and recharging of emotional energy. Emotional energy is what both motivates individuals and also links one situation to the next as individuals seek the satisfaction it brings. Collins adds, "Note the emphasis: the analytical starting point is the situation, and how it shapes individuals, situations generate and regenerate the emotions and the symbolism that charge up individuals and send them from one situation to another" (2004, 44). Despite his stance of methodological atheism, Collins has paradoxically offered a theory of emotional energy and ritual chains that can be applied to better understand the living out of godly love.

Although there are significant fundamental difference in assumptions between Sorokin and Collins, there are also relevant and noteworthy commonalities. Collins's "emotional energy" and Sorokin's "love energy" can be regarded as members of the same conceptual family. Sorokin's theory, complete with hypotheses to assess love, provides a more specific model to describe and assess the particularities of interactions reflecting godly love. Collins, on the other hand, has provided, although perhaps inadvertently, a more general microsociological framework that alerts researchers to the importance of the social situation in which interaction occurs. For both Collins ("emotional") and Sorokin ("love"), energy is a product of interaction that can be stored in cultural symbols, symbols that may be material or cognitive.

Our modification of Collins's basic model is simple. He demands an embodied copresence but his only focus is on situations that necessarily include at least two persons. Ironically, this claim is made as well by Pentecostals. It is the dyadic relationship between God and a person (embodied by possession by the Holy Spirit) that forms the reality that is congruent with Collins's interaction ritual. All that is needed is the acceptance of the possibility that God is real and can be experienced by persons that are equally real. In the Pentecostal tradition, the irony is that Collins's interaction ritual has been realized within the lived tradition for whom possession of the Holy Ghost has long been a central emotional experience in a religion that is better felt than told.

From New Paradigm to Emerging Church

BnF, always first and foremost a church and then a ministry, professed as a central tenet that loving relationships with the poor and homeless were an indispensable component of every Christian's life. It was this radical tenet that was a factor in moving BnF from a group of "new paradigm" churches to the network of emerging churches. BnF's history is rooted in what Donald Miller has described as a "reinvention of American Protestantism" through the development of "new paradigm churches" (1997, 1). As Miller describes such congregations, "Appropriating contemporary cultural forms, these churches are creating a new genre of worship music; they are reconstructing the organizational character of institutional religion; and they are democratizing access to the sacred by radicalizing the Protestant principle of the priesthood of all believers" (1997, 1).

New paradigm churches are the places of worship for many of the boomer generation; leaders of the emerging church movement contend, however, that they remain modern creations that hold little appeal for the post-modern children and grandchildren of aging boomers (Kimball 2003; Anderson 2006). The emerging church movement thus claims to be more than another limited modernist attempt to reach younger generations. It arose out of a more general question raised in the mid-1990s about whether postmodern Christians could still be considered Evangelicals. Emerging church leaders came to believe that they and their followers remain *evangelical* in the broad historical sense, but they tend to reject the more specific Evangelical label. They may be resistant to old labels, but not to self-examination that leads to new alliances. At times, as when Brian McLaren noted that "in many ways" he had more in common with Catholics than with Protestants, foundational teachings of new-paradigm churches run counter to Evangelical assumptions (Gibbs and Bolger, 2005, 34–39). Scott Thumma has described the ideals of the emerging church movement as "sophisticated and well-reasoned analyses of contemporary society and the role of God and church in a changing reality" (2006, 192). While the structure of many new-paradigm churches has been said to focus on meeting the needs of their main constituencies, leading spokesperson Brian McLaren challenges those in emerging churches, saying, "It's not about the church meeting your needs; it's about you joining the mission of God's people to meet the world's needs" (2004, 120).

In 1997, Association of Vineyard Churches (AVC) founder John Wimber died. Shortly thereafter, David VanCronkhite, whose extensive and other-serving vision even in the 1990s resonated more with criteria marking the emerging church network than the "new paradigm" congregations, withdrew from this denomination. Like others in the loosely knit emerging church movement, BnF was gnawing at the edges of the once-radical "new paradigm." It had outgrown its Vineyard roots. Although still wed to a traditional and biblically based Christianity, including Wimber's understanding of the mysterious and miraculous "signs and wonders" reported in the Bible, a now-independent BnF was free to pursue its own creative path, one that was marked with a "generous orthodoxy" and a lifestyle of what BnF termed "extravagant giving." Like other emerging churches, BnF also promoted a worldview that decried the modernist great divide between the natural and supernatural. There were continual reports of "signs and wonders" at BnF; the miraculous was commonly the subject of testimonies; and, for many at BnF, the supernatural became a "natural" experience as they stepped away from the familiar and secure to "walk by faith." Theirs was not to be a privatized faith meant only for BnF's little circle of believers, but one that was intended to be taken out into the streets and parks to share with the poor and the broken. As with most other emerging churches, BnF sought to embrace its community and promised to bring the Kingdom of God first into the problematic and troubled daily world of Atlanta's addicts and homeless and then "to the nations."

An inner-city Atlanta church, BnF was founded by David VanCronkh-ite in May 1991. During this study, it was physically located on a 3.7-acre complex within blocks of the golden dome of the Georgia capitol building and the neon Coca-Cola sign on top of the soft drink maker's interna-tional headquarters. In contrast to the nearby neighborhood, increasingly one of this-worldly government and commerce, BnF was a church with a proclaimed vision of divine destiny, belief in activity of supernatural forces, and countless stories of divine "signs and wonders." Within its first decade and a half, BnF has demonstrated in microcosm the ebb and flow of a dynamic spirituality that has come in waves throughout the one-hun-dred-year history of American Pentecostalism. It is a spirituality seen to empower concrete and pragmatic goals (whether it be spreading Chris-tianity or meeting the needs of the poor) with spiritual gifts, including glossolalia, prophecy, miracles, and healing. BnF was about ushering in the Kingdom of God, first in Atlanta and then to the nations.

Religious narrative reflecting this vision is central to the BnF commu-nity—a vision that can be succinctly presented by the church's core values and its proclamation that "the Kingdom of God is at hand." Following the teachings of Jesus and narratives found in the New Testament, BnF asserts that the Kingdom is the demonstrated reign of God through supernatural signs and wonders. The gifts of the Spirit are seen as integral to the call to love God and neighbor. The empowering of the Holy Spirit is regarded as the force that enables the members to live out a neo-monastic lifestyle through a related BnF core value calling for "intense commitment to a relational community." As with other emerging churches, the community aspires to be a universalistic one that moves people out of their "comfort zones" in entering into committed relationships with others of differing economic strata, race, age, and gender. A descriptive statement about BnF goals ties this relational church into the larger world community:

> We are aware that the poor represent a visionless and hopeless people who when embracing a common vision and beginning to love one another bring life and joy to a city. . . . The poor, who are gifted and talented, when brought into relationship with one another, find the destiny they have al-ways hoped for. Some will go to other cities and nations that Blood-n-Fire serves, some will continue to serve Atlanta, some will be sent to new areas of the world by the Lord's direction to establish additional BnF locations. Many will "simply" be restored to their families, their jobs and their soci-ety. (http://www.bloodnfire.com; accessed February 15, 2003)

At the time that we formally began our research in January 2003, BnF was a beehive of activity. We had carefully designed our research agenda to include the existing ministry structure and to study the efficacy of the services offered (see appendix B). The physical site that was home to the church and ministry consisted of two old, once-abandoned buildings, one of which was known as the Warehouse and the other the Sanctuary. There were nightly events at the Warehouse, including "dinner, family meeting, and community time." On Sunday and Friday nights, religious services provided a context where spiritual gifts were learned and used in preparation for taking the BnF ministry to the streets of inner-city Atlanta. Dinner was served without charge nightly and after the Sunday morning worship service to anyone in need of a good meal; the number of those served at times reached five hundred. The adjacent Sanctuary served as lodging for those in need of a place to sleep; it also symbolically served as the place for Sunday morning worship. The number housed, including mostly men, some women and children, and some families, typically went down to one hundred or fewer in the summer months. During cold winter nights, however, the Sanctuary would be filled to capacity with two hundred fifty people; on the coldest nights an overflow could be found sleeping on mats in the adjacent Warehouse. Addicts in varying stages of the nine-month Training (drug rehabilitation) Program lived upstairs in the Warehouse, where they studied, prayed, and slept without significant contact with the outside world. BnF had became a well-known place among Atlanta's downtown poor where the needy could come for food, shelter, and clothing, as well as spiritual nurturing that promised them a destiny and future.

By the end of 2003, however, it became apparent that there was trouble at BnF. A power struggle for leadership, fueled partly by individuals seeking evidence of the fulfillment of BnF's vision, ensued during 2004. David VanCronkhite was for a time absent from BnF, but eventually he was restored to his original position of undisputed leadership. Although he won the battle, it seemed as if he had lost the war. When those who sought to hold VanCronkhite true to his vision dissociated from the ministry in sincere belief that their leader was a failed prophet at best, BnF lost more than half of its members. Many of these members had been actively in charge of the ministries in VanCronkhite's absence, and still others drifted away during the conflict and its aftermath. More importantly, BnF lost the support of the corporate-elite board of trustees, who had been the financial backbone of the BnF ministry during its most successful years. Many on the board sought some evidence of tangible results of VanCronkhite's vision. With news of the schism and the departure of its prestigious board, income was reduced to a fraction of what it had been during the previous few years. By November 2005, BnF was forced to suspend nearly all the services it had once offered to the poor of Atlanta.

BnF's ministry, regarded as a key component in building the Kingdom, was imploding before our eyes. There was no miraculous influx of money or means to do the practical things required to handle the needs of the poor. The family-like community had scattered—dissident members had departed, some potential supporters sat on the sidelines waiting to see what would develop, still others joined those who worked in the flood-destroyed city of New Orleans. The tragedy of New Orleans in late August 2005, where BnF staffers joined in the work at Victory Fellowship (Metairie, LA) to help flood victims, provided BnF with a temporary stay from the near destruction of the ministry in Atlanta. By the time we conducted our exit work, the hustle and bustle of daily gatherings for prayer, ministry, eating, sleeping, and recreation had been reduced to a small "house church" that met weekly. Meanwhile, the prophets and their prophecies continued to renew the promise that new life will spring from the ashes of this once-viable sign of the coming Kingdom of God as a dozen or so committed members faithfully work with VanCronkhite to rebuild BnF.

As we write this book, the buildings are being dismantled and sold for their antique bricks, and the property will also soon be sold. The BnF ministry as we knew it and studied it is no more, yet not everyone sees BnF as a failed experiment. If we are tempted to write an obituary, others seek to tell of a rebirth of godly love and perhaps yet another birthing of BnF. We make no predictions; rather, we end our story with the dismantling of the buildings on the 3.7 acres in downtown Atlanta that once provided a central narrative as well as the physical embodiment of BnF.

2

The Man, the Myth, and the Vision

And each time I heard "these people" tell their stories I so remember thinking, "I want a story to tell. I don't have any stories. I
want a story." Truth be known, it was one of the motivating factors
in my going to the inner city with sixteen bags of food following
three other men, none who had a clue of what we were doing . . .
or the cost. But you know, I got my story . . . and now I get dozens of stories every day . . . no seriously, dozens every day . . .
stories that are worth giving up on the American dream . . . . stories that are far more valuable than not going because of the fears
of what might happen in going after them . . . Stories of unbelievable miracles . . . unbelievable signs and wonders . . . big stuff . . .
blind seeing, deaf hearing . . . families restored . . . jobs supernaturally provided . . . fathers and sons miraculously restored . . .
you wouldn't believe the stories, even if I told . . . but I got 'em,
wouldn't trade 'em . . . for anything . . .

—VanCronkhite 2002, 3

The making of myths and the visions that they embody are
often treated as faits accomplis, and their content and outcomes are assessed without regard for the interaction process that brings myths into
being in the first place. What David VanCronkhite calls "stories" and what
we are calling "myths" are central for understanding interaction ritual in
an emerging church. The process of constructing myths is an example
of what Collins describes as "mutual focus" in which participants "develop a mutual focus of attention and become entrained in each other's
bodily micro-rhythms and emotions" (2004, 47). Myths provide a source
of emotional energy that propels subsequent interaction rituals (IRs) and
their interaction ritual chains at BnF. Each story consists of IRs, and these

IRs are linked to other stories that make and modify myths, myths that provide a "mutual focus" for lived religion. What is significant to note is that many of the stories VanCronkhite tells center not on interaction with other human beings (who may play supporting roles) but with God as a primary partner.

There are those who would see mythmaking as a cognitive process "arising from the evolution and integration of certain parts of the brain" that is basic to all humans and inherent to all religions (d'Aquili and Newberg 1999, 79). Regardless of whether humans are "hardwired" for myth, there is little question that mythmaking has been a basic cultural tool throughout the history of humankind going back thousands of years to the Paleolithic period (8000–2000 BCE). The forces of modernism, however, have not been kind to myth. Modernist thinking, with its roots firmly planted in rationalism and categorical logic, has been said to bring about the "death of mythology" (Armstrong 2005, 119). The focus on cognitive critique of myth by modernists is part of the reason that persons of faith have always found "myth" to be a pejorative term when applied to their tradition. Persons of faith experience and narrate their world in stories that for them are simply true.

It has taken post-modern critiques to remind us that science, with its proclivity for measurement and quantification, is itself involved in mythmaking (Cahoone, 2003). Unfortunately, scientists are no more willing to acknowledge that they are involved in mythmaking than are people of faith. Our use of myth is simply descriptive of a cultural process that is central to generating godly love; it implies no negative connotation. We concur with the psychologist Rollo May, who, in lamenting the dearth of functioning myths in modern society, has described myth as follows:

> A myth is a way of making sense in a senseless world. Myths are narrative patterns that give significance to our existence. Whether the meaning of existence is only what we put into life by our own individual fortitude, as Sartre would hold, or whether there is a meaning we need to discover, as Kierkegaard would state, the result is the same: myths are our way of finding this meaning and significance. Myths are like the beams of a house; not exposed to outside view, they are the structure which holds the house together so that people can live in it. (1991, 15)

Myths that allow humans to make sense out of a senseless world differ and involve different interaction rituals from the production of modern science, journalism, or literary works. As we will see in examples of significant myths for the BnF community, they are often produced, altered, and recharged in dialogue with the divine.

Although David VanCronkhite, the founder of Blood-n-Fire, loves to tell stories, he would not claim to be involved in mythmaking. His narratives are generally centered on his personal experience of an immanent and transcendent God who has given him a vision for BnF. Like prophets of old, VanCronkhite hears from God; and when sharing a divinely given message he may remind the listeners of his intimate relationship with God. "God always calls me 'David,'" he says, to reinforce the intimacy of his dialogue with the divine and the similarity of his prophetic relationship of godly love to that of the biblical King David with Yahweh. His myth-producing IRs are embedded in a Pentecostal worldview that is more Hebraic than Greek, one that minimizes the divide between Logos (i.e., logic/reason) and mythos (i.e., myth/mysticism) inherited from Greek philosophy (Armstrong 2005; Poloma 2003).

As VanCronkhite discloses his prophecies, they can be viewed as a series of narratives that relate a chain of interaction rituals. Some of them are told once or twice and then forgotten; others have achieved a permanence that provides meaning and motivation for pursuing things that David believes to be part of the Kingdom of God. VanCronkhite is generally not one to tell the stories of others (unless they have relevance to his own life and vision); his storytelling is personal, centered on God, the Bible, and the inspiration of the Holy Spirit. He encourages others to follow his example of listening for the voice of the divine but also cautions that not everyone is a prophet. IRs, although they often include God as a partner at BnF, more commonly occur between humans as the interaction ritual chain develops; prophecies not in accord with the current vision are quickly checked.

VanCronkhite's ascent to prophetic status within the community developed over time and within a particular situation. We begin his story where he often begins it—with his conversion and the birth of his vision of the coming Kingdom of God.

The Visionary in Social Context

Although David became an Evangelical believer in 1971 during a Christian seminar in Dallas, his vision about the Kingdom of God would come later through his affiliation with John Wimber and the Association of Vineyard

Churches (AVC). After seeing "dramatic response" to prayer in his own congregation in 1977, Wimber was launched as "a gifted leader and public speaker into a renowned national and international 'signs and wonders' ministry that has had a profound affect on tens of thousands of Christian charismatics and noncharismatics alike" (Wagner 2002, 1199–1200). Don Williams describes Wimber as being "driven by his understanding of the Kingdom of God" (2005, 167). For Wimber this understanding was rooted in Jesus, who "came in the power of the Spirit to evangelize the poor, heal the sick, drive out demons, liberate the oppressed, and build a people living under his lordship who will reflect his character and ministry in fulfilling his mission to the nations" (Williams 2005, 167). VanCronkhite was driven by a similar vision of the coming Kingdom of God, but his vision, much more than Wimber's, developed to emphasize the central role the poor and oppressed would play in the coming Kingdom.

David VanCronkhite remained affiliated with the Association of Vineyard Churches (AVC) until Wimber died in 1997. After Wimber's death, VanCronkhite elected for BnF to become an independent church and ministry, aligning BnF more closely with the emerging church movement than the AVC. One sign of his distancing himself from Vineyard structure and polity is reflected in the name David gave to his congregation. While all AVC congregations of the time were designated by the name of the city followed by the label "Vineyard Church," David called his church Blood-n-Fire, a motto that has long been associated with the Salvation Army.

The roots of BnF began to emerge in 1991, while David and his wife, Janice, were members of the Atlanta Vineyard Fellowship. Pastor Johnny Crist proposed developing an outreach to the poor in the inner city. At the time, David "was an affluent, born-again businessman. His wife, Janice, was a professional tennis player who associated with the likes of actor Clint Eastwood and tennis star Jimmy Connors" (Daigle 2003, 70). Exactly how affluent David was and how affluent he and Janice are today is unknown. At least one long-time member of BnF, now himself successful entrepreneur, has questioned David's story. He reported that he had repeatedly searched the Internet over the years but has been unable to find any traces of Integrated Health Systems Inc., the company for which David reported that he had served as CEO. Whatever David's social class, he did abandon some level of status and class when he first embarked on a journey to evangelize the poor that would eventually lead to the establishment of Blood-n-Fire.

None of the four men who left the Atlanta suburbs in search of "the poor" under Crist's leadership knew the terrain of inner-city Atlanta or what form their outreach might take. They simply headed south "with sixteen bags of groceries" to preach the Gospel to the poor. As VanCronkhite recalls the event, "Minister to the poor? Ha. We couldn't even find the poor. . . . [We] took off from white, very middle class Atlanta and headed south to find the poor. We drove for an hour and a half—we didn't even know where to go look. Most of us had never ventured anywhere into that part of America" (Bogart 1997, 22). David tells how they pulled into the parking lot of Capitol Homes, a housing development that was across the street from an abandoned warehouse complex on 3.7 acres. He would later purchase the warehouse site as home for his ministry.

One recount of its history on the BnF Web site (http://www.bloodnfire. com; accessed February 24, 2004) noted the change that occurred during that first year of visiting Capitol Homes as one in which the suburban visitors went from distributing "sixteen bags of groceries" to a "full-fledged ministry." The following excerpt details the kind of activities involved in that transition: "The bags of groceries became a weekly hot barbecued chicken dinner with a worship band set up in a vacant field in the middle of the housing project. Men and women from the suburbs mingled with the families of Capitol Homes, serving food, playing baseball, and offering hope and encouragement while being encouraged and blessed by those they shared their lives with. VanCronkhite called this outreach 'Blood-n-Fire,' a name he later discovered was the original slogan of the Salvation Army."

The visits to Capitol Homes that began in May 1991 would become a regular Saturday outreach for volunteers from the Atlanta Vineyard. VanCronkhite identifies the May 1991 date as the birthday of the ministry and the beginning of BnF. But it was October 31, 1993, that he said marked the beginning of his church. David succinctly recounts his perception of the change that occurred during those first two and a half years of BnF's existence until the BnF church was launched, one that reflects a common vision of emerging churches for inclusive communities: "It [October 31, 1993] marked the date our hearts enlarged from 'doing ministry to the poor' to becoming a community of 'displacement,' i.e. a community that includes black and white and brown, yellow and red, rich and poor; young and old." Markers of change are always flexible, and the change from "ministry" to "church" was probably not that clear-cut. What it does mark is a break from the Atlanta Vineyard and David's becoming the pastor of his own church as a prophet led by God.

Among VanCronkhite's stories told during this early period of BnF's development are prophecies that were given to him, including the often-told account of the prophetic prayer in which he and his wife were given the "William and Catherine Booth anointing." David told us that at the time of his prayer he had never heard of the founders of the Salvation Army. Whether this prophetic word was given before or after his receiving a name for the new ministry is not altogether clear, but it established a nominal spiritual link between the two ministries separated by two centuries. Like the rough and rugged early Salvation Army that affected the lives of countless destitute men and women in England and the United States, VanCronkhite envisioned BnF to be a revolutionary force that would change the lives of the poor in Atlanta as well as in other parts of the world.

Coupled with the prophetic proclamation that gave the Booth mantle to the VanCronkhites is a further clarification relating how God gave BnF its name. David had been praying about a name for the ministry. He participated in a March for Jesus in Alberta, Canada, in 1992, where he said he saw the words "Blood and Fire" on a banner. He immediately "knew" that God was answering his prayer. David searched the Bible and learned the name was biblically based: "I will show wonders in the heavens and on the earth, blood and fire and billows of smoke" was recorded in Acts 2:19, as the apostle Peter spoke the words of the prophet Joel (2:30). An account on the Web site goes on to explain the significance of the name and its spiritual ties between BnF and the Salvation Army: "The name signifies the blood of Jesus and the salvation that comes only from Jesus and the fire of the Holy Spirit." It was several years later that David was informed that Blood and Fire was the original slogan used by William and Catherine Booth, the founders of the Salvation Army. On finding this out, David noted, "Though there is no affiliation with the Salvation Army, we are gladly reminded that the Booths' heart for the homeless, the lost, and the poor is the same heart we have at Blood-n-Fire."

In the early years of BnF the imagery of an army fighting a spiritual battle with global effects was reflected in talk about revolution and warfare. The military language, however, would give way to the relational language of "family" as the second millennium drew to a close.

Spiritual Transformation

The Impartation

David describes his own spiritual transformation as being one that moved him away from indifference and ignorance and toward compassion and encouraging relationships with the poor. He notes that this transformation occurred during a neo-Pentecostal "conference" with worship, preaching, and prayer sponsored by John Wimber's Vineyard in Southern California: "Janice and I were coming out of what you might call 'the come late, leave early' crowd of our church. Yet, we were fortunate enough to have been invited to attend our church conference. As I recall, we were excited not so much about the conference but that we were going to hang out with new friends in church leadership" (VanCronkhite 2002, 32). It turned out to be a gathering that David said changed his life. He describes this change as an "impartation."

The agent of David's spiritual transformation was a middle-aged missionary to Hong Kong, who as a nineteen-year-old new convert left her native England in response to a divine call (Pullinger 1980; Brookes 2008). Her name is Jackie Pullinger, and David commonly referred to her as "that woman." David often would verbally share his story about spiritual impartation, and in 1998 he wrote it out as a newsletter testimony that he sent to invite recipients to the "If I Have Withheld" conference at BnF. Jackie Pullinger would be a featured speaker for the event.

In the written account David tersely describes Pullinger's message and his reaction to it: "She quickly began what was one of the hardest messages I had ever heard preached. It was a fiery, passionate message about the poor and compassion for the poor. But frankly, it left me very angry. Angry at her for telling me the truth about who I was in regards to the poor and where the Church was in regards to the poor. I didn't think I much liked that woman!" (VanCronkhite 2002, 32).

The conference with some ten thousand people in attendance was a revival-like ritual (not unlike a Billy Graham crusade) that invited attendees to respond to the message and to "come forward, repent and receive impartation for this thing called 'compassion for the poor'" (32). Although David reported that he was still angry with "that woman" and did not intend to go forward for prayer, "Something caused Janice and me to finally get up toward the end of that prayer of impartation and meekly ask God to give us what 'that woman' was talking about, this thing called compassion for the poor" (32). In other accounts David shared how he was unable to approach the prayer with open hands that would be a sign of full acceptance; the best he could do was to extend his hands and lift up two fingers.

David said that nothing seemed to change at the time of the prayer, but something did happen over the next few weeks that he claimed "ruined" him for life.

> But over the next weeks and months I would suddenly find myself seeing things I had never seen in the city or on the streets. I would notice people I hadn't noticed before and I would have this sense of urgency to help them, to speak to them, to share hope with them, to get food and shelter for them or to share Jesus with them. I found myself falling in love with the poor, the harassed, the oppressed. I found myself looking for ways to reach out and help men and women I had never even noticed before. I found myself weeping over people I had never cared about before, never even noticed. I knew then what happened. God had changed a heart. He had miraculously changed a heart of stone to a heart of flesh (Ezek. 11:19 stuff). God had actually used "that woman" Jackie Pullinger to break both Janice and my hearts. We were literally "ruined." (32-33)

Despite the centrality of "that woman" in David's story of personal transformation, Jackie Pullinger's name was not heard as often over the last several years. Once said to be David's "spiritual father," this title now rests on a minister from Florida whom David calls "Papa Jack."

Jack Taylor, a Baptist pastor for more than twenty-five years and founder of Dimension Ministries in Melbourne, Florida, is an evangelist with a message about personal and corporate revival. His life and ministry "took a dramatic turn with increased manifestation of the power of Holy Spirit" during a visit to the revival at the Toronto Airport Christian Fellowship in August 1994 (http://www.coffeewithjack.com). Papa Jack played an important role in supporting David as he would struggle to retain control of BnF.

The Call and the Promise

At the time that the VanCronkhites felt their hearts being transformed David began to critique modern Christianity's blind attraction to the American dream. A reporter for the *Atlanta Journal-Constitution* offered the following description of David's evaluation of the dream in relation to the Kingdom of God: "As he talks about the passion of his life—building relationships with the poor—he chooses words carefully, not so much speaking as thinking aloud. And what he thinks is that the dream he once lived is an enemy of American Christians. 'There's this competition for the Kingdom of God and it's called the American dream,' he said. 'And they're in conflict with one another because they both demand 100 percent commitment'" (Daigle 2002, B1).

David VanCronkhite was no stranger to the American dream. He tells how he once earned a high-six-figure salary as a CEO at a hospital information systems company based in California. The salary "afforded him a BMW, Porsche, Mercedes convertible, and regular cruises and exotic vacations," along with other material rewards granted by the dream (Daigle 2003, 70). In 1993 he was offered a job that would have given him a "huge increase" over this existing salary. David recalls that he was trying to "sort out his life" when he heard God speak to him: "David, I'll bless you in the business world, but I'll bless you even more if you'll go to the poor." David interpreted these words as an invitation rather than a command, and he chose to say yes. Although he would continue to critique the American dream, untangling himself from its hold was never easy. It was years later that he would finally sell his house in the suburbs, and even then he found himself living in downtown gentrified Atlanta rather than with the poor.

David says he likes to "hang" (out) with the poor, but he has never actually lived in their midst. Although some of his followers made their primary dwelling among those they served, David's main residence was never with the disinherited and displaced. For years after establishing BnF, David and Janice remained in suburban Norcross, and their beautiful home stayed on the market for over five years. VanCronkhite often expressed a puzzled wonderment as to why his house wouldn't sell when other homes in the area sold so quickly. As he often does when in a quandary, he posed the question to God. According to David, God replied, "If I let you sell the house and you move into the Warehouse, you would expect everyone else to do the same." He said that God wanted to soften his heart so that he would not judge those who chose not to live among the poor, and it took years to finally bring him to that place. When David did sell his suburban house, his plan was to move into the simple accommodations of the Warehouse (as one of the two buildings came specifically to be known) with some of his followers and recovering addicts who already lived there. But the plan took a turn when he was offered a lovely, newly built condominium overlooking the pool area in a gated, gentrified community not too far from the warehouse complex. Reportedly, in submission to Papa Jack, David made the decision to accept the offer of a wealthy benefactor to live rent-free in this upscale community. As we rode with David to visit the condominium during the initial site visit prior to formally beginning our research, the electronic garage door opened to reveal a large dog eagerly rushing out to greet the car. Ralph quipped, "David, I have the title for your next book—At Least the Dog Is Black." The remark was met with silence, but it clearly reflected Ralph's skepticism that BnF was actually about transforming the lives of the poor.

Around the time of our visit David had the opportunity to purchase a lake house an hour-and-a-half drive outside Atlanta from a BnF leader who was about to begin an affiliate community in Asheville, North Carolina. David's detailed story about the acquisition of the property would appear on BnF's Web site when the VanCronkhites moved out of the condominium and took up more or less full-time residence in the lake house. The story of "Diamonds on the Lake" began with a dream that his wife, Janice, had in 1999 about seeing herself on the deck of a house that looked out over shimmering water, "like diamonds on the water" (http://www.bloodnfire.com; accessed December 15, 2004). David Kula, a former successful corporate attorney from Chicago, and his wife, Val, bought a lot in "the beautiful retreat on Lake Oconee" and had a large home built on it when they came to work with BnF. It turned out to be the house of Janice's dream; when Janice would visit, she noted how the shimmering lake seemed studded with diamonds. When the Kulas decided to move to Asheville and begin a new BnF ministry there, they offered to sell the home to the VanCronkhites. David, who admittedly had been critical about the Kulas living in such luxury, was originally reluctant to purchase the property. Perhaps ironically, David felt persuaded that God swept away his doubts and creatively showed him the way to enjoy the beautiful lake house without abandoning the vision that was so critical of the American dream and its opulent lifestyle.

Two divine proclamations were given to the reluctant and confused David—one to him personally in prayer and the other through a well-known prophetess, Cindy Jacobs. In both God told David that he was to "get the house"; it was "Janice's dream house," not his. A deal was made and financing was "miraculously" provided (as was a later refinancing at a lower rate of interest); the property was titled in Janice's name. But David remained uneasy and made excuses for purchasing the house. He shared his dilemma as follows: "My message proclaimed: 'Leave the American dream, leave the riches of the world; go after the poor and the have-nots. Be voluntarily displaced from the riches to be in relationship with the poor.' Yet my wife owned a beautiful lake house in a wealthy resort area. Talk about hypocritical!"

Once again God spoke to him with a command that "was firm and to the point." David heard God say, "David, quit cursing what I have blessed you with." After this word, David turned to the Scriptures and was able to quiet his qualms about fine living in the midst of a ministry to the poor: "Jesus was the One who said, 'Seek first the Kingdom of God and all these things will be added to you.' Regardless of my embarrassment or my concern for what man will say or think, He is God. If He wants to bless in ways that seem contrary to me, He is still God."

Yet former members of BnF as well as outside observers who questioned David's lifestyle shared Ralph's cynicism about whether it was really God who instructed them to live so well and beyond the pale of mundane financial consequences. Duane Crabbs, founder and pastor of South Street Mission in Akron, Ohio (who attended one of VanCronkhite's conferences), wrote the following assessment after reading an earlier draft of this manuscript:

> In the prophetic, the coherence between the message and the messenger is especially critical. It is called integrity. In challenging the dominant social structures of a society (principalities and powers) it is critical to be as free as possible of the influence of those structures. We are to be in the world but not of it. When David did not sell his house and move among the poor, I believe he disobeyed God. All of His words of knowledge and inability to submit to any authority become self-serving rationalizations in the midst of his rejection of the truly prophetic call to a radical lifestyle. Jeremiah, Hosea, Jesus and the apostle Paul all exhibit an unbalanced extreme message, but it was shored up by their equally unbalanced extreme commitment in their personal lives. David has sacrificed much and still has a prophetic gift, but the major disconnect between his life and his words has emasculated the work. God is no longer speaking to him for he quenched and grieved the Spirit. (Personal e-mail to Margaret, March 12, 2007)

A person who served as a model for Crabbs when he moved into what he calls "the 'hood'" in Akron ten years earlier came from VanCronkhite's turf. Bob Lupton (2005), founder and president of FCS Urban Ministries in Atlanta, believed that urban ministers needed to reside within their communities. Lupton also served as a BnF board member. Although David once taught the importance of living with the poor for those who would turn their back on the American dream, he came to reverse his position. More and more of his time would be spent at the lake house and less and less at the downtown warehouse. While our empirical evidence does not permit us to accept or reject VanCronkhite's accounts of divine revelation, we do note the effects that this change of the original vision had on the interaction rituals within BnF.

The primary stories are David's and they were told and reinforced in IRs within BnF's inner circle of followers. For his close disciples, David's stories assumed myth-like properties that provided a source of emotional energy supporting the godly love that was lived out by many followers, who themselves reported frequent IRs with God. In varying degrees they renounced the American dream as they gave up potentially lucrative careers, aspirations for advanced degrees, and lives in suburbia to live out their understanding of the vision at BnF. Few of the poor and homeless were involved in the IRs that shaped and reshaped the changing BnF vision, and they were not energized by the emotional energy these rituals generated within BnF's inner circle. Although many of the homeless heard the stories, they failed to find the vision presented by David to have much relevance for their daily lives.

God, David, and the Warehouse

Perhaps no single story is more central to BnF's interaction rituals than the acquisition of the warehouse property. It became a tangible symbol of David and God's partnership that gave BnF its mandate of a radical commitment to the poor.

During the earliest years of BnF's existence its base, as we have seen, was the Atlanta Vineyard, from where suburban volunteers came to the city each Saturday to pass out groceries, to pray for those they visited, and to "take the ministry to the streets." Vineyard leaders in California had learned from the Jesus People Movement in the 1970s how to take the Gospel and their new worship music to the beaches and the parks where the people played (Di Sabatino 1999; Jackson 1999). While there are no beaches in Atlanta, the band from the suburbs soon learned that inner-city neighbors can be brought together with music and food. Some defectors have asserted that this period of street ministry without property ownership represented BnF in its purest form. This was a time, they noted, when the emerging BnF community played and prayed in the projects and parks where the poor and homeless lived. Certainly the scope of the ministry could never have developed as it did without something like the warehouse complex; but, whether viewed through the eyes of nostalgia or reality, those who noted the change in the ministry believe they have a point. There was a price to be paid for the growth of the ministry as more energy was put into the acquisition, development, and maintenance of the warehouse property. During the time when "street ministry" was emphasized, BnF was forced to interact on the turf of the poor and homeless rather than "inviting" the poor and homeless to be "guests" to the BnF "home."

But VanCronkhite and his followers believed that the acquisition of the warehouse was not the product of human striving but rather a gift from God. When in 1993 David learned that the warehouse complex across from Capitol Homes was for sale, he reported to his followers that God told him, "That is your building, go and get it." God even told him the amount he was to offer for the property. Accounts in print are more likely to use the words "I was impressed" rather than "God told me," but in verbally telling the story David often says, "God told me," "God led me," and "God says." According to David, God told him to offer $550,000 for the property, a fraction of the appraisal price. The offer was turned town. Reportedly the complex was sold a couple of times, but none of the transactions went through. VanCronkhite continued to repeat his offer, telling the owner that was what God told him to pay for the property. As time passed and deals fell apart, the owner finally called him one day and said, "Come and get your property." David arrived with his attorney, and the owner asked for a down payment. David didn't have the money. In total frustration the owner reportedly worked out a financial deal that gave VanCronkhite the property in a settlement that required periodic payments, which if not met, would result in the return of the warehouse buildings to their former owner. That arrangement kept the saga going for years until the final payment was made. As due dates would arrive and BnF bank accounts were empty, the needed money would arrive just in the nick of time. For David and his followers, it was an ongoing miracle.

Margaret visited BnF the week before the final payment for the warehouse property was due in spring of 2001. During lunch with David and some other followers, David commented that he needed over three hundred thousand dollars the following week or BnF was going to "lose the warehouse." Margaret asked where he was going to get it. David replied, "I don't know; I certainly don't have it. It's God's problem. He's the one who told me to purchase the property; He's going to have to provide." Margaret heard nothing more about the situation until she received a newsletter dated August 2001 with the following account:

> There was this letter . . . arrived in the mail addressed to Mr. Crokite [*sic*] . . . , "Dear Mr. Crokite, enclosed please find a check in the amount of $100,000" . . . from an anonymous donor . . . when added to the other $203,000 so generously given by the business community of Atlanta, we were able to pay off the balance of our debt on the Warehouse . . . right on time and paid in full . . . without a fund-raiser, a mass appeal (though in my "strong faith" I certainly entertained the thoughts more than once). In 1993 God said, "that's your building, go get it" and he has provided in every way ever since.

We see the story of the purchase of the warehouse, abbreviated by David to stress the role of the supernatural in the transaction, as a mythic symbol for BnF followers. It demonstrates the process described by Collins in his theory of interaction ritual chains, a theory that we modify to include perceived interactions with the divine. It provides a detailed illustration of how God spoke to David, how God provided for BnF, and how things work in the Kingdom of God that takes seriously accounts of religious experience. It became one of the stories that was central for BnF's vision and values, an example of an element Collins has defined as central to IRs—where "participants develop a mutual focus of attention and become entrained in each other's bodily micro-rhythms and emotions" (2004, 47). The myth of the warehouse is not simply an ethereal account but included a solid reminder in battered brick and decaying mortar of God's promise to make the Kingdom of God tangible in the city of Atlanta.

Centrality of the Kingdom Value

In discussing the development of Kingdom of God theology in the emerging church movement, Eddie Gibbs and Ryan Bolger present the following short description of its central thrust: "Emerging churches embrace the gospel of the kingdom as revealed in Mark 1:5–16. At the outset of the gospel narrative, the good news was not that Jesus was to die on the cross

to forgive sins but that God had returned and all were invited to participate with him in this new way of life, in this redemption of the world. It is
this gospel that the emerging church seeks to recover" (2005, 54).

Although John Wimber and the new-paradigm churches began a new
emphasis on the now-present Kingdom of God, David VanCronkhite, and
leaders of other emerging churches, "stress the Kingdom of God much
more than their new-paradigm/purpose-driven/seeker parents ever did"
(Gibbs and Bolger 2005, 54). David's succinct summary of the BnF journey toward ushering in the Kingdom can be found in his Sunday morning worship e-mail of January 28, 2006, a time during which he and his
followers sought to rebuild the schism-ravaged BnF: "It's done! 15 years
of daily searching have brought us to the simplicity and the practicality
of Blood-n-Fire Church Atlanta . . . from redux through consolidation
to reconstitution. The restoring of the simplicity of who we are as a community of believers, the simplicity of the God-given vision and mission,
and the practicality of walking out another facet of the local body called
Blood-n-Fire Church Atlanta. And most important, the singularity of the
values; i.e., all encompassing value—the Kingdom of God is at hand!"

According to David, BnF is now entering the third phase of its "journey as a body of believers." The first phase involved "soaking in the reality
of a faith walk, the reality of the supernatural for us today." The account
of the acquisition of the warehouse properties provides, as we have seen,
a central myth for this period. The second phase "was about relationships
within the family of believers and the awareness that relationships are difficult even when they begin with him." We will develop this phase, already
noted as marked by a transition from "army" to "relational community,"
more fully in the next chapter. The third phase focuses on "the simplicity and practicality of the supernatural lifestyle becoming natural in the
context of called community walking out the very practical day-to-day
lifestyle." For David, as for John Wimber, Kingdom living is accompanied
by "signs and wonders" that empower believers to bring the Good News
to the world.

Proclaiming that God's kingdom is at hand, as we have seen, has been
the central teaching of BnF, rooted in biblical texts and as taught by John
Wimber and the Association of Vineyard Churches that he founded. The
"Vineyard Statement of Faith" contains numerous references to the Kingdom of God, as reflected in the following statement: "WE BELIEVE that
the whole world is under the domination of Satan and that all people
are sinners by nature and choice. All people therefore are under God's

judgment. Through the preaching of the Good News of Jesus and Kingdom of God and the work of the Holy Spirit, God regenerates, justifies,
adopts and sanctifies through Jesus by the Spirit all who repent of their
sins and trust in Jesus Christ as Lord and Savior. By this they are released
from Satan's domain and enter into God's kingdom reign" (Jackson 1999,
411). Many orthodox Christian believers could affirm this statement of
faith. As with most creeds, however, dissention comes in the details.

David's understanding of the details about the Kingdom of God has
been tweaked throughout the years, particularly as it relates to the role of
the poor and marginalized in ushering it into being. In assigning the poor
a central role in this vision, David seemed to radicalize Wimber's original position. This version of the vision was toned down and seemingly
restored to a Vineyard-like "radical middle" during the schism at BnF.
Each modification of the vision brought with it repeated calls for "repentance" or turning away from the old and toward a new way of viewing the
Kingdom. In one of his stories, David recounts how he experienced the
call to "get back to the Kingdom of God"—to make it central to all BnF
values and teachings. David had been talking with some youth in one of
Atlanta's projects and felt that they were asking him to provide something
that would compete with the "highs" (drink, drugs, and sex) of street life.
In a talk later with his "spiritual papa, Jack Taylor," he told Taylor of his
frustration and discouragement:

> They say help, but I've got nothing . . . a church service . . . they're not
> interested; a teaching . . . heard em; a church program . . . they've been
> there . . . so, I said, "Jack, what do I do?" He pondered all of a few sec-
> onds, made a statement and asked a question, "Well, David, you have to
> get back to the Kingdom of God!" He said, "We often make the mistake
> of treating it just like another subject to be taught." Then he warned me,
> "Don't bring the Kingdom of God down to the level of another teach-
> ing. There is the Kingdom of God and Jesus and there is nothing else of
> its magnitude. Everything else fits into the kingdom or outside the king-
> dom!" (VanCronkhite 2002, 38)

Values of the Kingdom

There is a certain underlying sameness we sense in the modifications
and different expressions of values and vision over BnF's history that reflects the abstract nature of the concept *Kingdom of God*. When we first

explored the possibility of doing research at BnF in the summer of 2002, David presented us with four "values" that were essential to Kingdom building. While these values remain implicit in the newer expanded list found on the BnF Web site, there are modifications that suggest shifts in focus (http://www.bloodnfire.com; accessed January 29, 2005; again February 1, 2006). The six values listed in 2006 as ones for which BnF has "a call and anointing" include

Power Evangelism—Proclamation of the Kingdom of God and demonstration of its power
Poor and Oppressed—Compassion and justice in the city
Creative Combustion—intimate, yet fierce, raging worship
Twelve—intense commitment to relationship
Giving Lifestyle—extravagant giving at all times
City Presence

"Power evangelism," a term made popular by John Wimber, has been used with or without being explicitly identified with Wimber since BnF's earliest inception. It is the force behind David's vision of the Kingdom and all the other values on this particular list. It is through the power of the Holy Spirit, as made manifest by the paranormal Pentecostal "signs and wonders" (including glossolalia, prophecy, healing, and miracles), that believers are empowered to powerfully proclaim the coming Kingdom of God.

"Creative combustion" (at least in its present form and nomenclature) was a newcomer to the list in 2006. It reflects another related core criterion (Kingdom theology being first) of emerging churches, namely "transforming secular space." As Gibbs and Bolger note, "Emerging churches tear down the secular spaces, times, or activities. To emerging churches, all of life must be made sacred" (2005, 66). In new-paradigm churches, this core value was often limited to adopting and adapting a different style of worship service, often held in secular-appearing structures. (The mall-like characteristic of many mega-churches is a good illustration of this new-paradigm principle.) For emerging churches, however, creative worship is more radical by "arising out of local cultural contexts" (Gibbs and Bolger 2005, 75) that reflect a "whole-life spirituality" that seeks to effectively dismantle the great divide between the sacred and the secular.

Creative combustion is but one marker of BnF's attempt to make the community culturally relevant, especially to the youthful volunteers. With the feel of a rave party, church gatherings designated as "creative combustion" were an attraction for many who had tired even of new-paradigm services. The "fierce raging worship" included the trendy sound of club music, use of candles, and exuberant dance. It also included a spontaneous use of a wider range of the arts in worship, especially painting and poetry. The new interest in "the arts," as we will later see, paralleled Janice VanCronkhite's developing career as a religiously inspired artist.

The remaining three BnF values—"extravagant giving," the "twelve," and "city presence"—are rooted in an interrelated core criterion for emerging churches, namely, living as community. Gibbs and Bolger describe the quest-for-community criterion as follows:

> Emerging churches believe that the church should shape its corporate life in accordance with the practices of the Kingdom of God that Jesus inaugurated in his ministry. . . . Emerging churches create a space for the Kingdom of God to enter their midst. They commit to the community that follows this King and lets their other loyalties take a backseat. . . . They display a willingness to abandon old church forms as they dramatically restructure their communities. They abhor the idea of church as a meeting, a place, a routine. Clearly, for these communities, church is a people, a community, a rhythm, a way of life, a way of connectedness with other Christ followers in the world. (2006, 115)

VanCronkhite's values of the Kingdom took on new dimensions over the years, expanding beyond John Wimber's emphasis on power evangelism to weave in other elements, including family-like relationships within BnF, use of the arts in worship, extravagant giving, and purchasing property that would give BnF a visible presence in Atlanta. From its earliest days of coming to downtown projects from suburban communities to deliver groceries, host street parties, and pray for those who came to receive, however, the poor and homeless were at the heart of this vision. According to David, the Bible demonstrates that God has a special love for the poor and broken—developing relationships with them was not an option for those who called themselves Christians.

Relationships, Community Building, and the Twelve

Although BnF may have begun its journey using army metaphors, by 1998 there was a shift underway toward becoming more relational—toward becoming a family. The "family" under discussion was not the nuclear one of the American dream but the spiritual family of God's Kingdom. And the poor and the broken were envisioned to play a central role in this extended family of believers.

David noted that when he first began his ministry, he had his own preconceptions about what it would look like: "I pictured myself compassionately proclaiming the Kingdom of God, evangelizing, teaching, inviting signs and wonders, and providing food, clothing, and temporary shelter for the homeless and rejected" (VanCronkhite 2003, 1). David goes on to tell how his perspective of ministry changed:

> Something didn't quite add up. As I began to spend time with the homeless and hurting on some of Atlanta's worst crime and drug-infested streets, I realized that seldom did the "poor and needy in the land" complain about their lack of food or shelter, and most knew the Bible pretty well. I rarely saw a man or a woman cry because they had no meal to fill an empty stomach, or because they had no comfortable mattress to lie on at night. But I had dozens weeping in my arms because they believed no one loved them and that they were alone in an unjust world where no one cried if they lived or died. They were inconsolably hopeless because they had no family or meaningful relationships. (VanCronkhite 2003, 1)

David recognized that the people on the streets took and were grateful for the material needs met by providers, but he became aware of what he believed was a root problem that beset not only the poor but all of America. David writes: "I learned that we have often mislabeled the people on the streets as homeless when, in fact, they are relation-less. . . . What they really want is what most in America really want—to belong to a family that cares, listens, demands, and gives one to another. In other words, they want to be part of a family that will just love them. Such, it seems, is the plight of not only the inner city of Atlanta but also our entire nation" (VanCronkhite 2003, 1).

David believed that he had a God-given solution to the problem, one that came to be known simply as "The Twelve." The seeds for the Twelve were planted during a God encounter in March 1998—seeds that took several years to sprout and grow into a plan to change BnF into a more relational community. As David tells the story, "The worship band is playing, and the aroma of barbequed chicken basting on the pits entices the passersby, prostitutes, and strangers in this Atlanta neighborhood to come and join us. . . . 'Ministry' is happening all around us" (VanCronkhite 2003, 4). David goes on to report: "Suddenly I hear it. And I know it's God. 'David,' He says, "it was about midnight and Paul and Silas were in prison, and they were singing songs and praying to Me. I heard them, and I did some signs and wonders and set prisoners free. If you will sing songs and pray to Me where the prisoners can hear, I will set them free. I will do signs and wonders. Signs and wonders are nothing for Me. But David, where will they go?" (VanCronkhite 2003, 4).

David says that he "didn't understand the depth or the implication of the question for several years" because he was "so caught up in the signs and wonders and in trying to understand the grace and favor of His promise to set prisoners free, which He did every week" (VanCronkhite 2003, 4). David credits God's beginning "transforming relationships" in his own life that cast light on God's call for BnF to become a relational community.

The change going on within VanCronkhite began a radical move that resulted in a seismic shift for BnF, taking it further away from the new-paradigm churches and toward the emerging church movement. Although located in an overwhelmingly black community, BnF's worshipping church had attracted largely white suburbanites. They gathered faithfully with the community and generously supported the church and its attendant ministry for the poor. One day David announced that Sunday services would no longer be held at the warehouse. Reports that reached Margaret in Akron, Ohio, indicated that David told the suburbanites to "take their checks and leave." It wasn't until several months later in talking with David that she learned the rest of the story. When asked about the exodus David said, "I never told them to take their checks; they could still send them if they wanted. I was concerned that these people came to the city and to BnF to 'feel good' on Sunday mornings; they never came during the week to enter into relationships with the poor. BnF still worships together; we just don't do it on Sunday mornings. If the suburbanites want to be part of what we do, they'll just have to come during the week to be with us as we are with the broken and the homeless."

Relationships and community were important to David, and this seemingly rash move cost BnF thousands of dollars each month. With income falling from about fifty thousand dollars to three thousand dollars and attendance dropping from between four hundred and six hundred each Sunday to less than one hundred who worshipped with BnF during the week, many former Sunday attendees did leave and did indeed take their checks with them. In a story he titled "The Cash Cow" David tells of a "revelation" ("like a prophetic picture, a movie") that he received about the larger Christian church that strengthened his resolve. It involved a greatly loved masterpiece painting that was the "cash cow" for the museum that owned it as people came from far and wide to view it. When the directors learned that there might be even a better picture underneath the top painting, they faced a dilemma. Could they afford to risk losing their "cash cow" to a mere possibility?

> Then I realized, this was a revelation about the Church. That over the centuries we have added so much tradition and custom to the simplicity of the Gospel and to the gathering of the "saints," that we "believers" have forgotten what the picture was intended to represent. And we are scared to make drastic changes because it could alter our "cash cow" . . . the Sunday Service and its supporting programs. We have people more than willing to support a structure that fits their schedule and their perception of what Church should be . . . what tradition cries out for, but will they support a more authentic cry for relationship with God and one another? (VanCronkhite 2002, 18)

David showed a willingness to sacrifice his "cash cow," initially at great cost to BnF. As is often the case with David's stories, this one too had a happy ending. The departure of a large number of white suburbanites changed the racial composition of the Sunday morning services (which resumed two and a half years later) from heavily affluent and white attendance to primarily poor and black. And as the story ends, the Sunday collections slowly made their way back up to earlier figures. The "cash cow" was clearly worth sacrificing for the vision David had for BnF as a "church of the poor."

David believed he heard clearly about the importance of relationships that included both the poor and the rich, but he remained in a quandary about how to bring substance to the vision. Then he heard of a program developed in Bogotá that provided him with the key to building the Kingdom through developing relationships. As a friend told him about the Group of Twelve (G-Twelve) that was making its way from Colombia in South America into the larger U.S. charismatic movement, David again knew that God was speaking to him about change in the community: "I began to dream about a relational community where one person invests his life in twelve others who, in turn, invest their lives in twelve others. In the span of a few breaths, my heart dramatically changed from one focused on ministry and numbers to one committed to building a community through what I now call BnF (Blood-N-Fire) Twelve" (Van-Cronkhite 2003, 6).

The Twelves were in place when we began our research at BnF—for those who belonged to the BnF church as well as the poor who lived in the Sanctuary and the recovering addicts who lived in the Warehouse. David and Janice were at the center with their Twelve (in fact, more like thirty or forty people were involved in this "inner circle"), and each of these "leaders" were to establish a Twelve of their own to disciple, and these disciples were to establish Twelves of their own. David saw it as the biblical way to build communities in which to live out other Kingdom values, including evangelism and "extravagant giving."

But the real purpose of the Twelve was relationship, the lifeblood of any truly emerging church. As David saw it, "When the purpose of Twelve becomes anything other than relationship, it is no longer Twelve. It becomes a program. It becomes purpose driven, not relationally driven. Relationship has a singular purpose—love" (VanCronkhite 2003, 19). While relationship remains a basic BnF value, David has more recently critiqued his early understanding of Twelve and the way it operated in the pre-schismatic BnF. The intimacy fostered in the Twelve sometimes had erotic undertones. This phenomenon is common in females attracted to charismatic male leaders (Jacobs 1989) and it would create problems for BnF, as it has for some other emerging churches (Gibbs and Bolger 2005). In the case of BnF, we heard no direct allegations of any specific sexual abuse, but some of the members did question David's relationship with his spiritual daughters. Ex-members were especially likely to report stories to demonstrate the subtle but real hold that David had on his women disciples. After the schism, when David worked to reestablish himself as BnF's sole legitimate authority, he "repented" mostly nebulous "sins" that he perceived brought about the serious crisis facing the community. One particular yet vaguely described subject of repentance was David's having "perverted" the Twelve in allowing his "daughters" to assume a place that rightfully belonged to his wife in the community.

City Presence and "Watching Atlanta"

One meaning given to "city presence" (as implied in some of the quotes used in this chapter) is the presence of BnF as a ministry to the poor and broken. It was about compassion; the VanCronkhite often said, "We have learned to do compassion, but we have no idea what it means to do justice." Although more mention came to be made of justice issues as the homeless find themselves driven from their homes and from the parks of Atlanta through gentrification and restrictive legislation, we believe BnF still showed little understanding of how it might be effectively involved in securing justice for the poor. David's vision only occasionally touched on "structural inadequacies" and poverty that underlies homelessness. The vision seemed to reflect the larger American framework on poverty that focuses on "individual deficiencies" rather than "structural dynamics" (Rank 2005).

"Taking Atlanta," however, remains for David a prophetic promise. Increasing attention has been paid to developing this narrative and establishing it as BnF's central myth. David has a twofold vision for Atlanta. The first involves seeing Atlanta transformed; the second is seeing this transformation spread to other cities around the globe. David shares his revelation of the first promise as follows:

> Ten years ago as Janice and I went to the inner-city, we had a vision of rebuilding cities that included "doing the stuff"; ministry, evangelism, worship, prophecy, signs and wonders, intercession and the basics of feeding the poor, giving shelter and clothing. . . . Then our heart [*sic*] was captivated by new pieces of the vision stirred by prophetic words. We started with the simple understanding of "rebuilding cities by planting churches of the poor in the inner cities" which came from a proclamation of seeing stadiums filled with youth and poor, lines miles long, with people trying to get in to hear nameless and faceless men and women of God proclaiming the Good News with unbelievable healings taking place . . . Atlanta was being transformed. I still believe it's going to happen, ten years later. (VanCronkhite 2002, 14)

VanCronkhite states that God has repeatedly said, "David, go take Atlanta," and he developed at least one plan for putting flesh on the vision. It began with an area around the state capitol known as the "capitol corridor." This vision for "taking Atlanta" included the purchase of properties in each of the four areas that made up the corridor. As David wrote in the newsletter of February 2002, "Blood-n-Fire has new places to 'go and take' . . . 4th Ward, West End, Broad Street and Simpson/Ashby. If one is familiar with our inner city, one will understand why we are to go there. There is so much we still do not understand but He just said go and give away His love wherever we go. So it's back to the streets (thank you, Lord) and it's getting more buildings for more community presence."

With these buildings now sold in the financial crunch after the schism, there is no longer much talk about the "capitol corridor"; but the original prophetic word to "go take Atlanta" remains very much alive. Atlanta is seen as a strategic city for the spread of the Kingdom of God and BnF an important player in the vision of ushering in the Kingdom of God around the world. David's narrative of the lake house ("Diamonds on the Lake") concludes with a statement that demonstrates his view that BnF's story was beginning anew at a time during which former members and outsiders were asserting that BnF was but a dying remnant of the former community. In a post-schism encounter with the divine, David heard God saying: "David, if you go to the poor I will bless you more than corporate America ever could in every way . . . That 3.7 acres of land you call the Warehouse is yours . . . David, get that lake house for Janice . . . David, look at Atlanta and be amazed for I am going to do something that you would not believe even if I told . . . The diamonds on the lake . . . the story is just beginning" (VanCronkhite at http://www.bloodnfire.com; accessed February 2, 2006).

Myths constructed through IRs between David and God are central for understanding the interaction ritual chains that supply an important "mutual focus" for the community. They provide a vision for living out religion in this emerging church and in its church-based ministry. After the schism and the breakdown of BnF's viable ministry, the vision would become more ethereal as greater emphasis was placed on "taking Atlanta and the nations" for God and less on familial relationships with the poor and the broken.

3

An Emerging Church Family and the Family Business

Emerging churches raise basic questions about the nature of church. Is it the place where weekly worship services are conducted, or is it a network of relationships? Emerging churches utilize the gospel both to dismantle and to rebuild church forms, marking a significant shift of emphasis from church to kingdom. The practice of inclusion creates a new kind of family. If a church begins to look like a family, then all its institutional practices will undergo change. Church as family is primarily about relationships.

—Gibbs and Bolger 2005, 96–97

The BnF narrative that we began in the last chapter embodies a simple story line. David VanCronkhite hears from God. We describe the relationship between David and his God as an interactive ritual (IR) commonly known as prayer (Poloma and Gallup 1991; Poloma 2003). As social scientists we choose not to dismiss divine-human IRs, to reduce them to "self-talk" or "thought chains," or to reframe prophetic prayer experiences as "the social process of thinking" (Collins 2004, esp. ch. 5). In accord with a methodological agnostic stance, we take VanCronkhite's descriptions seriously and explore possible empirical outcomes related to his IRs with what David knows to be God. It is this interface of perceived divine action with human actions that we are calling godly love.

A straightforward reading of VanCronkhite's stories reveals a God who has been intimately involved in the development of BnF's vision and values. Without dismissing David's belief in encountering God, we nevertheless find examples of human IRs in all of the stories. David's reported transformation experience began with an IR at a religious conference, his vision of the Kingdom of God is rooted in John Wimber's AVC, the BnF name was confirmed at a rally in Canada, and the Booth anointing came through the prayer of another prophet. Throughout the BnF story we see both perceived divine-human and human-human IRs linked together, producing and recharging emotional energy within this emerging church.

IRs, as Collins has stressed, are variables and not constants: "They do not always succeed; they range from mere ingredients to high solidarity" (2004, 219). In the case of BnF, the "success" or "failure" of its IRs are mirrored less by any ethereal vision than by its church and ministry. Whatever else it may be, Blood-n-Fire has always been first and foremost a church with a mission. The story of the "killing of the cash cow" presented in the last chapter marked a seismic shift for BnF, away from its new-paradigm origins toward becoming an emerging church. During the two-year period when Sunday morning services were suspended, the congregation and its ministry changed its focus from a central weekly common religious ritual toward a focus on familial relationships, relationships that would include Atlanta's poor, homeless, and marginalized. This structure consists of two important, interrelated components—components that came to be called "the church family" and "the family business"—both of which were central for putting institutional flesh on an otherwise abstract vision.

BnF as an Emerging Church

Meaningful relationships, especially relationships with the poor, were a core value for the BnF vision and mission. Abandoning the army metaphor for that of loving relationships and family, David provided the vision and the leadership for interpreting what it meant to be part of this intentional community. The metaphor of BnF as family could be heard by the mid-1990s when Margaret attended the "If I Have Withheld" conference, which over the next three years gave rise to the BnF Twelve. By early January 2003 when we formally began our research project, the Twelve was regarded as the specific God-given plan for living out familial relations. David described the "heart of BnF Twelve" as follows:

> Above all, BnF Twelve stands for intense commitment to relational community. It means daily personal investment in the lives of individuals who are building trust and love for one another. It is to know and be known. BnF Twelve is a revelational process of building life-long relationships. BnF Twelve is also a very slow process for growth and, thus, not easy

or popular. It requires a huge, upfront investment of life, just like Jesus modeled for us through his life, death and resurrection. It is one day, one meal, and one phone call at a time. (VanCronkhite 2003, 10)

The plan was described in newspaper article in the *Atlanta Journal-Constitution* under the headline, "Saving Souls—12 X 12," referring to the number of persons set for the ideal-sized small group (Daigle 2002). Like many programs espoused by BnF, this plan was fluid; its guidelines, abstract; its boundaries, permeable. Change rather than stability is basic to BnF plans and programs, forcing the structure to quickly modify to reflect David's visions. David's flexibility was somewhat frustrating to some family members who appreciated the role that set norms and expectations have for normal life.

A by-product of this openness to change and fluidity of structure is an absence of simple formal elements like membership lists or formal criteria for becoming part of the family; BnF relies instead on affective signs and symbols to provide permeable boundaries. Talk about love flowed freely and genuinely at BnF, as it does in many charismatic communities.

It was David who was able to bequeath the familial status on those outside the immediate community, and he who verbally adopted many "sons" and "daughters." David frequently radiated both passion and compassion in reaching out to others with his message about family. We observed that middle-aged adherents were often less enthusiastic about the family nomenclature than were younger members, who appeared to be searching for genuine and lasting family relationships—or perhaps for a powerful father figure. While David encouraged younger adult members to call him "Dad" and his wife "Mom," middle-aged followers were less likely to accord David this parental role. For the homeless whom BnF served through its family business, *the Twelve* and *family* were terms they simply ignored (if they were at all familiar with them).

This is not to imply that the poor failed to appreciate the work that BnF was doing on their behalf, but only that they were unable to identify with its emphasis on being a "church family." For example, Phil, the longest continuous "shelter" resident of BnF, told us that BnF "saved his life." He was grateful for whatever BnF believed—as long as it led members to support the shelter. He had a bed to sleep in and food to eat in a place that was a temporary shelter for most but a permanent residence for him. Phil observed the frequent flux at BnF from the sidelines and remained noncommittal when tensions periodically developed within the church family. It seemed that whatever was going on, Phil had seen it before and watching without comment was the safest stance to take.

The familial love talk could be both confusing and inspiring. It might take a while for visitors to realize that the homeless black man that David had his arm around and introduced as a "son" was someone who showed up from time to time but had no significant ongoing relationship with David. Being David's favored "son" was a tenuous position, whether the person was poor and homeless or a committed leader and member of the BnF community. Middle-class young adults, many of whom seemed to covet David's approval, could be basking in "sonship" one day only to find themselves marginalized as new "sons" and "daughters" moved into favor. Godly love's ideal qualities of intensity and duration are perhaps humanly impossible to balance to everyone's satisfaction. Intense familial love can be shared with only a limited number of people, and the BnF members who valued David's special love often found themselves playing a game of musical chairs. The homeless seemed to take in stride this dissonance between talk about love and the realities of social distance between David and his spiritual offspring. As Larry, one long-time homeless shelter resident who has come, gone, and returned again over the years, commented to Margaret, "This is a big family. Just like in other very big families, you don't always get to know everybody. If you have many brothers and sisters, you know what I mean. David has a lot of people around him. He is in the center, and I am on an outer ring. I can't expect him to have time to stop and talk with me."

David's theology about loving relationships was simply that "we cannot become all God intends us to become without the continual life, love, and nurturing of others pouring into us. There is just no way anyone can walk out his or her salvation, no matter how dramatic and powerful the conversion and revelation of Jesus, without a family to spiritually mature in" (VanCronkhite 2003, 11). The story David once liked to tell to demonstrate the importance of the BnF family involved an encounter that Chris Franklin, then chief of staff for BnF's ministries, had with a Muslim drug dealer during an outreach trip to London (where BnF once had an established ministry). Chris met Charlie in Piccadilly Square, where Charlie became "impressed with Chris's authority and forthrightness in declaring the power of Jesus Christ." Chris and Charlie hung out together for two days, after which "Charlie finally declared his desire for Jesus in his life." He rejected his Muslim faith and drug dealing, asking "Jesus to change him and make his life meaningful." As the story goes, "Immediately Charlie began to exhibit physical manifestations and gifts, including speaking in a supernatural language (tongues) that undeniably expressed God's love and sovereignty in his life. He had what many would consider an uncommonly dramatic and supernatural encounter with the risen Jesus" (VanCronkhite 2003, 11–12). David has little patience with non-Christian religions. He perceives his commitment to Jesus to require an absolute rejection of other faiths. Followers of Islam may be fed, but if they cannot accept Jesus at some point, they will be asked to leave the shelter. BnF is about the Kingdom of God, and commitment to his only begotten son, Jesus. Two years later Chris returned to London and found Charlie "still in Piccadilly Square." Charlie's conversion proved to be short-lived. Although he still remembered his "dynamic conversion experience," his "life was in a worse state than before." David questioned how this could be and then provided the following didactic response: "The answer is pretty easy. Charlie had no family or community walking out a supernatural life of love and power with him. There were none willing to say, 'Charlie, come be in my family. Let's walk out this supernatural life together. We love you as you are, and we will do whatever is necessary to see God's destiny in you fulfilled'" (VanCronkhite 2003, 12).

While the vision of family as a relational community remains intact in BnF, the structure and practices that emerged at BnF Atlanta would eventually be a cause for "repentance" and change in the aftermath of the schism. In observing the Twelve in operation during our study, we noted that it had an onion-like quality of layered and stratified interaction. Some members were much closer to David than others, and we perceived this to be a function of personal attractions. David and Janice's Twelve was decidedly larger than any other (twenty to forty followers might be present for a gathering), and those linked to the family directly through David were seen to be in a more privileged position. None of the homeless or addicts could be found in David's Twelve, although some members from the core group might include them in the next layers of family or in a Twelve created within the shelter. Despite ministering to primarily poor African Americans, the bulk of the homeless in inner-city Atlanta, BnF is composed largely of white Christians ministering to African American homeless who identify with BnF's practical mission but not its vision.

Social Stratification, Shifting Norms, and Amorphous Constraints

Given the amorphous structure of the BnF family, it is not surprising that it was difficult to tell who was *in* the family at a particular time and who was not. In asking about the status of particular individuals, doubts about their position were sometimes subtly seeded—doubts about whether they really had BnF's "DNA" or whether they accepted being David's "son" or "daughter." These same doubts were raised about some of the BnF leaders and their followers outside Atlanta.

The composition of the Atlanta family and BnF International has always been in flux. Both the London BnF and Paris BnF disappeared from the radar screen as we began our research and were replaced with BnFs in Alaska, Amsterdam, and Prague, all of which remain little more than a hope and a promise. (Other BnFs on the wish list that never materialized during our study included Tijuana, San Diego, Nashville, and Toronto.) The BnF in Columbia, South Carolina, closed its doors in 2003, and Houston's one-person BnF moved to Odessa, Texas, around the same time.) When we would request information on a specific international BnF, answers were generally ambiguous. Some BnF ministries outside Atlanta were presented as having the DNA of BnF Atlanta and others were in question. The BnF family both in Atlanta and in other locations, like natural families, could be messy and have black sheep lurking in the shadows. Furthermore, it has never been clear to us how many shadowed sheep there really are.

At the head of each Atlanta BnF Twelve was a "father" (who could be female or male; husbands in the families headed by married couples were referred to as "Dad" while their wives were "Mom"). Some visitors to BnF raised their eyebrows when they heard David being referred to by adult followers as "Dad," noting that this practice seemed "cultish." Yet David has always been the central father figure, even when he is called by his given name. In principle David was under the authority of his "Papa Jack," as he came to call the Florida-based evangelist Jack Taylor. Dissidents would later refer to Jack Taylor as an "absentee father" because he was never an integral part of BnF daily life. Similarly, sons and daughters could be disowned, as they drifted away or as David's number-one spiritual son, Chris, was disavowed during the schism.

As Kathleen Jenkins has noted, "The institution of family is an icon of relationality. Social scientists, medical and psychological professionals, government officials and politicians, and religious leaders have often held family up as a model of interdependence" (2005, 45). Evangelical teachings, including Pentecostal-Charismatic, have embraced this cultural norm. The emphasis on a need for spiritual fathering at BnF is a particular religio-therapeutic practice that reflects a cultural marriage between religion and pop psychology. It is based on popular teachings in charismatic Christianity that trace personal problems and social ills to a lack of "fathers" in the larger culture. The religio-therapeutic problem is a simple one: biological fathers have failed to live up to their God-given calling. For many involved in this teaching, the "cure" is usually limited to prayer and prophecy that promises to "heal" the father-child problems through a relationship with Father God. For BnF disciples trying to live out David's teaching about Twelve, the spiritual father was seen as a kind of midwife for birthing a deeper relationship with God. Divine intimacy and fluid familial relations are a contrast from the autocratic "shepherding" found by Jenkins in her ethnographic study of "awesome families." The establishment of "spiritual fathers," however, did serve to preserve the structure of the BnF community with its charismatic leader at the center. David remains ultimately the head of the BnF family with all others, regardless of their age and social status, in submission to him.

Although BnF preached that the poor were invited into loving relationships, promised to all who participated in a Twelve, in practice they were never integrated into the dominant middle-class BnF culture. The homeless would be ushered into a "family" led by someone from David's group (or often another subgroup), rather than David himself, and confined to a Twelve established in the homeless shelter or rehabilitation program for addicts. Despite creative attempts to develop Twelve for the poor (such as referring to the shelter as "home" or serving people at tables during the evening meals for the homeless with a BnF member), community as envisioned by David failed to emerge. It is sufficient to say that even though the dining situation was amicable and the food was good, few dinner tables demonstrated signs of any lively interaction. Most "guests" ate quickly and often quietly, leaving as soon as they were finished. As with many of David's charismatic-driven programs, few of the poor and homeless "guests" showed any interest in playing "family" at the nightly dinners.

David himself seemed aware that many went through the motions without really hearing the vision. During one of his interviews with us, David was lamenting how BnF "became a shelter" rather than a relational community. He then told us a short story demonstrating his disappointment in the BnF's failure to reach the poor with David's vision: "I'll never forget two or three years ago, we were doing a tour; and I stopped and asked one man, 'Willie, what's it that we do here?' You know what he said? He said, 'We speak in tongues and we do Twelve.' [David laughs] 'Where'd you get that, Willie?' But he was right on. Whenever he was there, it was about the value of tongues and getting in the Twelve. For him, that was the right answer. He didn't speak in tongues, and he wasn't in community; but he knew what to say" (June 28, 2004).

More recently (at a conference in March 2006), the homeless once again were being thanked for having opened up their home to host a small gathering of the elite. At one point when David stopped speaking and asked if there were any questions, a homeless resident raised her hand and stated, "We have opened up our home to you and tried to make you as comfortable as we could. When are you going to invite us to your home?" Silence fell over the small group for a very short time. Then David simply shook his head and pensively replied, "I don't know; I really don't know."

The poor and homeless were less enticed by promises of an intimate relational "church family" than were David's young middle-class followers. When asked, "What do you like most about BnF?" in an open-ended question, "relationships" was quickly given almost inevitably as the first response by middle-class followers. Equally telling was the answer to a question about what the respondent found most difficult about BnF; again the answer most often given was "relationships."

BnF's Intentional Family in Sociological Perspective

BnF's emphasis on familial relationships can be viewed as an "intentional community." Members of intentional communities share a commitment to each other that goes beyond ordinary church membership and involvement. The charismatic movement, which experienced the Pentecostal perspective spread to historic churches during the 1960s and 1970s, gave rise to hundreds of intentional communities similar to BnF, but these communities had virtually disappeared by the turn of the millennium (Poloma 1982; Csordas 1997). Paralleling the rise of religiously based intentional communities were the more secular efforts at communal living associated with the counterculture (Rozak 1968). The sense of collectivity (being "one in the Spirit") that gave rise to charismatic intentional communities, and the effort at communal living associated with the counterculture, soon gave way to a more individualized spirituality in which many identify themselves as spiritual but not religious.

BnF's model of "family" provides a contemporary example of another move toward "commitment and community," which has a long history in America; one of the largest waves occurred in the 1840s and another strong wave developed in the late 1960s. Rosabeth Moss Kanter noted the sociological themes that can be found in this quest for community as follows: "The initial impetus for the building of American communes has tended to stem from one of three major themes: a desire to live according to religious and special values, rejecting the sinfulness of the established order; a desire to reform society by curing its economic and political ills, rejecting the injustice and inhumanity of the establishment; or a desire to promote the psychosocial growth of the individual by putting him into closer touch with his fellows, rejecting the isolation and alienation of the surrounding society" (1972, 8).

These three themes—religious and spiritual values; desire to reform society; and rejection of the isolation found in society—are all found in BnF, just as they were central to charismatic communities that dotted the United States in the 1970s. These communities also demonstrated the characteristics of what Marc Galanter (1999) has called a "charismatic group"; these characteristics include a shared belief system, a high level of social cohesion, a capacity to strongly influence members, and a leader imputed with charismatic (or sometimes divine) power. Taken together these sociological themes and charismatic characteristics are underpinnings for living out relationships in intentional communities. It is also these themes, especially the focus on a single, charismatic leader, that distinguish religious intentional communities from the secular, more democratically structured countercultural communes.

BnF is first and foremost a church, albeit one whose vision and qualities of an emerging church bear closer resemblance to a sect than a denomination. Sects are religious groups emanating from a dominant religious institution (i.e., Christianity in the United States), but they are distinguished from more established religion by the degree of tension that exists between their vision and the larger culture. Sects experience much more tension than do established denominations that have acclimated to the prevailing culture

An example of such tension can be found in the conflict that exists between the "supernatural" Kingdom of God and the materialistic American dream that David believes permeates the wider secular culture. Sect-like emerging churches are in conflict with churches rooted in modernity. This tension is reflected in the image emerging church leaders have of themselves and their constituency: they consider themselves "evangelical" but not "Evangelical." BnF sees itself in tension both with larger secular culture and with established "dead religion," as reflected in David's description of the BnF Twelve:

BnF Twelve is foremost about our loving Him with all and then loving one another as ourselves. Jesus declared this to the world when a religious expert of the day asked Him the "trick" question. "Teacher," the legalist baited, "which is the greatest commandment in the Law?" Jesus answered: "Love the Lord your God with all your heart and all your soul and with all your mind. This is the first and greatest commandment. And the second is like it: Love your neighbor as yourself. All the Law and the Prophets hang on these two commandments" (Matthew 22:26-40). (Van-Cronkhite 2003, 12)

He then adds: "It amazes me that 2,000 years later our greatest spiritual goals seldom include relationship with Him and each other. We idolize our goals of building a teaching institution, establishing our ministry, or parading our power gifts as the ultimate expressions of our Christian faith. We'd rather have the temporary acclaim of man for what looks good on the outside than having relationship with each other" (VanCronkhite 2003, 19).

In sum it is the relational church/family, with David as the charismatic leader/father, that has served to guard, activate, and empower the BnF call to serve the "poor and the broken." With his emphasis on relationships, David regards the church as a living organism—a relational process, if you will—for ushering in the Kingdom of God as envisioned by him and promoted by his followers. While the organic analogy works well to describe BnF from one vantage point, looking at it from another stance reveals a chasm between the providers and the beneficiaries. To continue the organic analogy with a focus on the real rather than the ideal, we see the hierarchical structure of BnF's family with mainly white middle-class followers of David at the head of a body in which the homeless are at best distant limbs.

Over time, BnF was destined to move away from its emphasis on street ministry to operate a multifaceted faith-based ministry in two adjacent warehouse buildings that David called the "family business." The smaller building was known as the Sanctuary and the multilevel structure next door as 188 or simply the Warehouse. Distinguishing the "family" from the "family business" has always been somewhat difficult and perhaps even illusory. Core family members were the ones who operated the ministries that composed the "business"; few of the homeless ever became an integral part of the business. If it was the top of the BnF hierarchy that was involved in the business, it was also structurally the source of great stress. There was an innate tension between the supernatural worldview of the Kingdom expressed within the context of familial relations and the institutional developments in and requisites of the family business. The heightening of this tension sowed the seeds for a schism that nearly destroyed BnF and likely contributed to David's own psychological crisis.

The Family Business

In talking about the ministries that made up BnF, David always insisted that BnF was about "more than three hots and a cot," referring to the meals served and the beds provided for the homeless. A bit of the background was presented on the BnF Web site in early 2004: "During BnF's first decade, VanCronkhite learned that the most important thing that he and his ministry had to offer was not food, shelter, clothes, or drug rehabilitation, but relationship. All of Blood-n-Fire's programs today reflect that discovery" (http://www.bloodnfire.com; accessed February 24, 2004). Despite David's lofty vision, what most of the homeless sought was a safe haven, a warm cot, and a decent meal. Most never shared in David's utopian vision of BnF as the family of love that would somehow "take Atlanta" for the Kingdom.

Those who worked in the everyday ministry found themselves with specific tasks to do, crises to handle, and bills to pay to keep the ministry operating. Bolstered with the success story of having "miraculously" acquired the warehouse property, we perceive David's vision blinding him to the pragmatics of actually making BnF work for what most of the homeless sought. Certainly some of the disciples were dedicated to "becoming family," but many whose contributions paid the bills and volunteer work sustained the outreach became more absorbed with details about the functional goals of the ministry than the vision that birthed it. If the "family church" was about relationship and vision, the "family business" was about faith-based ministry in which some workers would later report they felt like "stepchildren," more certain of God's than David's love for them.

There were three major facets of the BnF ministry—the Sanctuary or shelter, Sobre La Mesa and the feeding program, and the Training Center for drug rehabilitation—all of which required daily diligence. Other programs included providing transportation, a clothing center, street evangelism/prayer, and even a motorcycle repair business. Details about the latter illustrate the disjuncture between the BnF providers and their beneficiaries that often surfaces as we describe the family and the family business.

David has a fascination with motorcycles—not just any motorcycle, but Harley-Davidsons. As one biker who sheltered at BnF said, "Other bikes are merely a 'hardly.'" David's fascination with everything Harley assured some biker presence at BnF. Considering that the average income of a Harley rider tops seventy thousand dollars per year, the once-rebel riding Harley biker is now more likely to be a professional, even a "yuppie." David's own custom "chopped" Harley is just one among many expensive Harleys to be seen at BnF. At one point, Ralph showed Margaret an area filled with about a dozen bikes belonging to BnF members, saying, "There is more than a quarter of a million dollars sitting right here." Interestingly, we never saw the homeless in any of the huddles admiring the fancy motorcycles or enjoying rides on them; they represented personal enjoyment by some BnF family "elites" that was often rationalized as a means to connect with the poor. The only connection we saw was that both the bikes and the homeless were safely sheltered in the same building.

This observation is not meant to disparage the genuine faith-based ministry sacrificially carried out by many members, but only to illustrate the disconnection that often appears at BnF between vision and action. Just as many faithful disciples seemed oblivious to the social distance erected by the fascination with Harleys, talk about love and "being family" filled the air, but the reality of caste and class spoke louder than words.

The Sanctuary

The Sanctuary of Blood-n-Fire was always intended to be more than a mere homeless shelter: it was meant to be a genuine home. It was the building that once served primarily as a place for Sunday services, being the first building to be cleaned out and fixed up for use. David describes the building's transition from being a place for religious worship to the dual-purpose of worship and shelter as follows:

But, we found it could be used so much better to provide "sanctuary" seven days a week than as a place for teaching one day a week . . . So the church decided to provide "emergency shelter" to those in "emergency need." For the last five maybe six months we have been honored to have 150 to 450 real people with real needs come and stay with us every night of the week. And these men, women and children are wonderful people; hurting yes; alone yes; many abused, many running from something, but just as many running to something . . . all needing relationship, all hoping there is really a God who really "hears the cries of the poor." And for a moment some actually believe that the "Sanctuary" might be a place where God shows Himself through our love for one another . . . that love your brother stuff the poor have been hearing so much about. (VanCronkhite 2002, 49)

The numbers served by the Sanctuary fluctuated from less than one hundred in the summer months to more than four hundred in the winter months. The higher numbers reflect nights of severe cold when, in addition to cots, mats are placed on the floor so that more can be sheltered from the winter elements. Visitors found the Sanctuary impressive, not because of its simple ambiance but because of the order and peace that seemed to permeate a place that could have been filled with turmoil and violence. The volunteers were for the most part very young and inexperienced (as with other things at BnF, work positions changed often), but they were caring and committed to trying to demonstrate the love of Jesus to the poor.

The amenities of the Sanctuary bordered on primitive. The lone exception was the expensive sound system used to play music that was as foreign to poor black culture as the Harley-Davidsons parked nearby. A stage dominated the front section, folding chairs for meetings and worship were in the center, and neatly made beds filled the rest of the large room. There were signs that some had made the Sanctuary a more permanent home: touches of folk art and personal items placed neatly on top of some beds. As the Sanctuary opened its doors to women and children, a section of the large room was curtained off to provide some private space for these families. In time Sunday worship would be moved over to the Warehouse; but whenever the BnF community used the Sanctuary facilities, David would be certain to remind "the church" to thank the residents for the use of their "home."

A rule for the Sanctuary that was dissonant with the insistence that BnF was to be a "home for the homeless" was the requirement that the residents be "in by 7 p.m. and out by 7:30 a.m." There were some exceptions— like a few elderly permanent residents or some women and children—but, regardless of the weather, residents were forced to leave "home" without having enjoyed breakfast and could not return until 5 p.m. (and no later than 7 p.m.). In one of our interviews with David we asked him where the homeless went once they left the Sanctuary early each morning. He seemed intrigued with the question—as if it had never occurred to him— and then replied, "I really don't know, but I am going to find out." To the best of our knowledge David never did find out, and the rule remained in force. Resources became harder and harder to come by after the schism, and at the time of this writing, only a handful of residents are living in the Sanctuary as guardians until it is sold.

The hierarchical structure in place between those who operated the family business and those who were served by it is also mirrored among the homeless. These few who were permanent residents and were "in charge" of taking care of the Sanctuary during the day while the rest went into the streets were an elite class of their own. Often they seemed to lose touch with their previous struggles in finding food and shelter. Phil, the oldest and most permanent resident of the Sanctuary, told us that he often felt as if intruders were violating his space when the Sanctuary was filled to capacity during winter nights. Phil, like David, presently has no strong relationships with or knowledge of the problems of the street homeless.

Despite all the compassionate talk about "relationships" and "family," attempts to put institutional flesh on the talk often failed. The homeless would be present for the mandatory worship and teaching each evening (there was no place else to go after the 7 p.m. lockdown) and would sit at tables as part of a Twelve once this program was introduced, but the Sanctuary failed at what it considered its primary mission of providing "relations for the relationless." Residents usually gave BnF's Sanctuary high marks as being a "safe place" and one in which they were treated with dignity. For instance, each assigned cot is a person's private and largely personal space. Watches, radios, books, and other personal items are regularly left on cots, and few instances of thefts occurred, which is no small thing for a homeless shelter. Homeless women, usually not accepted by most urban shelters for safety reasons, were even more grateful that BnF accepted them and their children. In spite of BnF's attempts to simulate "family" and encourage "relationship," however, for the vast majority who came through its revolving doors, the Sanctuary never became "home."

Sobre La Mesa

> Life happens around a table filled with good food. Each week Blood-n-Fire prepares around 3000 of the best plates in Atlanta for staff, the men in the Training Center, and the men, women and children living in the Sanctuary. This is where deeper relationships frequently begin, crossing social, generational, and racial barriers. (http://www.bloodnfire.com; accessed January 19, 2005)

When Sobre La Mesa (hands across the table) first opened in a renovated section of the Warehouse, it consisted of a coffee bar and some couches; it was designed to encourage BnF members to meet there rather than at Starbucks, where community members regularly hung out for fellowship. Indeed one of the ironies of BnF is that often after a worship service or serving the homeless an evening meal, David and select staff members would go to trendy Atlanta restaurants to eat and sometimes end the meal with a stop at Starbucks. Sobre La Mesa never really took much patronage away from either the local restaurants or coffee shops. Within a short time, it came to apply to the nightly meals open to the public with no strings attached, served in the large room adjacent to the café. The café became a hangout for those volunteers living in the Warehouse and for men in the Training Program who also lived in 188. Because patrons were charged for drinks, the café was not a place for the homeless.

As the name Sobre La Mesa implies, relationship building (with each other and with God) was regarded as more important than food and drink. This may have been true for some volunteers who were residents of the Warehouse, but this vision seemed to elude the homeless. They patiently stood in line waiting for the doors to open at 5 p.m., sat down at assigned tables, ate the meals served by the volunteers, and then quietly left—having had little interaction with each other or with BnF volunteers. The volunteers would sometimes take it on themselves to facilitate interaction (like learning everyone's name, serving as a host at one of the tables, or praying with individuals), but many of these efforts were short-lived.

The meals were generally very good—perhaps the best offered the homeless in Atlanta. David always sought to serve the best food finances would permit, beginning with the fried chicken dinners that followed the Sunday service and noteworthy meals sometimes featuring steak, pork chops, and fish during the week. David contended that his critics told him that hot dogs were "good enough," but he replied that these critics didn't want hot dogs for dinner and neither did the poor. The famous Sunday southern fried chicken dinner was served after the morning service, and those who came to the service were assured of first admittance. Those who came only for the meal had to wait until all church attenders had been seated. Although there was a common fear that there would not be "enough food," as a general rule, all who came (regardless of whether they had attended the Sunday service) were fed. If BnF had a reputation among the homeless, it was not for David's vision of the Kingdom of God, but rather for serving good food. That, too, was to change after the schism.

Finances became a critical key in the shutdown of the ministry. New possibilities for expanding the feeding program came when the old kitchen was replaced by a large, new, "state of the art" kitchen, a gift of Chick-fil-A, in 2002. The new board of trustees (which included Chick-fil-A's chief operating officer, Dan Cathy, among other prominent Atlanta business leaders) brought in unprecedented donations that allowed BnF to serve quality meals to nearly five hundred persons in one evening. Donations, however, were reduced to a trickle after the schism of 2004 and the public meals were discontinued in 2005. "BnF on Wheels," a mobile kitchen also donated by Chick-fil-A, never got out of the Warehouse lot and onto the streets. The business community of Atlanta had been generous with its provisions to support BnF's ministry to the poor. Some donors would come to question the wisdom of their generosity as the ministry shut its doors for the last time, while others claimed that they had no regrets. Meanwhile, David would come to describe this period of increased dependency on corporate offerings as "the time when my faith was stolen." His mistake, he told us, was to rely on the board rather than God's supernatural provisions for the ministry's daily needs.

Despite creative attempts to create community in Sobre Le Mesa, the visionary goals proved to be elusive. The volunteers, both those within the BnF community and those who came from outside to help, worked hard to make sure that the meal was tasty and served hot, and that guests were treated with dignity. They met together nightly before the meal to pray for the guests, and some contended that this prayer was why there always seemed to be a peace (or at least little conflict) blanketing the dinners. We did not perceive, however, that any of the systems that were put in place produced lasting relationships among homeless.

It is significant that neither the Sanctuary nor Sobre La Mesa appeared on some of the earlier BnF Web sites or in models of BnF. As important as these two programs were for generating service (and financial support), in retrospect they now somehow seem to have been tacked on rather than being central to the BnF vision. They represented a ministry to the poor—one in which workers attempted to build community with little success. The hope for bringing the poor into the BnF family seemed to rest in the residential Training Program for addicts.

Training Program

The BnF Training Program seemed to be in a nearly constant state of flux as leaders sought better ways to heal and restore addicts to the community. The following description of the Program could be found on the BnF Web site during the first year of our study:

> Blood-n-Fire offers a four-phase program for men in the Training Center to restore lives broken by addiction. Through the foundation of the Kingdom of God, the men are equipped spiritually and with the practical life skills as they are restored to relational community. Here, while living in a safe, accountable environment, they can begin to address and process individual issues. Those completing the program have the opportunity to become leaders among the poor and the poor in spirit in Atlanta and demonstrate a faith that is relevant and life changing. The Training Center's year-long program has four phases: The Portal, New Beginnings, Transition and Restoration. (http://www.bloodnfire.com; accessed on February 24, 2004)

Many if not most of the homeless men who sought shelter and food at BnF had alcohol or drug addiction problems or both; crack was the most common hard core drug addiction among homeless African Americans. The Sanctuary and Sobre La Mesa provided fertile ground for recruiting candidates for the Training Program. On paper and in initial interviews with key staff members before we began the project, the Training Center promised to provide a drug rehabilitation program worth investigating. We soon learned that a structured program of any duration simply did not exist. Ralph's desire to empirically assess the success of this Training Program was quickly dashed.

Although the Portal was not regarded a part of the official Training Program, it was the screening place: "The Portal was to be an opportunity for addicts to encounter God while detoxing and getting free from all life addictions. It was to be open to any man willing to change and to believe that there is a supernatural God who offers the love and power to heal" (http://www.bloodnfire.com; accessed February 24, 2004). One criterion was an openness to accepting the baptism of the Holy Spirit and speaking in tongues, a characteristic of churches in the Pentecostal-Charismatic traditions. The length of time in the Portal was to last from three to ten days, and the applicant was isolated from family, friends, and even others in the Training Program. It was to be a time to connect with God in solitude with an expectation of a Damascus-like experience that might prove to be life changing. At the completion of this phase, leaders might extend an invitation to the man to become part of the next phase, New Beginnings. While empirically assessing the effects of the Portal experience would have given us hard data, the shifting sands of the Training Program and eventual collapse left us with only anecdotal accounts.

New Beginnings was a thirty-one-day "investment" for those men "desiring to become part of community and to make positive social behavioral changes." About the cloister on the third floor of the Warehouse, the BnF Web site reports, "Participants vigorously address and deal with their addictions in a highly structured daily life schedule. As this phase's completion, the men better understand God's destiny for their lives with a developed sense of belonging, family and accountability" (http://www. bloodnfire.com; accessed February 24, 2004).

Upon the completion of New Beginnings, the participant was to be evaluated and moved into the Transitional phase of the Program, lasting one hundred fifty days. Still confined by the Program to the Warehouse, "The Transition phase offers the men in the Training Center the opportunity to build upon their commitment to Jesus and their decision to 'change kingdoms.' Each individual is challenged by daily transformation in his life as he learns more about the Kingdom of God and its call to a supernatural lifestyle and community where he is asked to love others as himself" (http://www.bloodnfire.com; accessed February 24, 2004).

In the Restoration stage of the Training Program, the man was to have "the opportunity to be restored to the outside community." He was to secure and maintain gainful employment while retaining accountability to the community: "At the completion of Restoration, the men may move to a new place and continue outside employment or pursue becoming part of the Blood-n-Fire ministry team at the recommendation of the staff" (http:// www.bloodnfire.com; accessed February 24, 2004). The program changed in some significant ways over the years under the direction of rotating and inexperienced staff. Some of the men we talked with who were in the Program during the time of our interviews reported that they had been through earlier versions that were quite different. Despite the improved structure and clarified expectations of the latest version, few made it through this yearlong program and even fewer have become part of the BnF family. Our desire to empirically evaluate what we mistakenly thought to be an established structure for the rehabilitation of the poor proved to be impossible.

Margaret once shared a conversation with David as they sat on a rock outside the Warehouse early one evening. As a record number of guests emerged from an exceptionally good evening meal, David turned and said, "There has to be more than this." She looked perplexed, thinking that he would have been delighted with the success of the public meal program that was commonly credited by the poor as serving "the best meals in Atlanta." David then began to lament about the number of years he had been with BnF and the few "sons" he had to show for the efforts. "I can count them on one hand," he said. His normally upbeat and positive visionary stance was eclipsed in that conversation by despondency and frustration. That conversation came back to me when I learned a few short months later that David was exhausted and taking a sabbatical. In time we learned that he suffered from clinical depression. The vision rested heavily on the visionary even when the ministry seemed to be at its peak and donations were coming in as they never had before. Clearly serving the masses in a successful faith-based ministry was not David's vision.

As of early February 2006, a new, stripped-down Web site no longer contained information about the Sanctuary or Sobre La Mesa, reflecting the shutdown of the ministry that began some months earlier. The Training Program was no longer described in terms of the four phases and even had a new name (Harvest House) with a simple statement of purpose. It promised to "restore broken lives through the foundation of the Kingdom of God and teach spiritual truth and practical skills allowing men to successfully return to relational community"—by invitation only. Two weeks later the Web site was stripped down further, and there was no sign of either the Training Program or Harvest House. For a short time several of the men from the Training Program/Harvest House temporarily relocated to New Orleans to assist with BnF outreach to flood victims, hoping that construction work would be made available to them. At the time of this writing, those few who are still "hanging out" with the BnF church are involved in demolition rather than construction, as the old Warehouse is being dismantled for antique bricks and beams for sale to the highest bidder.

The Family Business in Sociological Context

BnF is not only a church, but also a congregation that successfully offered an array of social services to the poor and homeless in downtown Atlanta. As Unruh and Sider have demonstrated in their excellent work *Saving Souls, Serving Society* (2005), church-based social ministry is both extensive and

complex. Depending on the particular study, the percentage of congregations that report to sponsor social services in the United States ranges from
57 percent to 87 percent (Unruh and Sider 2005, 5). Most of these ministries
lack the depth demonstrated in the BnF family business; these programs
tend "to be short-term and oriented toward emerging or one-time needs"
(Unruh and Sider 2005, 30). Most provide "relief service" without affect-
ing the larger social structure or transforming the lives of recipients. The
relationship between faith and ministry also varies in religious intensity,
ranging from "faith-permeated organizations" that "extensively integrate explicitly religious context" into their outreach to "faith-secular partnerships"
with a base that is more secular than religious.

As can be seen in our discussion of the family business, BnF represents
a "faith-permeated organization." A Pentecostal-Charismatic religious
worldview is foundational to its vision and mission; faith-based activities
are evident at all levels of mission, staffing, governance, and support. BnF's
mission can be described further as "holistic-complementary," where "telling people about the gospel and demonstrating one's faith through social
action are seen to have equal intrinsic value, and each has more value in
association with the other" (Unruh and Sider 2005, 141). BnF thus reflects
a "whole person anthropology" that recognizes the "totality of human beings" who are "not just physical, emotional material beings, but also spiritual beings in which all these aspects are intertwined" (Unruh and Sider
2005, 175–76). The BnF vision includes what Christian Smith has called
"engaged orthodoxy" that demonstrates a "genuine heartfelt burden for
the state of the world, a tremendous sense of personal responsibility to
change society" (1998, 44). The way this change is believed to be effected
is through "relationship"—or what Unruh and Sider term "expressive relationship," maintaining that "the only truly effective way to change the
world is one-individual-at-a-time through the influence of interpersonal
relationships" (2005, 179).

BnF thus represents but one type of church-based ministry, one that requires great commitment to its vision. Only by clarifying VanCronkhite's
vision for BnF and by putting its ministry into the larger context of faith-
based programs is it possible to assess godly love as found there. As Unruh and Sider astutely note: "Religious practitioners often have different
standards of success than those who study the success of their ministries.
Many ministry leaders profess an interest not just in particular quantifi-
able social outcomes, but in the 'whole person'—a unit of assessment that
is difficult to define, let alone measure" (2005, 214).

Toward an Assessment of Godly Love

Sorokin, in what we consider to be the most thorough social psychological theory of love to date, presented and developed what he called the "five dimensions of love." They include its intensity, extensity, duration, purity, and adequacy, constructs that each warrant detailed analysis as they are intertwined in human activities. Because much of what we have presented in this chapter includes materials that can be used in evaluating or assessing love at BnF, we propose to conclude with a brief discussion of what Sorokin calls *adequacy of love* and its potential relationship to the remaining four dimensions.

Adequacy is evaluated in terms of subjective goals to love and its relationship to objective consequences. For example, we have noted David's vision to create loving familial relationships between the homeless and middle-class BnF members—the vision is lofty. At the same time, we have observed that objective situations in both the family and family business often fell short of the vision. Sorokin provides a theoretical description for the two possible forms of discrepancy between the subjective goal to love and loving manifestations:

> *The adequacy* of the subjective goal of love to its objective manifestation ranges from a complete discrepancy between the subjective goal of love actions and its objective consequences, up to their identity. *Inadequacy may have two different forms*: (a) love experience may be subjectively genuine in the loving person, but the objective consequences of his love actions may be very different from, even opposite to, the love goal; (b) a person may have no love experience or intensions subjectively, yet the objective consequences of his actions, though motivated by something else than love, may be most beneficial for others, similar to the effects of genuine love. The first sort of love experience and activity is altruistic subjectively but not objectively. The second sort of experience and action is not altruistic subjectively but is altruistic objectively. (1954/2002, 17)

The discrepancies between the ideal of godly love presented in the BnF vision and the reality of living out the vision provide a measure of "success" or "adequacy." This measure, however, is far from absolute or straightforward. BnF deserves high marks for the clean, safe shelter of the Sanctuary and the good food served with respect for all in Sobre La Mesa. Despite this seeming success, by David's own criteria BnF was to be about more than ministry. BnF's mandate is to train disciples to usher in the Kingdom of God, first in Atlanta and then across the globe.

To further untangle the Gordian knot of love adequacy, the other dimensions noted by Sorokin must also be considered in relationship to a consistent love that is both subjectively genuine and objectively adequate. Questions may have developed in the reader's mind about the degree to which love at BnF is *intense*—and intense for whom? Judging from interpersonal interactions we observed during the course of our research, it seemed that love for those within the largely white BnF middle-class family was more intense than for the poor and homeless. Sorokin suggests that "when the manifestations of intense love in its overt actions and instrumentalities are accompanied by wisdom and knowledge, then love intensity is positively connected with its adequacy" (1954/2002, 29). In other words, it is difficult to love well what one does not know. Open communication between the poor and the providers at BnF would seem to be a minimum requisite for adequate love, and this we failed to perceive.

We have also suggested that the BnF vision itself puts limits on the extensity of love that would make it more "adequate" for some groups than others. We reported a middle-class culture that permeates BnF despite its verbal opposition to the American dream. We also noted that as a faith-permeated ministry BnF is guided by an Evangelical Christian religious worldview limiting its extensity to persons willing to accept Jesus as their personal savior.

Sorokin's theory has pointed to the relationship between adequacy and another dimension of love, namely *duration*. He observed that "adequate love is likely to last longer than inadequate love." Sorokin further states: "The unlovely and harmful consequences of an objectively inadequate love weaken and sometimes kill not only the love of the loved person, harmed by inadequate results, but even that of the loving person himself, made resentful by the 'ingratitude' of the other party or shocked by the harmful results of his own love activities" (1954/2002, 35). As we provide details of the schism and its aftermath in a later chapter, we will explore some of the problems with inadequacy that surfaced during that critical period.

Finally, Sorokin reminds us that pure love is rare given how love is often subjected to "emotional blindness" and always has some "soiling elements." Having issued that cautionary note, Sorokin suggests a positive relationship between the purity and adequacy of love: "Pure love contains an element of true wisdom or cognition as to the best means and ways of its manifestations. It implies a notable lack of emotional blindness, and a notable knowledge of the adequacy or inadequacy of its manifestation" (Sorokin 1954/2002, 35). It is probably safe to say that no altruistic endeavor is without its warts and blemishes. The question to be wrestled with is how much these deficiencies affect the adequacy of love.

4

Charisma and Spiritual Transformation

Faith based organizations representing a variety of religious traditions continue to provide a great deal of social services to many of the most needy in society in some of the otherwise most neglected communities. But from a social science perspective, we don't know much about the variables that influence a person's decision to become a volunteer in the first place, as well as the factors that help to mobilize and sustain so many volunteers. What do we know about the altruistic work of religious or spiritually motivated workers and volunteers to combat anti-social and egotistical behavior on the one hand, and to promote pro-social or conventional behavior on the other hand? What is the extent of the other-directed love dispensed by faith based organizations?

—Post 2006, 18

In seeking answers about factors and forces in religiously motivated altruism it is necessary to go beyond reductionist theories of evolutionary biology and rational choice theories in social science (Post, Underwood, Schloss, and Hurlbut 2002). Human emotions in particular have found little place in popular theories of altruistic behavior. Collins's interaction ritual theory emphasizes emotion energy (EE) and provides us with guiding hypotheses, which, if expanded to include godly love, do shed light on the questions that Stephen Post raises in the epigraph.

Collins critiques rational choice and the "cost-benefit model" by pointing out three main difficulties: "First, there are classes of behavior that seem to escape from cost-benefit analysis"; "there is no *common metric* that would make it possible for actors to compare costs and benefits among different spheres of action"; and "there is a good deal of evidence that individuals in natural situations do very little calculating" (2004, 143–46). In an effort to address these shortcomings of rational choice theories, Collins places EE at the center of his interaction model: "IR theory provides a theory of individual motivation from one situation to the next. Emotional energy is what individuals seek; situations are attractive or unattractive to them to the extent that interaction ritual is successful in providing emotional energy. This gives us a dynamic microsociology in which we trace situations and their pull or push for individuals who come into them" (2004, 44).

Emotional energy (EE) is a heuristic but abstract construct that requires testing against empirical observations in concrete situations. We have already presented accounts demonstrating how godly love is a source of EE for David VanCronkhite, which in part generated the vision, values, and structure of BnF. If the primal drive behind human behavior is EE, as Collins hypothesizes, it often took the form of godly love for those who joined the BnF family and worked in the family business. Their stories included encountering the divine before coming to the community; many are baptized into the Pentecostal-Charismatic worldview with experiences of godly love. The form of EE that they seemed to be seeking and found satisfying at BnF was generated by spiritual encounters and familial ties with like-minded believers.

Pentecostal-Charismatic or neo-Pentecostal (P/C) Christians, especially those touched by the ongoing renewals and revivals, are "Main Street mystics" who report a wide array of spiritual gifts and transcendent experiences of God (Poloma 2003). Like David VanCronkhite, they are unlikely to see themselves as "religious" (a term that generally carries a negative connotation), preferring to regard themselves as "spiritual." One leader, a young woman who had been with BnF for six years at the time she was interviewed, spoke of how at BnF the "Spirit of God has been given such freedom to move and speak, in its prophetic words to people's hearts"—a freedom that is "pretty much against most religious systems." She added: "One of the things that we do to keep in check and in alignment with the Holy Spirit is (to acknowledge for) the difference between ninety-nine percent flesh and one percent Spirit—the difference is that the one percent Spirit makes God smile. It's learning to grow that one percent into ninety-nine percent—training, guiding, and learning. In other places I've been it's always been "Did you see that ninety-nine perfect flesh?" instead of "Did you see that one percent Spirit?" Here we tend to emphasize the Spirit rather than the flesh."

Capturing the Voice of Pre-schism Family Members

The primary voices in this chapter are those of David's committed followers before the schism that fragmented BnF and created a Tower of Babel. At the time the interviews with BnF community members were being conducted, David's disciples seemed to be of one mind as they spoke of their love for God, David, the BnF family, and the poor. The story that was unfolding was much like Margaret assumed it would and Ralph hoped that it might be. Blood-n-Fire appeared to be a unique faith-based church/ministry with a vision and committed followers that in ways were reminiscent of religious movements of the 1960s. BnF had a dream propelled by godly love, and many members seemed willing to sacrifice all for it. The interviews were designed in part to explore the faith and faith experiences of the respondents with a special focus on spiritual transformation and how it related to altruistic love as lived out at BnF.

Questions were guided by Stephen Post's astute query that opened this chapter. What was it that drew members to the BnF family? How did changes in their spirituality interface with their work with the poor and homeless? How successful was David in imparting his vision to his followers? What was the role of personal spiritual experience in activating compassion and altruism in the volunteers? The in-depth interviews with BnF family members each lasted from forty-five minutes to more than two hours. With the permission of the respondent, each interview was taped and transcribed. Although many of these respondents were interviewed a second or third time by Margaret as she conducted additional interviews with other relevant parties after the schism unfolded, in this chapter we are limiting ourselves to exploring the process of spiritual transformation for the fifty-two respondents who were working with BnF in 2003 at the pinnacle of the ministry's success.

Using a structured questionnaire (see appendix B-1) we also collected survey data from members in early 2004 at the BnF International gathering attended by local family, a dozen or so leaders from other cities, and some of their disciples. This same questionnaire was also given to local family members who openly chose not to attend the gathering. By this time we recognized that a possible schism was brewing despite talk of repentance and reconciliation by all parties. The survey yielded a total of 105 responses, including those loyal to VanCronkhite, others eventually labeled by us as dissidents who boycotted the annual meeting, and still others who at the time of the gathering were trying to stand back from the fray. The survey results used in this chapter provide a statistical skeleton for the BnF community that is fleshed out with reports from the qualitative interviews with the pre-schism faithful. This same survey was completed by 117 Sanctuary residents, whose responses will be utilized in chapter 6 to present the voice of the homeless service recipients.

Descriptive Facts and Figures: Comparisons and Contrasts

At the time of the interviews, the clear majority of BnF members were not employed full-time outside the church ministry. (Of the survey respondents, 53 percent indicated that they were working at BnF "full-time" and another 8 percent, three-quarters time.) Before coming to BnF, however, interviewees had worked in a wide range of largely middle-class occupations, including business management, office work, construction work, computer technology, teaching, social work, hairdressing, and medical sales and technology. A few put their previous occupational experience to use in the family business as they served in the Sanctuary (homeless shelter), Sobre Le Mesa (feeding program), or the Warehouse (drug rehabilitation). Some continued to work part-time outside the ministry for self-support (including as a physician and a hairdresser) or relied on the income of an employed spouse. As encouraged and modeled by David, most had learned or were in the process of learning how to "live by faith," relying on God (or personal benefactors) to do the "miracles" needed to meet their daily needs without paid employment. A minority of members did receive somewhat regular subsidies (although reportedly not regular salaries) from BnF as needs were presented and funds were available. (Twenty-one percent of the survey respondents indicated that a significant percent of their income came through the family business, while 27 percent said it came primarily from "paid employment"; another 28 percent said it came from "contributions of family and friends.") It was only later that we would learn of the favoritism practiced in disseminating BnF funds—favoritism alleged to be based on closeness to David rather than contributions to the ministry or objective needs.

The vast majority of the original interviewees were self-described members at BnF Atlanta, including four black males who had graduated from the Training Program, two other men who were in the Restoration (final) stage of the Training Program, and two interns. Seven other respondents were leaders of BnFs in other cities but most had been with BnF Atlanta for some period of time. Interview respondents tended to be committed

Evangelical Christians before coming to BnF, mostly from P/C churches. (For the expanded survey sample that included members who had not been interviewed, over 50 percent were raised Evangelical or Pentecostal-Charismatic, another 20 percent were mainstream Protestants, and 8 percent were Catholic; 14 percent said they had "no religious background" while growing up.) Slightly over half (n=28) of the interview respondents were female; nearly half (n=24) were male. (In the survey, 52 percent of the respondents were male; 48 percent, female.) Caucasians (n=43) greatly outnumbered African American respondents (n=9) in both the interviews and survey sample, in which only 15 percent were African American. The African American respondents were likely to have entered the BnF family through the Training Program, having sought help from BnF for addictions. They represent the handful of graduates of the Program who managed to find a permanent position serving BnF.

Interviewees ranged in age from nineteen years to sixty-four years; the average age was 40.5 years. (Survey respondents had a slightly lower mean age of 37 years.) Eighteen held at least a college degree; all but four of the remaining respondents completed high school. (The modal survey respondent had some college or vocational training beyond high school, and 31 percent reported graduating from college, of which 9 percent had some post-college education.) With the exception of three or possibly four interview respondents, the overwhelming majority reported that they had not done previous work with the homeless or with those suffering from addictions. (Of the survey respondents, 65 percent reported that they had little or no contact with the poor, and 85 percent had little or no contact with addicts before beginning work with BnF.) At the time of the interviews, subjects were with BnF anywhere from less than a year to twelve years; the average length of time was 5.2 years. (In the survey the mean for length of time working at BnF was 4.7 years.)

All the voices presented in this chapter were committed BnF members before the schism. The passion of their commitment is evident in that despite persistent probes, none provided critiques of the family to which they belonged. We approached the interviews with particular questions in mind, including those dealing with the respondent's introduction to BnF and the decision to join the community, narratives of primary conversion experiences (usually predating contact with BnF), and spiritual pathways that developed through BnF modeling and teaching. We were particularly interested in exploring godly love. Godly love includes a vertical relationship with God and horizontal relations with others. These two interrelated components—love of God and love of others—will be discussed in terms of pathways of spiritual transformation and attendant IRs within the BnF community.

Pathways of Spiritual Transformation

Psychologist Kenneth Pargament has defined *spiritual transformation* primarily as a "fundamental change in the place of the sacred or the character of the sacred as an object of significance in the life of the individual" (2004, 8). For members of BnF, as for other P/C Christians, this "fundamental change" took place in being *born-again* and later followed by *Spirit baptism*, an intense spiritual experience usually accompanied by glossolalia. Moving into the ranks of the significant minority of American Christians who profess to be born-again involves accepting certain basic tenets of orthodoxy (resting on the Bible as the authoritative word of God). But as Christian Smith has noted, professing right doctrine alone is not sufficient: "Right theology has to be individually personalized through conversion and firm personal commitment" (1998, 25). Thus, being "born-again" involves both intellectual assent and the will to commit one's life to the person of Jesus Christ. Nearly all the interviewees professed to having taken the first step in the transformation process before coming to BnF, although some (especially those who entered the BnF family from the Training Program) had "backslidden" (causing them to question the depth of their initial commitment). Most had also experienced Spirit baptism, giving them a taste of the fruits of mysticism. Nearly without exception, respondents were drawn to the spiritual powers that they saw exercised at BnF, which moved beyond those expected in the average P/C church.

For P/C Christians, being born-again is a most important first step, but only a first step, on their spiritual journeys. Being baptized in the Spirit, usually with the sign of speaking in tongues (glossolalia) is another primary marker of spiritual transformation. The experience of tongues and other charismata is believed to empower the believer in seemingly extraordinary ways. It serves as an example of what Pargament has identified as a "secondary" form of spiritual transformation that marks a "fundamental change in the pathways the individual takes to the sacred" (2004, 8). The pathway is no longer limited to reason and human assent but moves the believer into mystical experiences of God. For P/C Christians the cognitive assent in accepting the divine grace of salvation is frequently complemented by an experiential and intuitive encounter with the Holy Spirit that enables them to speak in tongues. This experience of Spirit baptism in turn opens the door to other charismata, including divine healing, prophecy, and a "faith to move mountains." Of the fifty-two interviewees, only one—an intern from Africa who had been with BnF only a couple of months—reported that he had not experienced Spirit baptism. It is worthy to note here that David VanCronkhite often speaks in tongues, not only while preaching but also in face-to-face conversations with his followers. He also interprets dreams and lays hands on followers, continually modeling the charismata that are the fountainhead of his ministry.

David played a major role in the conversion of a few respondents that seemed to contribute to their unwavering loyalty to him and to his ministry; for others, he exerted a less personal role. While some were undeniably (at least at first) drawn to the charisma and person, others seemed to be attracted primarily by particular facets of VanCronkhite's vision, including the BnF family, the "signs and wonders," kingdom living, the music band, and relations with the poor. Their stories, a few of which we present below, suggest that spiritual transformations generally consist of an array of motivators interwoven into unique IR patterns. Moreover, they are not constant and often change as pilgrims continue along their spiritual journeys.

BnF as a Catalyst of Spiritual Transformation

Some interviewees, especially those who came in on the ground floor of BnF's founding, had not yet made a commitment to a spiritual journey before meeting David VanCronkhite. Drawn to his charisma and charm, his passion for the emerging and ever-changing vision, and his caring and concern, they were able to make a deep faith commitment that they attributed to the person, the testimony, and the ministry of David.

Ned, now a leader of a small international BnF in Cape Town, serves as an example of someone who began his spiritual journey as an adult under David's mentoring. Ned was one of David's work colleagues when David was still employed in the corporate world and before he walked away from the American dream to begin BnF. Ned tells his story as follows:

> My wife and I were friends with Janice and David in the corporate workplace. We were very good friends and were involved in sales in hospitals. I was actually involved in a rather large endeavor in Florida that went sour and was escorted out of the boardroom at a drop of a hat. I was

devastated. David, who was vice-president of sales, came into my office and asked how I was doing. I said, "Oh, I'm doing fine." He pressed, and I finally broke. "I am not doing well. I am not doing well at all. I am tired of all this; I am tired of feeling like I have failed; I'm tired of having country clubs ripped out of my hands." I was sad for myself. David said, "I think I know what you need." He began to tell me about Jesus Christ. I was skeptical. He patiently pressed. I finally asked what I could do. He wrote out a prayer on a piece of paper. I then said it by myself after he left. Janice and David then invited us to their church, and we became part of the Atlanta Vineyard.

Not only was Ned born-again, but together with David he sought a deeper commitment for his newfound faith. Ned had been part of the earliest teams to leave the suburbs of Atlanta to take groceries and knock on doors in attempts to reach the poor. He and his wife had also been with David and Janice at the Jackie Pullinger conference in Anaheim where David received an "impartation." Like David, Ned believed something happened at the Pullinger conference, bringing "heart changes" that affected their new ministry. He noted, "I would categorize that what we were doing before the conference as a sort of 'helps and friendship.' After the conference the outreach became true compassion." Although many of the others who began this journey with David have long since moved on from BnF and their stories not easily retrieved, Ned has never forgotten the key role that David played in his spiritual life. Together with the other leaders of BnF International, all of whom had sacrificed the American dream for a life of service to the poor, Ned stood with David during the schism. (Dissidents would later tell us that David was less than approving of Ned's work in Cape Town—the small group that left from Atlanta just before the schism was sent by David to monitor the activities in South Africa.) David was undoubtedly instrumental in spiritual life changes of many, but not all have stood with David as Ned has.

David's niece Kathryn was another person whose life was changed dramatically under David's influence as he reached out to his natural family just as he did to others who were not part of his biological kin. Kathryn believes she was "saved" or born-again at age twelve, but "it never took hold." She proceeded with her conversion account: "By the time I was eighteen, I was into a lot of trouble. This was just before BnF was founded, but when Janice and David were involved in the Vineyard. I went to their group home meeting (with the Atlanta Vineyard), and my spirit was just stirred after that for something more than I had. That's when I actually dedicated my life to the Lord. I went back to Texas and got my things and came back."

She reports that "relationships" have been her greatest source of satisfaction at BnF over the years—especially her relationship with David and Janice. When asked about the earliest days of BnF when she walked with David as he pioneered the ministry, Kathryn replied:

> It was real exciting—especially when you follow someone like David. He is a visionary, and without saying anything, he can somehow gather people around him. So when you are following someone that charismatic who so believes in what they are doing, it's fun. It's hard but fun. Of course, when it came down to when he was going to quit his job (he made very good money), I went, "What are you doing?" I thought it was amazing! Wow! You must be serious. This isn't a Saturday thing any more, giving up his job and all the comfort that went with it.

Although many of the others who had gathered around David over the years "came, saw, and left," Kathryn, with her "revelatory prophetic gifting," ministered front and center with him for years. Although she expressed deep gratitude for all David and Janice had done for her, it was apparent during the interview that she was seeking to find her own path. She said she was being "called" to Europe; but at the time of the interview, she either could not or would not articulate any details. Within a short time after the interview Kathryn became engaged to a young European and married him the following year.

Rose Bigelow is another young woman who has walked with David nearly since BnF's inception and who now leads the struggling community. Rose was raised in a household where occult practices were normal routine. Influenced by a young friend, she had a born-again Christian experience as a young teenager but did not immediately become a member of any church. It was when she began attending the Atlanta Vineyard a few years later and met David's niece Kathryn (who was still attending David's old church) that she was led to her spiritual home. Rose was spiritually affected during the first visit to the Atlanta Vineyard, which she describes as follows: "The minute I walked in the room the first time that I visited, the presence of God hit me so hard that I burst out crying. I cried the entire time I was there the first visit just because I was overwhelmed by His presence." Rose was satisfied there, but Kathryn kept encouraging her to visit BnF. Rose eventually visited the old dilapidated building for a Sunday service. As Rose continues the story of her journey:

> But Kathryn kept harping on me to go downtown—and this was right after they had gotten the building. I finally acquiesced and one Sunday came downtown. The minute I walked in the door, I was just overwhelmed by the Presence. And I sat in the back—this is just when I was in a tiny little corner of the Warehouse. The whole area was filled with junk. And there were all these homeless guys in there. I sat in the midst of all these homeless guys and my heart just broke. It just really broke. I cried the entire time that I sat there.
>
> I just said (to the Lord), "You know, I don't know what this is but I want to be a part of it." So I made a commitment in my heart to go to the Vineyard every other Sunday and to BnF on the other Sundays. And that probably lasted for about a month—it just didn't work out. I kept wanting to come downtown more. It was a draw to be part of what God was doing—to be involved with the poor.

Although Rose has been a favored and faithful daughter to both David and Janice, it would be a mistake to attribute David's following solely to natural friendships, family ties, or David's personal charisma. The stories are more complex than that. The open-ended interviews (including Rose's) usually said very little about David, but much about the spiritual paths of the respondents that led them to BnF. It was intimacy with God that followers sought, and most already knew or were in the process of learning to hear what they believed was God's voice. Most asserted that they were divinely led to BnF and had stories to tell (much like Rose) of being spiritually moved by the divine presence they experienced, both in the place of the BnF warehouse and the space of family relations. They took comfort in that they were where they believed God wanted them. It was through this sense of divine leading and divine presence at BnF that led them to believe that they had found their personal destinies.

A Tale of Two Cousins

We begin this tale with Jeff, a high school graduate in his late twenties at the time of the interview, who walked with David from the earliest days of BnF. The son of a missionary, Jeff had set out on the journey of a prodigal son before David entered as an instrument of change. Jeff began his story as follows:

> Well, I am a missionary kid, so I grew up in Mexico. At eighteen I left home for good. Because of the way I was brought up (very religious— very performance oriented), I basically didn't have any knowledge of Jesus. I knew the Scriptures and could tell people how to get saved. My dad would count the heads I would bring in for salvation. I could lead someone to the Lord in less than two minutes. But it was all not real to me. So by the time I was eighteen I started messing up real bad, and I got into lots and lots of trouble.

Eventually he was invited by a cousin (Matt) to come to live in Atlanta; but because he was still abusing drugs, he was soon forced to leave his uncle's house. Jeff now was self-reportedly "miserable and on my own." He returned to school where he met Joel, a friend who invited him to a BnF Saturday street outreach. Jeff accepted the invitation, but reportedly he did so only because Joel promised Jeff that he would be able to play drums in the worship band. Jeff recalled the following about his initial meeting of VanCronkhite: "We pull in and there was this guy with his curly hair, cowboy boots and T-shirt. He came directly over to us—and Joel and he just started hugging. Then he grabbed me. I was sure I reeked of alcohol and marijuana and who knows whatever—I was really messed up. He grabbed me and hugged me and said 'I love you.' I was captured. Here was this guy whom I didn't even know—I just met him. And he tells me that he loved me! I was hooked."

Jeff was invited by David in these early years to walk with him, even accompanying him as David journeyed to purchase the warehouse property. At one point Jeff lived with David and Janice in their suburban home. He reported that over the years his relationship with his own father has been restored because of David: "My dad's come a long way; and I have come a long way as well. God used David to restore that relationship." In reading in between the lines of Jeff's story, it is apparent to the authors that his friend Joel and his wife (who invited Jeff to move in with them at the onset of this spiritual journey) also played an important role in Jeff's transformation. Joel is one of many names occasionally mentioned whose story about leaving BnF is unclear. Jeff told us that he rarely sees Joel anymore.

Two years after first coming to BnF, Jeff invited his cousin Matt to join him. Matt grew up in a Pentecostal church and experienced Spirit baptism (and glossolalia) when he was eleven. After two years of rebellion around the age of fifteen, he realized he needed to make a decision—"Either God was real or he wasn't." Matt described the intense experience he had at a Pentecostal summer camp in the midst of "one of those bizarre Holy Spirit revivals" where he spoke in tongues (and was unable to speak in English) for three days. At the same time, he soon found that although his Pentecostal church may have professed to believe in the supernatural, at least in Matt's opinion, "Nobody was willing to take it for face value; this is real." Matt said: "I really turned off my church when I came back from that youth camp. The chairman of the deacon board came up to me after I gave this incredible testimony (two days of healings and emotional healings) and said, 'You'll settle down and get into the groove of church pretty soon.' That was it for me; I went up to my dad and said, 'I want to leave this church; if that is the extent of reality, I'm done—I don't want to be here.'"

He succinctly described his draw to BnF as follows: "The attraction was people who were dumb enough to believe that it [the supernatural] was all really real." After introducing Matt to BnF in 1993, Jeff withdrew from BnF for ten months in the mid-1990s. It was Matt's turn to bring his cousin back into the fold; David welcomed Jeff as the prodigal father welcomed his son in the often-told biblical story. "I was a wreck—an absolute mess," he says of his time away from BnF. Jeff briefly described his return as follows: "So Matt brought me back. This was in 1995, and I remember walking into the Warehouse. David was up in his office. I remember walking in and collapsing in his arms. And I have been there ever since. I've had my ten months of being a prodigal."

As did his cousin Matt, Jeff married a young woman he met at BnF. But marriage and especially having children bring new responsibilities that often change existing relationships. Matt and his wife wrote a memo to BnF family members just before the schism broke wide open sharing how they "felt led" to spend more time with their growing family. When they first withdrew from family gatherings, it was with David's blessing; but they were soon to learn that this highly unusual blessing was but a façade. Withdrawal from the BnF family meant that followers would be discouraged from associating with those who chose to leave the community. That situation had not changed, as Matt soon learned when his former church family ostracized him. Matt would spend the next three years watching his business flourish and his family grow, but he missed the spiritual community he once enjoyed at BnF. While putting finishing touches on this chapter Margaret received a message from Matt in which he reported that he and his wife are planning to be a part of a church plant in Atlanta that will be affiliated with Bethel Church in Redding, California, a church known for its experiences of the supernatural and being at the forefront of neo-Pentecostal revival.

Jeff and his wife remain with BnF, but for a time they had seemingly distanced themselves from the thick of the schism fray. They had taken paid positions with another ministry, bought a house, and were expecting their first child by the time we had completed the formal interviewing phase of the study. The move to suburbia, purchase of a new house, and paid jobs might have caused David to make innuendoes about their choices in less tumultuous times, but they were able to ride the wave and retain his favor as he regrouped his band of loyal followers. At the time of this writing Jeff is managing a Web site for the "harvesting" of the bricks and beams of the dismantled warehouse. Opposite a photograph of the warehouse beams taken when the structures were still intact is the following text:

> For your Review
>   Absolutely stunning . . . these structures begin to tell a story on their own by the fact they are so well preserved . . . you see, the structures never really sat empty or abandoned . . . the roofs were well maintained over the decades and the buildings were kept very well due to years and years of commercial business activity and then on to very real life changing ministry . . . So many of Atlanta's homeless have come through these structures and their lives have been forever changed . . . (http://www.225harvest.com; accessed September 6, 2007)

Jeff and Matt had other siblings and cousins who were drawn to BnF. Prior to the schism they seemed to be on the sidelines, working the sound system and playing in the worship band. Their names could be found on e-mails that went out to family members after the schism indicating that they retained some level of involvement. At least from the distance from which we observed the restructuring of the BnF church, it appeared that these young men were drawn to David and the countercultural church he proposed for youth more than to David's vision of ministering to the poor. While single, they joined in the street ministry when music and the "supernatural" was an important part of the action. When demands became more stringent (e.g., giving up paid employment), they could retreat to the margins for a spell and return when conditions changed, as Jeff done (unless David chose to ban a former follower from coming to family events, as he did in the case of Matt).

David Selects a "Son"

Although David has a biological son, until the schism when David "repented" of having failed him, D.J. was on the margins of David's life. (It wasn't until after the schism that the authors ever saw him with David.) David admittedly had put the BnF family and his committed followers ahead of biological family ties. As BnF moved away from the "army" metaphor toward one of "family," it seemed important, however, for David to beget a special son to whom he could pass on his mantle. Chris Franklin, in his mid-thirties at the time of the interview, proved to be inspired by David's journey, attracted to his passion, and drawn to his vision. He became David's number-one son and was given the day-to-day operations of the family business.

Chris had been a successful sales person (making a high-six-figure income) before he and his wife, along with their small children, followed David's example of walking away from the American dream for a life of ministry and service. Like many other disciples, Chris's spiritual transformation began before he ever met David. He was raised in a fundamentalist Christian home and was baptized when he was twelve; despite that background, he says, "I never met Jesus until about seven years ago." Chris gives the following account: "When I met Jesus, everything in my life changed. I was chasing money; I was out for the next thrill. But He showed up in my bedroom one night and spoke to me—and it just wrecked my life."

During an interview Margaret queried how Jesus appeared in Chris's bedroom and how He spoke to him: "Was it a dream? A vision?" Chris quickly responded and continued with his story:

> It was not a dream. I was wide-awake. I'm not sure what to call it. Jesus was there! The presence was in the room, and I was weeping. At the time I was reading the Bible in preparation for a Bible class I was teaching. And Jesus said, "Chris, it is all true. And you can do everything that is in there if you want to." So Linda [Chris's wife] and I got on this trek of chasing Him. So wherever He would show up at meetings—where there were a lot of signs and wonders—we were there.

It while Chris was on this "chase" that a pastor friend suggested that he and Chris visit Blood-n-Fire to attend a prophetic conference. During the first two days of the conference, the teachings and prayers of the conference leaders spiritually touched both men. It was on the third day of the conference that Chris would make life-changing strides on his new spiritual pathway. David VanCronkhite was scheduled to "do the thing that morning." Chris had never met David or heard him speak before. At this point in the interview, Chris interjected another "conversation" that he had been having with God off and on for some eight months before coming to the conference. According to Chris, the conversation went something like this: "I'm going to give you a dad." I would say, "I have one, thanks. My parents live." And God would say, "No, I am going to give you one." So I would say, "OK." On and off for the next eight months I would say, "Tell me about that dad thing." And God would say, "I am going to give you one."

Chris then proceeded to describe what happened the Saturday morning in 1999 when David addressed the conference:

> David said, "On Thursday night we talked about the Holy Spirit and how He came in power. Last night we talked about the Son and how He came in Power. But this morning we are going to talk about the Father—and He is going to come in power to deal with some fatherless people." I sat in the very front pew, in the far corner. I turned around to look—to see who God was going to touch. I thought it was awesome that some fatherless people were going to be touched. In my wisdom, I didn't recall that God had been telling me for eight months that He was going to give me a dad. So I didn't consider myself fatherless.
>
> I turned around, and that was the last thing I remembered. I didn't hear another word that David said. An hour or so later I got off the floor in snot and tears. I don't know what the Holy Spirit did, but I felt the power. It was that deep intercession, groaning thing. And as I tell people, "Hey, you can fake tears, but you can't fake snot." [laughs] I was just a mess.

As Chris got up off the floor after having been put there by what he regards as the power of the Holy Spirit, David came over to him and instructed him not go anywhere. For the next few minutes David proceeded to talk with people who were waiting to speak with him. Finally David said to Chris, "The Lord said to tell you that if you want a home, you're home."

Although Chris's wife, Linda, was at their home taking care of their small children and was unable to attend the conference, she too received a divine visitation that tied her to Chris's experience. She shared how she had been in the shower crying out to God while Chris was at the conference, "Please give us a home. Please let somebody tell us, 'You're home.' When Chris called and told me what happened, I cried, 'God has answered my prayer. We've got a home.'"

For the next several months Chris continued to work in the corporate world. When he was offered an opportunity of a promotion that would require a move from Georgia, he sensed God was leading him in another direction. Although he believed God was leaving him free to pursue this job offer, like David who had walked this path before him, Chris also believed that God had a "better plan." Following David's modeling, Chris quit his lucrative position in sales and began ministering to the poor in the area of his home in Douglasville, Georgia.

Meanwhile, Linda was praying that an opening would develop at BnF for Chris to work in the Atlanta ministry. As Chris reported, "I never had any inkling that's what God was going to do. But two weeks to the day after I left my job and Linda was praying, David called. He said, 'Hey, I've got something I want you to pray about, but don't pray long. We're in a mess.' So I went down to Atlanta, and David put me over the food ministry."

At the time of the interview in the spring of 2003, Chris was functioning as the CEO of the family business, overseeing the BnF shelter, drug rehabilitation, and food ministries. He was totally committed to David and to David's vision, reporting that he "would be happy simply to be carrying David's briefcase." In fact, however, in many ways Chris was outdoing David in living out the BnF vision. Not only was he functioning extremely well as the CEO of the family business, but he seemed to be surpassing David in bringing a younger generation into the ministry and vision. He and Linda took them into their home and welcomed them into their daily lives. This new generation was calling Chris (not David) "Dad." It was Chris's spiritual transformation story, his newfound walk in the supernatural, and his mentoring that became central for many of these new disciples.

Call to the Poor

The interviews shared thus far with some of David's followers suggest that different people were drawn in differing degrees to different parts of David's ever-changing vision. We continued to observe the ongoing modifications of the vision as God reportedly led David down the twist-ing road of His Kingdom. It appeared that not only would a follower's understanding of the vision be expected to shift to align with David, but commitment levels to following David on these twists and turns varied. David's ever-changing vision would leave some followers on the margins and cause others to withdraw from involvement with BnF. The account of a mass exodus after David discontinued the Sunday worship services (found in chapter 2) describes one example of such a withdrawal. Those who remained with BnF, however, now knew that personal engagement with the poor and homeless was a core value of BnF that was not (at least at that time) negotiable. Nonetheless, relatively few of the inter-viewees reported the ministry to the poor as the primary draw to BnF. Some seemed to be inspired by David the charismatic leader and were eager to become his son or daughter. Others were taken with the su-pernatural "signs and wonders" that seemed to be a part of daily com-munity life. Still others were drawn by the BnF "family" and its neo-monastic lifestyle.

One of David's disciples who emphasized the importance of the BnF mission to the poor as a draw to the community was Carol, a twenty-nine-year-old single white female who had been with BnF for three years at the time of the interview. She was "saved" at a Pentecostal church at the age of twenty-three and Spirit baptized shortly after. Carol was attending one of the ministry schools that came out of the P/C revivals of the 1990s when the school sponsored a ministry trip to BnF. Carol recounted her first reaction to visiting BnF as follows:

> Actually, it just shocked me—because I had never seen anything like this with homeless people. I am from Wyoming—I am from a small town. We don't have homelessness like we do here. Wow! Here is something I have never seen and now it is right here in my face. And someone is doing something about it. When I returned to school, it was hard to go back to a regular church and everyday life because of what I experienced here—just knowing that there were people who didn't have anywhere to live; just knowing that God was working in an atmosphere like BnF. So to go back to my school and my home church and just get caught back up in the social club of religion—it was hard. God really opened my heart to knowing that church is more than what is going on inside the church walls; it is going out to the streets—to the people—and building relation-ships. That is where it all starts—with relationships with the poor.

Carol returned to school to finish her degree, and for ten months made a five-hour drive monthly to visit BnF. She then added: "I felt that God was showing me that this was the place where I was to be. It was just the timing of it; it took me ten months. I hesitated a lot—just the fear of coming here and not working—not knowing what the future was financially— or the stability of it all. So that leap of faith kind of scared me! That's why I hesitated for so long. But God told me, "You need to go; if you don't go now, you never will go." So I moved here in 2000.

Carol had served in varying positions at BnF Atlanta before moving to one of the BnF International sites for ten months. When she and the other members of the visiting team returned to Atlanta from Cape Town, their spiritual family was split by the schism. Carol chose to stay with David and his changing vision, which would gradually move the cause of the poor to the back burner. Carol continued to work with what is left of the Atlanta ministry, at times in administration and at others for post-Katrina New Orleans.

Like Carol, twenty-seven-year-old Autumn came to BnF from a revival school in Florida where she had learned about and experienced many of the gifts of the Spirit. Autumn jovially relates that she was a "little scared" about the visit to BnF because she heard there were rats in the Warehouse building where they would be staying. Rats or no rats, it was a visit that changed her life:

> After being there a couple of days, my whole life was changed. I heard about the Kingdom of God for the first time—His kingdom—not just an encounter with Jesus. I saw this whole new way of life, and it was awesome. And the poor—oh, the poor. The one thing that stands out is being in the Sanctuary (we slept in the Sanctuary with the people). I just remember being there as we were worshiping, and God was just breaking my heart. I've never experienced anything like it. I was just lying on the floor—I didn't care what germs were there—just crying, saying, "God, I really want to see you. I want you. I want to see you. I feel this is totally different from anything I have ever experienced."

Autumn returned to the revival school, but (like Carol) she found that something was missing: "I think it was after I came to BnF and then went back that I realized how relational God is and how relational BnF is. It's not only Jesus—that's only part of it. My relationship between me and Jesus is going to reflect my relationship with people."

Autumn became one of David's special daughters, often included in the group that ate together after services and listened to "Dad" as he shared his ever-changing visions diagramed on the yellow legal pad that he carried along with him. At times David would walk down the street holding her hand and she might, on occasion, sit on his lap. Autumn treasured the spiritual father-daughter bond. She was quick to embrace each new vision, and she seemed to have a special ability to connect with the poor who sought food and shelter at BnF. Autumn made an effort to learn the name of each "guest" (as the homeless were called) and listen to and address their personal concerns, and she was quick to pray with them. She was part of the faithful group of followers who walked with David through the schism, which separated her from many of her former family members. Until recently her artwork was for sale, along with the paintings of Jeff's wife and those of Janice VanCronkhite, on the BnF Web site.

In both Carol's and Autumn's interviews, illustrations are readily found that demonstrate the interface between growing in the love of God and loving the poor in accord with David's vision at the time. Colin, a forty-seven-year-old African American man from a solidly middle-class family, provides another illustration. Colin first came to BnF with a twelve-pack of beer, looking for some fun after hearing there was a block party in the area. He reported, "I heard music playing, and where I'm from, this means a block party—with barbecue and music and people coming together." Although the music sounded like dance music, in fact it was the worship band. About a half hour or forty-five minutes later, the worship broke and David began his ministry. Colin continued his story:

> Pastor David brought everyone together in prayer, and then he began to speak. He was speaking out of the book of Psalms and made a very, very profound statement that really touched my heart. At that time he said, "To someone here I want to say that Jesus loves you tonight." And when he said that, I had such a tremendous conviction over myself. I knew that he was speaking to me, and I just started crying. I knew that word was mine—and I grabbed it. I grabbed it. Pastor David prayed with me and whatnot. Then I spoke very briefly with him and said, "I am ready to change my life—I am ready to just give it up." And he said, "You need to come back with us tonight."

Colin moved into the Training Center. He shared how his attitude changed from thinking that "people who are poor are lazy" to "seeing the needs of the poor, learning more about them, and feeling compassion." He claims that "I now know my purpose," elaborating how he tries to treat each person he encounters with respect and compassion that he believes is not generally found in government-sponsored programs.

> I have a pastor's heart, and I pastor a lot of people just by my caring. God has given me an ability to be very good with names and birthdays and I can remember all kinds of stuff. And it is encouraging to people when I do—it makes it so personal. A lot of people who come to BnF to seek our services deal with state agencies and city services, and when they go there, they get handed a number. When they come here, it is all by name. And I will know their name three months from now when they come back. Yes, God has given me a heart for the people. My prayer for each day is more brokenness for myself—so that I can love God more and love people more. That is my prayer.

In observing Colin's performance in answering the daily phone calls requesting BnF's help and the drop-ins seeking food, shelter, or clothing, we saw someone who consistently treated the poor and homeless with concern and utmost respect. He saw his position as important—one that represented the first contact for many with the BnF family.

Colin had married another BnF church member (both reportedly independently heard God's call to marry the other) who, although drawn to the ministry, has always been employed full-time. While Colin served BnF, his wife worked in the marketplace. During the brewing schism, Colin sought to be a peacemaker, believing that reconciliation between the parties would eventually occur. Unlike most, who were less adept at navigating the troubled waters without choosing sides, Colin (one of the handful of black BnF family members) was able to remain with the BnF ministries under David and then Chris's interim administration. He continued with BnF when David was reinstated. During a visit in early 2006, however, one of the authors learned that Colin was no longer at his familiar post. A newcomer to BnF had replaced him.

During the time of the initial interviews, dedicated followers chose to focus on David's strengths. Some depicted David as "quick to listen" and "teachable" but also as an unquestionable heir to "God's special anointing." Katy, a forty-eight-year-old divorcée (who provided those short descriptions) called herself a "country mouse." She told of how awkward and out of place she felt when years ago she first visited David at his beautiful suburban home. Katy looked around at the fine furnishings and, in her discomfort, sat down on the floor. David, without missing a beat, immediately sat down next to her. Katy then added, "I had so much respect and awe for him even before he sat down next to me on the floor. But when he did that, I knew that I had found a man I could follow."

Katy had been involved with David (at least marginally) from the early Vineyard days until the mid-1990s, attributing her departure from BnF to personal difficulties within her family. She renewed and intensified her involvement in 2003. The following unsolicited comment speaks in a voice that resonates with those of other followers:

> You see, God calls David a man after his own heart. The reason that is because David is teachable. He is always ready to learn. I would sit in his office and say, "David, we have to do this." And he wouldn't see it. And I would just look at him and say, "Why can't you see just see this?" [laughs] But as we would sit there and talk, I would watch the light bulb go on in David. And as soon as David gets something, that's it. He's got it. Even if he doesn't get it right away, that's OK, because he wants to get it. And God honors that heart in him. That's why nobody else can wear his mantle. Nobody. Because God has placed that heart inside him.

Loving God, Loving Neighbor

Nearly all the respondents spoke about falling more deeply and more passionately in love with God and told of how their experience of God's love was the catalyst that deepened their love for others. Love of God and love of neighbor were intimately interwoven in BnF narratives. For example, Carol often heard God telling her, "Carol, there is more than you are receiving right now." What she believes this means is that "God loves me and that he expresses His love in different ways." Carol reflects on some of these ways that she learned during her journey with the BnF family:

> I know that God loves me, but at times it is different from his saying, "My daughter, I love you." Right now I am going through a rough time, and I feel that he is cradling me in his arms. Right now he is sharing a love that is different from a romantic love. It is more of a caring love. There are times I feel he is pursuing me and wants me to pursue him in a romantic passionate love. . . . When I first came to know him, I was introduced to church and to God, but I really didn't get it. I went to church and read

my Bible without understanding the relationship part of it. But one day it just clicked; it made sense. I am not living my life for me, but I am living it for Him.

Carol believed that knowing more of God's love empowered her to give her life to work with BnF even when the going seemed rough. When we asked Carol about the source of greatest satisfaction in being part of BnF, her answer reflected the answer we received from most of the interviewees: "I'd have to say it is the family orientation. The Lord says that He will put the lonely in families—and that is what he is doing. I have a family that is three thousand miles away, but I also have a family here. I have brothers and sisters—there is family every day." Spiritual transformation, according to the BnF vision, not only involved personal change, but also the development of new families—the Twelves—the structure of which was described in the last chapter. The interpersonal relationships fostered by the spiritual family were arguably the single most important draw for prospective members.

Transformation into Spiritual Families

Being a committed member of the BnF family was seen as essential for individual spiritual growth and for walking out the church's mission. In its earliest days BnF followers saw themselves as a spiritual revolutionary army, a twentieth-century American version of the Booths's Salvation Army. That model changed as David began to get "revelation" about the Twelve. Interviewees were quick to talk about the "family" and their "Twelve," commonly noting that "relationships" were what drew them to BnF and were what brought them the most satisfaction. The family referred to were primarily members like themselves who came to BnF to walk out their spiritual journeys with other like-minded, committed "brothers and sisters" under the authority of a spiritual "father." (Relationships with the poor and homeless, however, were qualitatively different, as our bringing the voice of the poor into the grand narrative will demonstrate.)

The development of the Twelve as a mechanism for living out family-like relations aligns with the literature that has demonstrated the importance of interpersonal relationships for converting, attracting, and maintaining members in religious groups. Janet Jacobs (1989) has suggested an analogy between conversion and falling in love, especially for conversion to groups like BnF that are led by a charismatic leader (Hood et al., 1996,

289–90). Occasionally respondents would volunteer a comment about "falling in love with the poor"; for most respondents, however, the vertical object of love was God while the horizontal love object took flesh in the family, specifically others who had committed to follow the vision and mission of David. Although David's ministry at the time emphasized the central place that the poor had in the Kingdom of God, only a minority specifically mentioned the poor and homeless as a factor in their joining BnF or in their spiritual transformation. Most frequently they talked of sensing God's presence and "walking in the supernatural," being drawn to David the prophet, and desiring to be part of a committed church family.

We have already seen how the Franklins, both describing themselves as having come from "functional families," were drawn to BnF as their new "home." Chris regarded David as his spiritual father who had introduced him to an abandoned pursuit of the Kingdom of God. Others—who lacked functional families of orientation, who experienced the breakup of families of procreation through divorce, or single men and women who were seeking something beyond themselves—seemed to welcome BnF as a spiritual family that they could claim as their own. Nan, a forty-five-year-old single physician, elaborated on why, after attempts to establish a BnF in her hometown failed, she left her successful career to live with BnF Atlanta for a time: "Everything I sought to do just fell to the ground. I couldn't understand it because the vision had grown and grown in my heart. The circumstances just weren't coming together to be able to pull it off. Then this summer I got this sense, 'This is my home—and I need to be going home.' Part of that 'going home' is the Twelve—there is not just ministry, there is also family. It's really nothing about the ministry per se; it's about relationships."

When asked what drew him to BnF, Randy, a divorced forty-five-year-old male who previously was employed as a store manager, responded simply, "The Holy Spirit—the unity, togetherness, community. I just knew I was supposed to be here." He elaborated on the difficulties he has had with intimate relationships:

> I never had any brothers or sisters. I was the only child in the family. My mother passed away, and my father is a very introverted guy. So understanding the connect between loving God and loving brothers as myself—knowing how selfish I have been—then trying to live with somebody. I now live with twelve guys that I would have never picked as roommates. So it has been a struggle. I can worship God all day, but until I can share

that love with others—until I can empty out . . . that's the hard part. Sincere love is something I didn't really understand. God had to show me, and he has shown me through my relationships here at BnF.

Some interviewees clearly put David at the center of the human relationship-building process; others put Chris Franklin or another leader at the center. Leah was someone who was drawn to David as her spiritual father and through him to the BnF ministry to the poor.

A friend at the school of ministry I attended had been to BnF and told me all about it. I really had no interest at all in it at that time. It's all about timing. Some time later David came down to the school. I didn't hear him speak, but my friend told me he was there and suggested we see if we could catch him. That was my first encounter with David, and he spoke some prophetic words over me. I still had no interest in BnF until a couple of months later when this friend and I visited BnF. As she gave me a tour of the warehouse I thought, "Get me out of here!" [laughs] But a month later we came back and I met with David. He began to speak of the Twelve, of relationship, of the Father's heart, and His desire to restore the hearts of children to the Father. My heart just leapt. I immediately had a connection with him. The Lord began to stir in my heart. I mean, that encounter with him at the warehouse just stirred a lot of desires in my heart for a father that I had no idea I had. So that began a relationship.

The interviewer asked, "So the draw seemed to be relationship?" Leah continued: "It was relationship only. I toured the facility; I heard what ministry was about, but my journey was David's heart—his heart to want to father and just the love that penetrated my heart." Leah not only wanted a father, but she also sought to live out David's vision of relationship with the poor. She quoted David saying, "If you are struggling or having a bad day or feel depressed, go to the poor and God will take all that away," advice that Leah found to be "unbelievably true." But Leah also shared her struggle with building relationships as she sought to establish a Twelve of her own that would model the love she experienced from David's. There was a young student, Anna, who came to BnF, and with whom Leah prayed—someone the Lord told her to "have a relationship with." Due to abuse and a lack of love in her life, the student was not particularly responsive to Leah's outreach. Leah asked David what she should do. David responded: "You know what you struggle with and what you have been through. You know how difficult it is for you. Multiply that by one hundred and you have Anna. Just be there—just be consistent. It could take two months or it could take twenty years. Just be consistent and don't expect anything." We observed many examples of disciples trying to live out this type of selfless advice, but they usually did so with very limited success and for a very short season. One telling example is found in stories related to David's teaching on "extravagant giving."

Modeling Extravagant Giving

"Giving extravagantly" was one of values frequently preached at BnF. There was a time, as David recounts events, when BnF "had become very un-extravagant" (*BnF Newsletter*, February 2002). As David went on to explain: "Coming face to face with the spirit of poverty everyday makes it easy to ignore. It's the thing that causes you to hold on tightly to the little (or much) out of fear of not getting it or anything else back. But we started giving again."

The recipients of extravagant giving were introduced by David as being designated by God and the sums collected given by God. As an example, the same issue of *BnF Newsletter* that commemorated the return to extravagant giving reported God's words to David about a visiting worship leader and musician: "I want you to *blow her mind away with extravagant giving*" (italics in original). The recipient was to be JoAnn, an evangelist musician who frequently visited BnF and who would later support David during the schism. JoAnn had also reportedly heard from God about this particular visit to BnF; God said to her: "I am about *to blow your mind away with my extravagant love for you*." In the newsletter account, David went on to commend the family members who "gave extravagantly even sacrificially" in obedience to David's vision. He recounted that the family sacrificed "motorcycles, savings accounts, guitars, shoes, boots, cash, watches, more motorcycles, more guitars and music equipment, jackets, more cash, silver candlesticks, family heirlooms, more motorcycle parts . . ." JoAnn left with an offering of $28,622, including her own 2000 Harley-Davidson Sportster. David ends this testimony with, "In four short days over $100,000 was given (not received). *Thank you, Lord*." JoAnn was blessed on more than one occasion with BnF's extravagant giving—so were other select individuals, churches, and ministries.

The criteria for selection were never clear to the authors, save for the fact that David stated that he had heard a call from God. Margaret was present in 2001 when over forty thousand dollars was allegedly collected from the small group gathered and given to support another BnF ministry in South Africa. Based on what we later learned from members of the board of trustees, we have reason to doubt that the entire amount came from the small group who gathered that night. David probably supplemented the collection with monies given to the general operating budget. This practice of supplementing free-will offerings of "extravagant giving" with BnF general funds occurred again just before the schism, when ten thousand dollars was given to the owner of a local diner. This woman was a nonbeliever and lesbian friend of David's biological son. She used the money not to save her livelihood but to remodel her living quarters, and the BnF construction business was paid to do the remodeling. The facts were woven into two stories, narrating a noteworthy case of selfless "extravagant giving" and God's miraculous provision of a project to help launch the new construction company. The diner closed, and remodeling the woman's house cost the new company far more time and money over the next year than anticipated.

When BnF was caught in the crunch of its own hard financial times after the schism, a story of a Sanctuary resident generously giving a check for five thousand dollars (his total life's savings) was widely circulated. It was said that "even homeless people have money." The man was to be recognized as someone who "gave sacrificially to the church."

David controlled both the collecting and the spending of money at BnF. It was he who selected the recipient and who appeared as the benefactor when the money was given. David liked to model "extravagant giving." He often picked up large restaurant tabs for visitors and the select family members who dined with him. He urged his followers to follow his example and to tip servers using the measure of BnF's value of extravagant giving. When the schism unleashed the critical voice of dissidents, extravagant giving became a choice target. As one family member commented, "David urged us to be extravagant with the little money we had, but he never used his own money for extravagant giving. It's easy to pick up tabs and leave big tips when you are doing it with church funds." Many others family members made similar comments to us.

Three Central Meanings of Love

The church/ministry of BnF provides a laboratory for exploring the complexity and varieties of love. The term *love*, as used in everyday language, includes a bewildering diversity of phenomena reflected in a wide array of literary, theological, and theoretical reflections. Classifications exist for defining love into types based on historical notions (including "courtly love" and "romantic love"); those based on theological and philosophical distinctions ("eros," "philia," "agape," and "caritas") as well as everyday common distinctions (such as "friendship," "romantic love," and "maternal love"). At its core, however, love can be said to be a relation between a subject and an object that positively inclines one person (the lover) toward another person or object (Johnson 2001).

Scholars have worked with this core understanding to produce scores of taxonomies, classificatory schema, and theories; but, as Rolf Johnson has pointed out, they still leave a major source of disagreement. These classifications often skirt discussions about the exact nature of the relation between the lover and the beloved, namely, "How the lover is inclined toward the object, what the lover's interest in it is, how he or she is apt to behave toward it, and the nature of the lover's feelings regarding it" (Johnson 2001, 3). Johnson proposes a classification that aims "to create a system that embraces all that we call 'love'—from simple attractions, to exalted passions, from self-sacrificial giving to all-consuming obsession" (5). The product is a typology that he calls "the three faces" or "three central meanings" of love—faces that he labels as *care-love, appreciation-love,* and *union-love.* These three categories of love serve a heuristic purpose in helping us work through the maze of affections reflected in the interview data presented in this chapter. Before love can be assessed for qualities like purity, duration, intensity, extensity, and adequacy, as we propose to do, it is helpful to know which face or meaning of love is being presented.

Johnson asserts that his three central meanings of love are "logically independent." Our interviews suggest that although it is questionable to equate *logical* independence with *empirical* independence, as Johnson seems to have done, the taxonomy is useful for a better understanding of love in terms of Collins's IRs. The three faces of love, often intertwined, as seen in the illustrative stories, are all potential sources of emotional energy; but the rewards provided by the different IRs—with others in the community, with the poor, with David and his vision, and with God—vary with different people and their particular spiritual journey.

Much of what we have illustrated in this chapter illustrates care-love. Johnson describes care-love "as concern for the good or the welfare of someone or something. To love, in this sense, is to care for or to care about the object" (2001, 30). Care-love can be regarded as the relational love depicted in the horizontal line at the base of the letter *L* that was often used at BnF to illustrate horizontal human love relationships. Two interrelated observations are worthy of special note with regard to care-love at BnF. First, care-love was central to David's preaching; both God and BnF are concerned, as David would frequently note, with loving care for the poor. It is also important to point out through the *L* (love) analogy that care-love at BnF is understood as being mediated by the love of God, a supernatural divine love that is the basis of David's continual prophetic statements.

The primary object of human love that forms the base of the *L* can fluctuate and change. For some David was the central figure; for others, another BnF leader or the "brothers and sisters" in the BnF family; for still others it was the poor and homeless. One essential parameter of such "directional love," however, was that it was mediated through the vision and language of concern and caring love for the poor. An important reason given by David for a relational church modeled after the family was for more effective ministry to the less fortunate.

Almost all respondents reported being attracted to the familiar relations that BnF promised through the Twelve. The vision of the Twelve proposed to link the objects of love in dynamic relationships; David would mentor his core group and each of these members would reach out to others (especially the poor, homeless, and young) to mentor their disciples in another ring of Twelves, who in turn would establish Twelves of their own. The Twelve, however, never worked as well in daily living as they did on paper. Some heard David's message about the centrality of the poor in God's kingdom. They were truly attracted to either the vision of and/or the reality of serving the poor. In their ministry there was genuine love for both God and the poor coupled with a desire to enter into relationships with the latter. Our data suggest, however, that often these relationships were of low intensity and low duration. Some care more easily for family than the poor; others care more for the poor than family.

In our assessment of David's actions during our course of study the love he modeled could be better characterized as appreciation-love than care-love. Appreciation-love is more aesthetic and abstract and also less active than care-love. As Johnson describes it, "The lover simply beholds the love object, appreciating it for what it is" (2001, 113). David could wax eloquently about his vision—about the kingdom, about love, and about the poor—but to us he seemed unable to model the living out of the quality of relationships to which he has challenged his disciples.

The significance of appreciation-love became increasingly clear to us as David's vision underwent a major adjustment after the schism. His post-schismatic vision continued to be about relationships, but it suggested that it was important to move beyond "compassion" toward more abstract goals including a renewed focus on "the Kingdom" and "justice." And while he continued to encourage the development of "relationships" within the community, the work with the homeless was decried as having focused on ministry rather than love relationships. We watched intently as David's beloved vision for the poor continued to increase in abstraction.

What Johnson says about appreciation-love and justice can be considered in light of David's vision of justice and his face of love for the poor:

> Does one, for example, intend the welfare of an ideal such as justice through loving it? In some sense, this might be possible. Lovers of justice would presumably practice it and thereby strengthen its existence in the world, influencing others to love and practice it. Or they might devote themselves to articulating its nature, and thus contribute to others' understanding of it. However, it is not clear that justice itself benefits from such care, nor even that its benefit can be coherently intended. . . . All that is required is the realization that one can love justice appreciatively without believing that doing so could contribute to its welfare. (2001, 122)

David's vision—whether about justice, the Twelve, or the Kingdom of God—is a primary face of love. The ever-changing vision can never be fully grasped, but it can provide a Quixote-like reality that is loved and nurtured. This meaningful but abstract reality can be assessed for its purity, intensity, extensity, duration, and adequacy but perhaps only in conjunction with the lenses provided by a more concrete care-love.

Although Johnson's discussion of union-love, the third face of love, focuses on romantic love, he does note the similar unitive nature of spiritual or mystical love. The object of union-love is attaining such a union or preserving, deepening, or extending an existing union, and this love object with which the lover seeks union is frequently divine. Johnson reports an interview between Jean Houston and Mother Teresa to illustrate this meaning of love, in which Houston asked, "Mother, how does it happen that you are able to do so much, and why are you in this state of joy?" The conversation continued:

"My dear," she said, "it is because I am so deeply in love."

"But, Mother, you are a nun!"

"Precisely," she said. "I am married to Jesus."

"Yes, I understand you are married to Jesus. All nuns are."

"No, you do not understand," she countered. "I really am. I am so in a state of love that I see the face of my Beloved in the face of the dying man in the streets of Calcutta. I see my Beloved in the day-old child who's left outside our convent, and in the leper whose flesh is decaying; and I can't do enough for my Beloved! That's why I try to do something beautiful for God." (Johnson 2001, 100–101)

Although Mother Teresa can be regarded as an exemplar—even an icon—in the practice of union-love, her response speaks to the importance of the unique intersect of the human and the divine that can occur in this face of love. What drew many followers to David was his ability, through personal charisma and vision, to ignite the flame of union-love within them and to provide the place where it could continue to burn. The EE generated by appreciation love or love of the vision can be seen as a kind of bubble around BnF in which family members as well as some of the homeless sought to live out godly love.

5

Godly Love as Emotional Energy

> We must be careful to distinguish EE [emotional energy] from
> other kinds of emotions that are displayed. First, EE is not simply a
> matter of showing a lot of excitement, agitation, loudness, or bodily
> movement. These are characteristics of the dramatic or disruptive
> emotions: shouting or lashing out in anger, squealing and gestur-
> ing with joy, shrieking or running around in fear. EE instead is a
> strong steady emotion, lasting over a period of time, not a short-
> term disruption of a situation. A general characteristic of EE is that
> it gives the ability to act with initiative and resolve, to set the direc-
> tion of social situations rather than to be dominated by others in
> the micro-details of interaction. And it is an emotion that allows
> individuals to be self-directed when alone, following a smooth flow
> of thoughts, rather than a jerky or distracted inner conversation.
> —Collins 2004, 133-34

In this chapter we continue to explore godly love as "a strong
steady emotion" that is found in the experience of the paranormal gifts of
the Holy Spirit or charismata. As characteristic of all EE, the charismata
"gives the ability to act with initiative and resolve, to set the direction of
social situations" (Collins 2004, 133-34). We use qualitative interview narratives and statistical findings from survey data to empirically demonstrate the effects of godly love on care-love and altruistic behavior.

As we have seen, BnF is a neo-Pentecostal emerging church that sought
to adapt traditional beliefs and practices of the historic Pentecostal movement into a language and form that resonates with contemporary society.
As Shayne Lee has astutely observed in comparing neo-Pentecostal and
Pentecostal beliefs and behaviors, "Neo-Pentecostals are more flexible and
emphasize a Christian's freedom to be led by the Spirit in all aspects of

life. Hence, neo-Pentecostalism offers a less costly faith than Pentecostalism by removing puritanical asceticism without sacrificing an emphasis on God's power and an appreciation for ecstatic experiences" (2005, 34). This flexibility is reflected in the revivals of the 1990s, especially in the Toronto Blessing (Poloma 2003). Pneumatologist and theologian Clark Pinnock described godly love found at the Toronto renewal that energized and revived American Pentecostalism as follows:

> The essential contribution of the Toronto Blessing lies in its spirituality of playful celebration. . . . What do people come to celebrate? Not raw experience or contentless mysticism, but the Father's love. They want to grasp, as the apostle Paul urges us, how broad and long and high and deep is the love that surpasses knowledge; and they want it to roll over them like ocean waves. It is not enough to express belief in it—knowing about it is not enough. Doctrine is no substitute for a love affair. In Toronto, the Bride of Christ wants to fall in love with Jesus again. (2001, 4–5)

Church, for David, was similarly a "playful celebration," far more than singing three old hymns, a Bible reading, and a dry sermon. It was a lively gathering that might have more in common with Hollywood than the "dead churches" that he believed were commonplace. David saw the importance of integrating the supernatural into the larger culture; he asserted that Hollywood has done a better job than the church of taking the miraculous seriously:

> If God were roaming about the earth today looking for someone to exile to the island of Patmos; someone to write a book about the heavens and the earth and its future; someone to see, hear and record unbelievable supernatural events; someone who could see it, believe it and would then be willing to be laughed at and ridiculed for writing about the supernatural; someone willing to tell it like "it is"; like they saw and heard it. Where would God stop as He searched for someone willing to do something like this? . . . No, He wouldn't go to the Church . . . but He might go to Hollywood . . . they know that despite what we say, we Americans want the supernatural! We are hungry for the supernatural . . . we have to believe that there is something more powerful than our money, our doctors, our counselors, our systems, and historically the only place we can turn for hope like that is either Hollywood or the comic books. The Church just doesn't believe there is a God who still moves the way He did 2000 years ago. (VanCronkhite 2002, 36)

While old-time Pentecostals had taboos against "worldly entertain-ment" (including movies, secular music, and dancing), BnF, reflecting the postmodernism of other emerging churches, would use contempo-rary music, dance, and other art forms for its outreach and worship. It was called "fierce raging worship" and it appeared to both of us to have more of the feel and sound of a rave than a Protestant church service. Hollywood was celebrated rather than condemned in BnF culture, and its creations could be used to support BnF's alternate worldview. A good ex-ample of how BNF used Hollywood to link popular culture to the BnF vision of the supernatural was its interpretation of *The Matrix*.

While *The Matrix* is a film about a world in which an artificial real-ity created by sentient machines attempted to subdue the human popula-tion, its references to religious ideas provided a popular medium through which to introduce BnF's world of paranormal possibilities. With post-modern lenses the Matrix can be seen as a prototype of the American dream, both being illusory realities that keeps the human population docile. Like Neo, the godlike hero of the film, Spirit-filled Christians can do the seemingly impossible in the war of good against evil once their eyes are open to their supernatural heritage. With this introduction to the paranormal comes an implicit promise that life could be as exciting as a Hollywood film for those walking on the Spirit-filled path.

The survey conducted among BnF followers and Sanctuary residents demonstrates that the respondents valued walking in the supernatural. It was rated as very important (70 percent) or important (17 percent) by an overwhelming number of the 105 BnF followers who completed the questionnaire (see appendix B-1 for a copy of the instrument). Sanctu-ary residents were less likely (43 percent) to report that walking in the supernatural was very important to them than the BnF family members (70 percent). This obviously significant difference is but one indicator that David's influence is far greater with his largely white followers than it is with the black poor they serve, an attitudinal difference that is mirrored the practice of speaking in tongues or glossolalia.

Glossolalia and the Kingdom

Over the past several decades, considerable research has been con-ducted in different disciplines on speaking in tongues. Scholars in the fields of theology, anthropology, religious history, semiotics, philosophy, linguistics, sociology, and psychology have all had their say about this phenomenon that has been found in diverse religions over the centuries and that has played a key role in Pentecostalism (Cartledge 2006; Spittler 2002; Mills 1986). Empirical studies have described glossolalia as "a mode of 'free vocalization' which nonetheless exhibits a degree phonological structuring greater than that found in comparable phenomena like baby talk and schizophrenese, while falling short of the complex suprasegmental sound-patterning associated with natural language" (Hilborn 2006, 111). For those who practice glossolalia in Pentecostal contexts, speaking in tongues is most commonly regarded as a prayer language, although for some it is also practiced as a form of prophecy in corporate settings (i.e., tongues followed by an "interpretation" in vernacular language), in conjunction with prophecy and/or prophetic prayer in private and corporate settings, and occasionally as xenolalia (i.e., someone speaks in tongues in a known language).

With the exception of one intern who had been with BnF only a few months, all the interviewees were glossolalic and most used their "prayer language" daily. Open-ended questions about glossolalic practice were included in a section of the interview about prayer. Some volunteered information about speaking in tongues as the topic moved to personal prayer, but most reported on tongue speaking only after being asked the direct question, "Do you speak in tongues?" Specific questions about tongues revealed that with the exception of two or three interview cases, all insisted that "praying in the spirit" or "praying with my prayer language" was a very important part of their lives. Some claimed to quietly pray in tongues on every possible occasion, believing that this was how they could follow the apostle Paul's instruction in 1 Thessalonians 17 to "pray without ceasing."

David's teachings about tongues departed from old Pentecostalism that stressed the doctrine of tongues as the "initial physical evidence" of Spirit baptism; he distanced himself from most old doctrine as much as he did from old religion. What he did emphasize through his teachings and his example is how tongue speaking empowers believers to walk in the supernatural. He strongly encouraged its use while providing a cultural setting where glossolalia was a normal part of daily life. Having been raised in a denomination where tongues was regarded as a bona fide spiritual gift for the early biblical church but one not intended for modern times, at first David was skeptical about glossolalia. It was only after a woman he met at church phoned and prayed in an "unknown language" for a back condition of David's (during which he was healed) that he was open to receiving this gift. He gives the following succinct description of the result of a minister praying with him for his spiritual language:

> I learned that day the gift of tongues was like every other gift. First, we must desire it. Then we must be willing to use it after we receive it. All we do is open our mouths; God does the rest. He will give the utterances. At first, I did not "speak fluently" as some do. I spoke a very "infantile" language, like baby talk. Ten years later I heard my friend, Jackie Pullinger of St. Stephens Society in Hong Kong explain it something like this: "speaking in your spiritual language is much like learning to talk in your natural language. You don't necessarily start with a full vocabulary. You start where you are with a few utterances, but, as you begin to speak, that language grows quite strong." (VanCronkhite 2000, 4)

With only a few exceptions, all the respondents claimed that praying in tongues had become a vital part of their daily lives since coming to BnF. The slight majority who prayed in tongues before their involvement in the community all claimed that they pray in tongues more now than they did before. Many of David's followers described their use of tongues within a set-aside prayer time, but nearly all noted that they pray in tongues frequently each day—as they are walking, driving, shopping, and going about other daily tasks and chores. For the BnF family, tongues is first and foremost described as a medium of prayer—of opening up one's being to the supernatural Kingdom with a power to change lives.

Autumn, a twenty-seven-year-old female respondent with post-college education whose transformation story we shared in the last chapter, provided the following description when asked what tongues means to her:

> I find it vital. I believe tongues is the key that opens up our spirits to the rest of the supernatural world. As far as personal tongues—the everyday speaking in tongues—it makes my spirit stronger. I use it for worship. It is a language that goes beyond my mind—*and my mind has a tendency to get in the way!* [she continued speaking with greater animation] I give thanks to God for tongues because it bypasses the whole brain. I go straight to God and this channel opens up in the supernatural. Like it clears all the static so I can get a good reception. It's the only way I know how to explain it.

This succinct statement makes some important points about glossolalia as prayer, which we assert is an empirical example of EE. Glossolalia is

perceived as a means of connecting a person to the spiritual world, opening up the channel and clearing the static so that the person can hear with
spiritual ears and see with spiritual eyes. It is also experienced as a medium for receiving spiritual empowerment.

Randy, a man in his mid-forties, began speaking in tongues shortly after he came to BnF. He described being Spirit baptized as his "most memorable spiritual experience": "When I was struck with the Holy Spirit, I
began speaking in tongues. I literally experienced the divine indwelling!
Being raised Southern Baptist, I had never really believed in tongues or
given it much thought. But when the Holy Spirit struck me, I actually
cried out in tongues. I experienced a breaking off of stuff and angels coming. It was awesome."

Visions of angels (and demons) were not unusual in accounts of glossolalia. Randy claimed that he spends the majority of his prayer time "praying in the spirit." It is while engaged in glossolalic prayer, Randy says, "that
I get revelation, I get discernment, I get direction." Through this account
we begin to see how glossolalia is intertwined with other paranormal experiences, including visions, words of knowledge, and spiritual direction.
Praying in tongues thus offers the pray-er a medium for direct two-way
conversation and communion with the divine.

Dawn, a middle-aged female respondent who became glossolalic only
after coming to BnF two years prior to the interview, described the interrelationship between the divine communion she experienced in glossolalic prayer as it related to her ministry in praying for others and in
giving prophetic words of knowledge (insights believed to come from the
Holy Spirit rather than natural ways of knowing) of encouragement and
support:

> I guess when I pray in tongues God has been asking me to pray for some-
> one, but I don't know what to pray. I believe when I pray in tongues that
> He knows that that person needs, and I don't necessarily have to know
> what their need is. My spirit knows and communicates directly with
> God.
>
> And also when I am praying in tongues, God will give me visions and
> He will give me specifics. Like when we pray in the evenings before the
> people come from the streets to eat, I will pray in tongues and I will have
> an urging. I know this is what I need to put into prayer. I don't always
> know what I should be praying or what I should be asking, but the Spirit
> praying through me does. And I am very visual—I get lots of visions that

apply to others. When I share the vision with the person for whom it is intended, people understand what the vision means for them and how it fits. Otherwise I would not have had a clue. When I report a vision, others will often say, "I get that. Oh, yeah. It's so right on."

Although speaking in tongues is generally thought of as a gift only for the pray-er, in the interview accounts we often noted a relational component. Some former addicts, for example, explicitly linked their addictions to a misdirected search for the spiritual and relational, both of which were partially met through the charism of tongue speaking. Evan, a twenty-one-year-old male whose drug addiction began while he was a student in a Christian high school, says he had always been religious—and guilt-ridden—about his drug problem. He reported doing drugs and frequently getting to a point where he would break because "I didn't want to go to hell!" He would then respond to his guilt by saying a prayer of repentance, but it failed to change his behavior: "I said it ever how many times. I didn't do good for very long; I would fall right back into my addiction." Shortly before coming to BnF he received the gift of tongues at an evangelical rally but claims that he did not immediately appreciate its value. He noted how the community at BnF provided the place for him to learn the power of his prayer language:

> Tongues wasn't a hard thing for me. Nobody taught me to do it. I heard about it a little—and I started praying in tongues. Then I went right back to doing what I was doing. I didn't pray regularly in tongues—just could do it if I wanted to do it. I still had no relationship to walk with. I knew it was real, but I didn't have relationship and my heart longed for it. I think that's why I did all the drugs—to numb the thing for relationship. That's all I was ever searching for.

This young man began "hanging out and doing the stuff" at BnF while still a high school student. He reported, "Wherever supernatural stuff was happening, I was up in the middle of it. I was drawn to the supernatural." At one point one of the leaders (Chris Franklin) prayed with him and then said, "Now you go pray for people." According to Evan, "I had prayed for people before, but not in that setting. And God just started doing the stuff through me—right then. That was when a switch flipped in me, I guess. It's not just the anointed man of God, but if you believe, it will happen through you! I was alive. It [the supernatural] became a lifestyle I could walk in instead of something that happens only in services. The same way I was caught up in the drugs—as a lifestyle. It's the same with the supernatural; it can be a lifestyle."

At the foundation of the BnF lifestyle is a belief in direct channel to the divine that is opened through experiencing intimacy with God through praying in tongues. Although commonly regarded as a personal gift of the spirit, it often has a social dimension for empowerment and service, through prophetic prayer, words of knowledge, and the ability to pray effectively for others in need. The empowerment takes on an interrelated but more controversial form when discussing the use of tongues for "spiritual warfare."

Warring Kingdoms

Not unlike the battle found in *The Matrix*, the supernatural Kingdom of God is seen as being at war with the kingdom of darkness. Thus glossolalia functions not only as a key to open doors to the supernatural but also becomes a weapon for waging war against evil in the spiritual realm. In a newsletter released in April 2003, LeAnn, one of BnF's longtime leaders, described what prayer has already done to this battle and its relationship to Atlanta's maladies:

> The prayer support has bombed the enemy's strongholds, but behind the places once known as places of comfort, familiarity, and peace, we find division, confusion, and strife. The homeless population is increasing. The economy is on the rocks. People are wounded by the systems of the world, by the discovery that "affordable housing" is not affordable, and skeptical of a city that says they are too busy to hate but in reality is the third meanest city in the nation. Atlanta is crying for compassion and justice. The trials of war are hard. Spiritually and naturally bodies become tired, sickness creeps in, and discouragement crouches at the door waiting for the right moment to hit. Blood-n-Fire has heard the call to go to war for the city of Atlanta. We know it is our call to take righteousness, peace, and joy in the Holy Spirit—the Kingdom of God to the streets. We are starting to face trials like never before.

Many respondents packaged the Kingdom of God, spiritual warfare, and tongues as a theme. Billy, a forty-year-old African American man in the Restoration phase of the drug rehabilitation program, said he knew nothing about the Kingdom of God and tongue speaking before coming to BnF. He was emphatic about the power of tongues to fight personal spiritual battles with the devil: "I think when I pray in tongues, things begin to happen in me—positive things. It makes Satan flee. It's like I can see Satan sitting right here [laughs and points to his shoulder] and as I pray in tongues I can almost see him leave."

The demonic is commonly believed to be manifest in negative emotions and addictive drives, which can be dissipated through the use of tongues. Kim, a twenty-nine-year-old white woman who had been with BnF for six years and married to Jeff (whose spiritual transformation story was told in the last chapter), had been involved in the occult before coming to BnF. She reportedly experienced both inner healing and deliverance from her past participation with a form of the paranormal condemned by the Pentecostal movement. Now a born-again, spirit-filled Christian, she describes herself as being a "seer or prophetically gifted" but also as one coming under "a lot of attacks from the devil." For her the gift of tongues plays an important role in deciphering the Holy Spirit from the devil. It also plays an important role in what neo-Pentecostals call inner or emotional healing. As Kim describes it: "Praying in tongues is very much a part of my daily life. Sometimes I can go into a room and someone will be dealing with major anger—and suddenly I find myself getting angry. It is allowing me to feel what the other person is feeling so that I know how to pray for them rightly. So I have to pray in tongues so that God can work in me and in the other person."

Those who lived in the Warehouse (the site of the Training Center for addicts) or the Sanctuary (the homeless shelter) were especially adamant about the importance of tongues for warring against evil and potentially dangerous situations. A forty-six-year-old African American male who was in charge of the Training Program at the time of the interview reported using tongues when he "doesn't have the right words to express to God what I am thinking and what I am feeling or what's in my heart." But, as do others at BnF, he prays in the Spirit "any time I feel threatened or under attack or when I am walking through circumstances that I can't control or I'm at that point when I am about to crack." He goes on to provide an example of how he prays in tongues when confronted with the possibility of physical harm:

It was just last night. One of the gentlemen in the house just had open-heart surgery about three weeks ago, and I had to go and pick up a prescription for him. So at about eleven o'clock last night I had to walk through one of the neighborhoods that is not one of the best. I always give a look over my shoulders to make sure nobody's following me or anything like that. I don't know—but just walking past some people, I found myself praying in tongues. It took away certain thoughts and things of that nature. It provided a kind of hedge of protection that I needed.

When trouble brews in the vicinity of BnF, whether it is a volatile exchange of words or weapons, we noticed that it was not unusual to see people gathered around the periphery quietly praying in tongues as other take measures to resolve the conflict. We heard occasional stories about the power of glossolalia to overcome violence—as when a drug dealer had a gun aimed at David, and it repeatedly misfired as followers prayed in tongues; but in everyday situations dealing with the homeless, the response could be quite different. On more than one occasion we saw David's followers seize a person who became violent and carry him (seldom her) outside, refusing him readmission to the Sanctuary.

Whether the warfare be interior and personal, interpersonal conflict, or against external urban problems, glossolalia was reported by interviewees to be an important spiritual weapon in the war between the kingdoms. Matt provided us with a detailed account of a BnF family gathering where many of the facets of glossolalia and the attendant gifts we have been discussing were experienced collectively. This account of a most memorable evening illustrates how perceived supernatural encounters can be seen as but another example of interaction ritual chains.

A Night to Remember

Matt titled his detailed description of the Twelve meeting at a family member's apartment on April 10, 2002, "A Prophetic Night." Only the day before, Matt had received what he believed to be word from God, which he had written down and shared with David. It came in a most unusual way, as a kind of "automatic writing." Matt received three words in his mind—he wrote them down and a few more came. Before long he had a coherent document that he believed he was supposed to share with the BnF family. As he began reading the "prophetic word of knowledge" at a gathering of David's Twelve, Matt noted that "a bunch of people started crying because the Spirit got real heavy." In an interview with Margaret, Matt gave Margaret a written summary of what went on during that four-and-a-half-hour meeting. With his permission selected texts from the twenty-page manuscript are woven into the narrative:

Part of the word that I got was "close your eyes and look into my Spirit." That word seemed to be something directed at me. When I closed my eyes and stood up, I didn't see the room. All I could see was what was going on in the spirit. And I saw hundreds of angels standing all inside the apartment. I saw some demonic spirits. Then God started speaking. It went on for four and a half hours of me speaking prophetically. It was not just "the Lord is going to bless your life," but like real specific—like "when you were 12 years old and dealing with this thing with your dad, and he wouldn't let you have a motorcycle and you put up a wall against him." Down to the money! And this was done for the whole leadership team. It was wild! Nobody moved for four and a half hours—we didn't get out until 11:30 that night.

My world was shook. I grew up believing I was a spirit living inside a physical body, but I had very little evidence of it. I had studied quantum physics and I understood that there's not really much of us actually here. My brother (the genius) studies God-consciousness. So I had an understanding of the basics of the philosophy—but suddenly I saw it. I stood face to face with angels and went head to head with demonic spirits. It wasn't just praying against them; we've been doing that here for years, and it's no big deal. But this was wild! It was seeing angels just walking around, and it seemed like it was just natural. I don't remember a lot of what I said that night; if people remind me, then I remember it.

Matt realized that things might appear a little odd, even to seasoned BnF members who gathered that evening, and he sought to put the group at ease. He told them of the experiences he had at church camp, including the visions, extended experience of tongues, and the miracles that he saw when he was fifteen years old. The unusual events unfolding at this Twelve meeting some fifteen later resonated with Matt's earlier experience. Then Matt felt that God was instructing him to pray in tongues. As he did, the following happened:

The Holy Spirit explained that these tongues were going to command angels to move. I stood up from the sofa and began to pray in tongues. I suddenly felt an authority in the Spirit that I had never experienced. I began to pray in tongues and saw angels moving in the room, and they seemed to be moving because of the directions that I was giving them while praying in tongues. I saw a large group of angels standing behind David. These angels had been with him for many years and were there to help him fulfill his calling at BnF. His angels also carried a lot of the anointing to minister to the poor. It was time for David to turn over the ministry of BnF Atlanta to the leadership at this meeting so that he can move onto the deeper things that God has called him to complete.

During the early stages of the schism in which Matt and his family were exiled from the BnF family, he would return to this vision. From his perspective, the vision was being fulfilled. God's anointing had lifted from David that night because of his failure to pass on the mantle as God had instructed. From the perspective of the authors there may be another lesson to glean. While David may be a prophet, he never claimed to be a mystic. In terms of the supernatural mystical gifts, Matt was outperforming his master.

Matt described his walking in the supernatural as a kind of gray area or, as he said, "the space between the words of the Bible." It represented the difference between the letter of the law and the spirit of the law. He knew that what happened that night was "not necessarily scriptural but that it did not go against or violate Scripture either." For him it was important for the family to dialogue with each other about what happened and to talk about anything they didn't understand. Matt then added, "Again, it was a family meeting and many things were able to transpire because of the closeness of the people in the group. It is my belief that theological-scriptural debates can become a real point of distraction if not walked out in prayer."

This memorable family gathering was filled with glossolalia, spirit beings (both angelic and demonic), some speaking words of knowledge, others seeing visions, and experiences of the prophetic. Some interviewees mentioned it to Margaret as one of the spiritual highlights of their journey into the supernatural; others were not certain what it meant in the grand scheme of things at BnF. Although David seemed open to what had transpired, he raised some doubts about its authenticity. It appeared to us that David managed the supernatural by permitting it to unfold; but when the paranormal occurrence did not enhance his vision or position, he would subtly sow seeds to plant doubts and to suggest possible problems.

The Prophetic as Words of Knowledge, Affirmation, Prayer, and Revelation

According to the Pentecostal worldview, prophecy is not a gift only for the spiritually elite; it is available to men as well as women, young as well as old, children as well as adults, rich as well as poor. Prophecy is more than simply a personal mystical experience through which God speaks; it is also a corporate one, having meaning only as its content is shared with another person or a larger community. As can be gleaned from the account just presented, prophecy can be likened to a bridge between the individual mystical self and the community. Prophecy is not truly prophetic, however, unless it is socially sanctioned. In BnF the sanctioning ultimately means the approval of prophecy by David himself.

As Gerald Sheppard has wisely noted, our "best efforts at description—in this case of something called 'prophecy'—are never timeless, innocent or constant from one epoch to another" (2001, 48). This is true for the functioning of prophecy within BnF as well as any comparison of prophecy within various streams of Pentecostalism or with intuitive experiences outside the Pentecostal movement. For example, private prophecies (such as those alluded to by Matt) as words of knowledge given to an individual are widely practiced in neo-Pentecostalism, but this phenomenon is seen much less often in more traditional Pentecostal circles. While private prophecy functions to sustain the individual with the spiritual community, it can do so only if it does not violate the community standards.

Sheppard correctly notes that a wide range of activities can be described as prophetic by Pentecostals and neo-Pentecostals. Prophecy may "take the form of 'interpretation' by one person in a familiar language immediately following incomprehensible tongues (or glossolalia) delivered usually by another person" (Sheppard 2001, 48). It can also include other variations, such as "anointed preaching, when the preacher feels like a channel of the Holy Spirit and words seem to flow in an effortless manner"; the words of a "'healing evangelist' [who] might sense special prophetic insights accompanying the healing manifestations of the Spirit"; and a "'word of knowledge' most pertinent to a single individual delivered by one person to another" (48). Although most Pentecostals and neo-Pentecostals share the belief that "prophecy does not typically predict the future, but gives assurance, confirmation, warning, or spiritual inducement" (64), some groups (like BnF) are more open to futuristic predictions than are others—particularly when they fit into David's latest vision.

Whatever the theological nuances, the various forms of prophecy need to be placed in a larger context. First of all, prophecy is a form of prayer—more specifically, a form of revelatory prayer that assumes intimacy with a living God (Poloma 2003, 215–22). It represents one end of a continuum between active, one-directional prayer and receptive, interactive prayer.

One-way discursive prayer rests primarily on the efforts of the pray-er; interactive, intuitive prayer assumes a dialogue with the divine, where God's activity increases and the pray-er's effort decreases (Poloma 2004).

Revelation—hearing from God prophetically—plays a big role in the day-to-day operation of BnF. It has always been modeled for followers throughout David's accounts of events and his teachings. This process begins with a sense or an impression of divine leading or guidance. For many who are visually gifted, divine communication also often comes through dreams and visions. Most followers have attended countless talks and conferences, usually given by itinerant prophets both at BnF and in other locations, to learn how to use this gift of the Spirit. An interview with Chris Franklin, former CEO of the family business, whose spiritual transformation account was reported in the last chapter, provides us with a good example of how he practiced prophecy in the daily life of the community.

Second only to David in authority when we began our study, Chris told us how his "spiritual kids" would share with him what they thought God wanted of them. Chris noted, "I don't have all the answers for them. I have to push them to hear from God. So my first question is to ask them, 'What is the Lord saying to you?'" At times he feels that God has "given me something for them," but Chris says that he "always waits until they hear for themselves; I am usually not released to share the words I hear until they hear for themselves—then I can confirm what the person is hearing." Chris assured us that he and his wife, Linda, prayed for all their spiritual children daily:

> That's the way I see teaching people to walk in revelation. God can give me a word for somebody, and I can call them instantly and say, "Hey, let me tell you." I don't usually do that because I may be out of God's timing. Just two nights ago I was able to say to a woman, "This is what I have been seeing for you for a year." Had I said that a year ago, she wouldn't be here today. She couldn't have handled it.
>
> So I think my job as a spiritual father is to say, "God really wants to be intimate with you—and God has you under authority. So you go hear from God." So when they hear, I can say, "I hear that" or "I don't hear that." In fact, I sometimes hear something totally opposite. Or I say, "I don't hear yet—let me go and see."

Once a person tells Chris that he or she heard something specific from God and Chris believes he has heard the same word, he holds them accountable. Chris noted: "A lot of people from the outside would look at me and my kids and say, 'He's controlling.' I don't tell 'em jack, but I do demand that they hear—and I remind them that they heard—and I demand that they walk out what they heard." Although Chris seemed sincere in his presentation on prophecy, some who walked with him didn't necessarily see it that way. One of BnF's leaders, who admittedly was more cautious than many at BnF about the way the gifts of the Spirit were being used, was conversing with Margaret about prophecy some time after she left the community. In hearing about Chris's protocol on prophecy, she replied, "That may be the way Chris sees it, but I saw a more directive and prescriptive use of prophecy. It was more like Chris saying, 'Don't you hear God saying thus and such?' To which the neophyte replies, 'Yeah, that's what I hear.' Then Chris, as promised, would keep the fire burning under the neophyte's feet until he did what the prophecy allegedly instructed. Chris and I had many go-arounds on the way prophecy was practiced at BnF." Clearly prophets often see differently and through the proverbial glass darkly.

A Statistical Supplement

Throughout the interviews we noted the important part the quest for God and the things of God play in bringing men and women to BnF. They were searching for a deeper relationship with a God who walks and talks with them within a community of fellow spiritual travelers. Complementary findings on the nature of this divine communication can be gleaned from the survey conducted with members of the BnF family, especially the responses to questions (using five options, ranging from "never" to "very often") that tapped how often respondents believed they heard God speaking through select media. The most commonly experienced forms ("often" or "very often") included "reading the bible" (66 percent), "through thoughts in my head" (54 percent), "personal prayer" (53 percent), and "through leaders in authority" (52 percent). Less commonly experienced forms were "through ministry to the poor" (45 percent), "through family and friends" (45 percent), "ordinary daily living" (45 percent), "during corporate worship" (44 percent), "visions and dreams" (35 percent), "through nature" (25 percent), and "through journaling" (22 percent).

In this same survey, the vast majority of family members indicated agreement or strong agreement (87 percent) with the statement "It is important for me to be walking in the supernatural." They also reported a strong sense of having found their personal destiny (81 percent). Nearly three-fourths of the respondents (74 percent) reported that they believed that they needed "to have relationship with the poor in order to live out my calling as a Christian." Taking these simple findings together, it would appear that many members of the family had found the spiritual path they were seeking at BnF.

Components of Divine Healing

Although Pentecostal and especially neo-Pentecostal healing practices include prayer for physical healing, healing is generally treated holistically and in an integrated context. Early Pentecostals believed that the Devil caused physical ailments and consulting a physician was to demonstrate a lack of faith; most contemporary Pentecostals envision allopathic and alternative healing practices alike as complementary to prayer for healing. The model of person found in most teachings on divine healing is an integrated composite of soul, spirit, mind, and body (Poloma and Hoelter 1998).

While believing in and praying for divine healing for physical ailments, BnF has placed more emphasis on healing the psyche than the body. This fact is reflected in the survey data that shows that only 2 percent of the family members and 12 percent of the Sanctuary residents had *never* experienced a "personal inner or emotional healing," while 30 percent of the Sanctuary residents and 19 percent of the BnF family respondents said they *frequently* experience such healing. The finding is in line with the ministry's focus on addiction, as found in the drug rehabilitation program and also in the emphasis on healing intrapersonal and interpersonal dysfunctions. Glossolalia, for many, once again held a key for this spiritual gift. Tongues was often mentioned as an important medium for personal therapy and personal empowerment.

Interview respondents elaborated on how glossolalia functioned as a self-therapy to relieve stress, deal with negative emotions, and to otherwise strengthen the psyche. Leah, a woman in her mid-thirties who reported praying in tongues "frequently throughout the day," made the following observation: "I do it as much as I can and as often as I can. I find that it edifies me. The Bible says to use tongues to edify yourself—to build yourself up. So sometimes I will pray just to build my spirit up. What I have said when I speak in tongues, I have no idea. I feel something spiritual and supernatural happens in my spirit that just builds me up."

LeAnn, a white woman in her late twenties who was given leadership responsibilities at BnF that went far beyond her academic training and credentials in overseeing the Training Program, tried to keep the stream of glossolalic prayer flowing throughout the day ("praying in the spirit on all occasions"). She noted how praying in tongues served as a spiritual tool: "That's how I view tongues. It's a tool that He gave us and it has great power. He said it would edify you, build you up and strengthen you. I don't know how we make it through the day if we don't do that. So it is very important." She likened tongues to having "an electric can opener versus a wind can opener," and proceeded to ask a rhetorical question: "If you have an electric can opener versus a wind can opener, why wouldn't you use the electric one when you've got the electricity?" In describing how she makes the myriad hard decisions that she faces each day, she added:

> There is very much developed in my life the "praying in the spirit on all occasions"—or "putting on the full armor of God" and then standing. And I would say that is what I do. Praying in tongues is a huge thing. That is where you get edified, and that is where God speaks to you. He can and does give me revelation. I don't know how many times I have gotten revelation in the shower or while brushing my teeth. Because He is right there in your heart is open and wants to hear. He is right there! Praying is ongoing.

Communication with God that brings a sense of intimacy with the divine is somewhat different from its use in spiritual warfare in that the results are usually more interior than exterior to the individual. Jim, a middle-aged, married man who has been with BnF for approximately seven years, describes it as follows:

> Tongues is our language to God that Satan does not understand. That it is unknown except to God gives us peace. It is a way that God can release his power in ways that normally wouldn't happen. In the natural some things wouldn't happen, but when you pray in tongues or intercede in tongues or do spiritual warfare in tongues, all those aspects of tongues can be seen as you see the kingdom of God advance.
>
> But tongues for me is communication with God—His giving us a language where we can communicate with Him. It's not about what I am thinking any more; it's about God's will for whatever is going on at the time. There are times that I have seen stuff happen—tragic stuff—that the

only thing I can do is pray in tongues. When the mind says, "You are not going to make it," but the supernatural says that I am praying in tongues because there is nothing I can do in the natural that will change what God's outlook will be. It's a way that God gives us to communicate with him so that the peace we have inside of us can come around full circle. It gives me peace about whatever happens—any situation, whether it is good or bad. I communicate with God on a level I cannot understand, and it gives me peace about whatever is going on.

Respondents described how anxiety gave way to peace, confusion gave way to wisdom, and weakness gave way to strength as they prayed in tongues. They believed that the use of their prayer language caused demons to flee and the presence of God to be made manifest. It was a source of personal edification and empowerment.

Accounts of and teachings on physical healing were far less common than were those on the glossolalia, the prophetic word gifts, or inner/emotional healing. Again we find a reflection of this general observation in the survey data, in which over half of the BnF family respondents rarely or never experienced physical healing and 71 percent rarely or never experienced God healing another person through their prayer. It is not without interest that the Sanctuary residents were significantly more likely to have personally experienced healing through prayer "often" or "very often" (38 percent as compared with 17 percent) and were more likely to have reported that God healed another person through their prayer "often" or "very often" (33 percent as compared with 14 percent).

Physical healing was not modeled with the same degree of attention that was given to the other gifts. Perhaps this was due to the premature death of David's daughter followed by the sudden death of a niece a few years later (both from a congenital heart disease). David rarely spoke of either death, although his niece Kathryn and his sister Katina talked freely about this double family tragedy. Certainly those who were seriously ill were prayed for with great fervor, including the wives of Papa Jack Taylor, whose first wife died shortly before the study began and whose second wife died during the schism. Jane Jones, who together with her husband, Phil, had been part of BnF from its earliest days and who founded BnF Costa Rica, died of cancer just after the schism despite the fervent prayers offered for her recovery. Janice VanCronkhite also suffered from cancer, but she was believed to have been healed through prayer and alternative medicine.

There was talk about a greater use of the gift of healing—specifically of establishing a healing center or "healing rooms" (Poloma 2006) in one of the BnF properties just down the block from Grady Memorial Hospital. This healing center was to feature a coffee shop where hospital visitors and medical staff could come to relax and where the BnF family could offer prayer for healing. The site was sold during the schism and the healing rooms never came into being. But, in general, there was never the same focus on healing in the community as there was on the prophetic. Prophets came and went with some regularity and BnF followers still seek out the prophetic, but conferences featuring healing evangelists and teachings were usually not on the BnF agenda.

Healing sometimes seemed to us to be relegated to the margins of the BnF community. With the arrival of Chris and Linda Franklin some of the more dramatic healing stories unfolded, including a healing of infertility of a family daughter and a report of a diseased ovary that was scheduled to be surgically removed. It was Chris's account of the healing of his spiritual son that was the most intriguing, a story that included a claim of resurrection. As can be gleaned from the accounts of Chris shared thus far, Chris was committed to "going all out for the supernatural" even before "being led" to BnF. Birthed by this desire for more of the supernatural, Chris reportedly told God, "I want to raise the dead." He believed that God responded, "You are going to raise the dead."

The narrative began when Evan came to live with the Franklins and Chris taught him how to ride his Harley. The near-fatal accident happened when Chris and Evan were going to get Evan's motorcycle license. Chris described the incident as follows:

> I was in the truck and he was on my motorcycle. We had gone about a mile—he was going about fifty-five miles an hour. All of a sudden his head dropped over, and he passed out. The motorcycle gently began to veer off, hit the shoulder, hit the grass, and then began to flip head over heels. Evan was flipping in front of it. With the first flip, he hit headfirst and the helmet came off. He continued flipping. By the time I got the truck off and stopped and got over to the ditch, his head was bigger than a basketball, and he took his last breath.
>
> I was desperate, and quickly called 911 (my faith wasn't big enough to do anything else). But I was just screaming, "In the name of Jesus, I command you to live; in the name of Jesus, I command you to live." I could hear every demon in hell screaming at me, "You killed him. God sent you

a son, and you killed him." The woman on the phone was saying, "Sir, you have to talk to me." I then told her where I was—but kept on screaming, "In the name of Jesus . . ." About this time, Evan went "whosh"—and his head went down like this. [showing a normal-sized head]

When the firemen got there, they said, "He's got severe head injuries and severe spinal cord injury." By the time the ambulance got there, they said, "He's got brain damage and spinal cord injury." By the time the lifeline got there, they said, "He's got brain damage and we don't know about the spinal cord." By the time he landed in Atlanta Medical Center, they said, "He's got a concussion."

When Evan got to the hospital, he was put into intensive care. They gave him no pain medication—no nothing. He was just out; his brain was bruised. The male nurse was no nice to us. He said, "Chris, they are going to make you leave." I said, "OK," but I lay on the edge of the bed with my hand on him praying in tongues. Then I see this big dark Muslim doctor come into the room. He asked, "How are you?" I said, "Blessed—and how are you?" He said, "You are blessed." And that's all he said.

Five minutes later the male nurse came in and asked, "What did you say to the doctor." I said, "I didn't say anything." He said, "You must have. See this." It was Evan's chart. "Look at this. He wrote that 'Chris Franklin cannot be removed from the patient's room for any reason. Patient shows marked improvement by his very presence.'" The doctor was the same doctor who was in the emergency room when Evan was taken off the helicopter.

Evan confirmed Chris's account in his interview, including the full recovery with no ill effects from the accident. He added, "The medical people thought I was going to have to go through therapy and all kinds of stuff. The doctor came in one day and said, 'Go home.' I've been fine ever since."

Spiritual Gifts, Liminality, and Community

Gifts of the Spirit, such as divine healing and miracles, often are reported to accompany tongues speaking at BnF. They are a reflection of what Victor Turner (1969) calls "floating worlds"—worlds that are "anti-structural" and "liminal." For Turner, "liminality" is a qualitative dimension of a process that often appears in efficacious ritual, operating "betwixt and between" or "on the edge of" the normal limits of society. Liminal conditions create an anti-structure that makes space for something else to occur.

Daniel Albrecht (1999) has utilized Turner's thesis to provide an innovative description of collective and public ritual practices that describes the spirituality of Pentecostal-Charismatic Christians such as those described in this chapter. Albrecht observes how rules of normal behavior are rejected during the most liminal domains of the liturgy. As these normative rules are suspended, space (as it were) is created for the emergence of *communitas*, that is ,"the relations among people under liminal conditions" (Albrecht 1999, 149). Albrecht goes on to state, "Pentecostal ritual not only brings its people together in a physical assembly, it helps to unite them emotionally and spiritually" (1999, 209).

The community-building interaction ritual chains found in Pentecostal-Charismatic spirituality discussed by Albrecht are not limited to church rituals. The supernatural played an important part in the ritual experience at family gatherings just as it did at the regularly scheduled worship services at BnF. The synergistic relationship between Pentecostal ritual and *communitas* can also take place outside these formal gatherings, as illustrated by an account told by Carlos. Carlos was a client in BnF's drug rehabilitation program when he experienced the use of glossolalia as a catalyst for community building. Although he prefaced his narrative by saying, "I always thought that tongues sounded stupid," glossolalia led to an unexpected relational encounter that illustrates the interface between liminality, empowerment, and community. Carlos tells his story:

> One day I was sitting on the floor praying in tongues. I was the only one on the floor and could see everyone's feet. I heard God say, "Do you want me to show you power? You heard how Jesus healed leprosy and all that kind of stuff." I said, "Yeah, that would be neat."
>
> I saw that one guy had pretty messed up feet. I wondered if I would lay hands on him—whether his feet would be healed right there. I got stirred up. So I got up and went over to him and began praying—really praying. Something overtook me, and I started praying in tongues. Then I took this man's feet in my hand! That's something I never expected to do. I thought I could never do it, but I did it and was filled with love for this guy. I felt love for somebody I didn't even really know! I didn't know what kind of disease he had—and I didn't care.
>
> When I finished praying, nothing happened. The guy's feet were still messed up, and I was kind of discouraged. So after a couple of days while I was praying, I said, "You know, God, you told me power and all that

stuff. What did you do? You were going to show me power and I didn't see anything."

God said, "It wasn't about healing—it was about the power of love. You were willing to hold someone's feet, even though you didn't know them. You did something that you thought you would never in your life do. You did it for love—the love that I put in your heart. It is so powerful you can do anything. People that you thought were human garbage—now you almost kiss their feet. You are loving them. They are your brothers. That is powerful! It makes you do stuff that you think you would never be able to do."

We can see from this incident the potential of glossolalia to move the pray-er into a liminal stance that is betwixt and between an altered consciousness and normal reality. While in this state, respondents noted that they often felt led to perform an action that ordinarily would have been unthinkable. There is often an increase in affect and a deeper bonding between the two persons. As glossolalics in this community prayed for and with others and followed the leading of the Spirit, we believe they can be fairly described as occupying a liminal condition. BnF developed *communitas* through experiences of godly love that molded BnF into a community of believers led by David VanCronkhite.

Glossolalia and other charismata can be a form of mysticism that often takes the pray-er out of his or her normal world and into the liminal world of the Kingdom of God. When glossolalia is practiced within the context of a community in which it is a normative practice, it has the potential to change not only the individual but also to affect existing social interactions and structures. Whether it functions to empower and unite is dependent on the context and manner in which this spiritual gift is presented and practiced. In the BnF context, glossolalia functions to empower the pray-er through a sense of unity with God, which in turn contributes to action that sustains and nurtures community life both within the family and within the family business.

What's Love Got to Do with It?

A review of our qualitative narratives suggests that charismata, including glossolalia, healing, and prophecy, can empower care-love. In accord with Pitirim Sorokin's discussion of love energy, we hypothesized that experiencing a loving God through glossolalia and spiritual gifts that accompany it in turn empowers compassion and loving behavior. We tested this hypothesis empirically against our qualitative observations and then through an analysis of survey findings. In our survey instrument (see appendix B-1) we included measures of the charismata, perceived relationship with God, acceptance of the BnF vision regarding the supernatural, and compassion or empathy for the poor together with altruism as an outcome measure. Our understanding of love is much broader than reflected in common discussions of altruism. Altruism can be conceptualized as one dimension of care-love, and care-love as but one face of love that can be complemented by union-love and appreciation-love. At BnF the union-love found in experiences of God and appreciation-love reflected in David VanCronkhite's vision are reflected in the enactment of godly love interactions and ritual chains. Many respondents told us that love begins with experiences of God's love and that believers at BnF are able to love each other and to serve the poor because God has first loved them. Our quantitative survey analysis (found in appendix C's statistical report) took such accounts seriously.

The main finding from our statistical analyses can be summarized as follows: based on our survey conducted in the context of the BnF community, there is statistical ground to support Sorokin's theoretical concept of love energy and its potential impact on expressions of human love. Those who experience more of the charismatic gifts of the Holy Spirit are more likely to report higher scores for reported empathic feelings and altruistic behavior than are those who do not experience God's presence and power in their lives. Although Pitirim Sorokin focused mainly on the social and psychological aspects of love, he never lost sight of its spiritual-religious aspects (Post 2002). He was convinced that more perfect forms of love hypothetically can be explained by an inflow of love from higher sources that exceeds that of human beings. Findings from BnF offer limited support for Sorokin's premised "love energy." Mystics who experience union-love with God were clearly more likely to report higher scores in care-love. This finding held true for both the family members and the homeless beneficiaries of their care-love, albeit with some important differences that we will note in the next chapter, dealing with the poor and homeless.

6

The BnF Family and
the Homeless Poor

If "love" is understood as a strong emotional sentiment which draws some people to others, there is no doubt that in most cases volunteers and paid workers at soup kitchens, homeless and battered women's shelters, AIDS hospices, child welfare agencies, and social service programs for the elderly are motivated by love. . . . Yet as a society we have become more skeptical about professions of love. We realize that whether in romantic love, political campaigns, advertising slogans, or religious appeals, words of love and sentiment come cheap. There may be no quick way to identify what "real love" is, but we do realize that an entire context is necessary to evaluate "love."

—Wagner 2000, 172

Like many intentional communities that have dotted American history, Blood-n-Fire professes to be all about love—love for God, love for family members, and love for the poor and homeless. Although details were ever changing, the vision and mission sought to bring God's love to the poor through the love offered by the BnF family. Members of the community hoped that in response to this love the poor and homeless would be drawn to the supernatural vision proffered by David's understanding of the Kingdom of God. It was also expected that they would then embrace the supernatural walk coveted by the BnF community to become true sons and daughters of David.

We have described David's vision within the conceptual framework of godly love, as encountering God's love and then loving the poor in accord with the personal and experiential love of God. This means that BnF is not simply there to service the physical needs of the poor but rather to bring the poor under the umbrella of God's love. It is with this understanding that we take on the challenge set before us by Wagner's opening epigraph. In an attempt to evaluate the love interaction between the BnF family and the people they served, with earlier chapters as a backdrop, we now turn to the voices of the poor, the homeless, and the recovering addicts served by BnF.

Sorokin's Attributes of Love Within Goffman's Total Institution

Pitirim Sorokin (1954/2002), the social theorist whose work is pivotal for any social scientific assessment of love, has proposed that love varies in dimensions or attributes, including in the intensity with which a person provides for the loved one. Low-intensity love involves minor acts, such as giving a few quarters to the beggar or relinquishing a bus seat for another's comfort; at high intensity, the lover freely gives things of greater value (time, energy, resources) to please the beloved. While Sorokin does not fully develop the different potential forms of intensity, his point remains clear. While the range of intensity is not interval (research cannot indicate how many times greater a given intensity is than another), it is often possible to see "which intensity is really high and which low, and sometimes even to measure it" (Sorokin 1954/2002, 15). This means that love can be measured on an ordinal scale, indicating that love is more or less intense. A question arising from Sorokin's discussion of intensity that we raise in this chapter is whether the BnF family's love for the poor and homeless is greater than, equal to, or less than the love held for family members.

This question intersects with another of Sorokin's dimensions of love, namely, extensity: "The extensity of love ranges from the zero point of love of oneself only, up to the love of all mankind, all living creatures, and the whole universe. Between the minimal and maximal degrees lies a vast scale of extensities: love of one's own family, or a few friends, or love of the groups one belongs to—nation, religious, occupational, political, and other groups and associations" (1954/2002, 16). Sorokin's extensity resonates with the classic Western discussion of the "order of love." How does one balance love for family and friends (the nearest and dearest) with love for the very neediest of all humanity? As an example of the widest extensity he offers St. Francis, who seemed to have a love of "the whole universe (and of God)" (17). Where do the poor and homeless who live in the Sanctuary and in the Warehouse fit in this "order of love" in the BnF community?

Sorokin has proposed an astute hypothesis on the interface of intensity and extensity that we will expand on in this chapter:

> Other conditions being equal, the *intensity of love tends to decrease with an increase of its extensity or the size of the universe of love.* Insofar as the empirical love of a person or a group is an energy of *limited magnitude,* the larger the love universe the thinner its spread. If a given reservoir of love supplies only three persons, its intensity is many times greater than if it supplies three thousand or three million persons. Herein lies the explanation of why frequently professed love for all humanity is so feeble in its intensity and rarely goes beyond a mere verbal declaration. (1952/2002, 21; italics in original)

While it is not possible for us to assign a specific rate to the level of love extensity represented by middle-class Americans working full-time to serve the poor and homeless, it would appear that the BnF family would rate higher on this dimension in their service to the poor and homeless than would the average American. After all, they have reportedly left behind the American dream to be players in the Kingdom of God in which all are God's children. Yet despite the vision of creating a "family" that integrates the poor, homeless, and addicts, as we have already noted, relatively little enduring personal interaction was observed between residents of the shelter and Training Program and the BnF family. In a sense, the residents ("guests" as they were called by BnF) were not unlike the residents of a mental hospital described in Erving Goffman's classic work on total institutions (1961). For Goffman a "total institution" was "a place of residence and work, where a large number of like-situated individuals, cut off from the wider society for an appreciable period of time, together lead an enclosed, formally administered round of life" (1961, xiii). This definition is particularly apt for the recovering addicts in the Training Program, who were confined to the Warehouse for the first six to nine months, only then to be released to assume paid employment outside BnF.

In this chapter we will include the voices of interviewees who were in various stages of the Training Program at the time of the study, as well as homeless men and women who lived in the Sanctuary. We let these voices speak for themselves as the reader seeks to assess whether BnF was an instrument of spiritual or social transformation for the minority of ever-changing Sanctuary residents who entered the BnF Training Program.

In the world of the old asylum, as with BnF clients, attempts were made to strip the patient of his or her old self and to create a new self that fit the new institutional situation. In this "stripping process," however, a new "underlife" developed that reflected both the patient's identity with the hospital and an opposition to it. The staff and the patients seemed to operate in parallel universes within the same physical space. Strictly speaking, BnF is neither a mental hospital nor a total institution, although the Warehouse does come close to the definition of a total institution; there are explicit rules covering everything from "lights out" to the necessity to request toilet paper, which was never freely available in either men's or women's restrooms. The interaction ritual that Goffman described in total institutions has been applied to other social groups and provides a frame for the survey data and interviews used in this chapter. The empirical evidence presented in this chapter points to "identification" with BnF vision and values for some clients while for others it suggests opposition to the front-stage behavior and identification with an underlife. Unlike the pre-schism BnF family members, the client/beneficiaries were clearly not of one voice.

Quantitative Findings

An examination of the correlations found in the top row of figures in appendix C-1 reveal important differences between the homeless and their volunteer providers on many points of interest to our discussion. Based on the surveys conducted at BnF, we see that the Sanctuary respondents are much more likely to be black (r=-.56; 73 percent vs. 17 percent), to be somewhat older (r=-.25; mean age of forty-three vs. thirty-six years), to be male (r=.16; 70 percent vs. 52 percent), and to have less education (r=.32; high school graduate vs. college graduate) than the BnF providers. Only 8 percent of Sanctuary respondents were married as compared with 46 percent of BnF respondents. In sum, BnF is a largely white organization providing services primarily to homeless, black, poor single men but also increasingly to women (and their children). The demographics presented by the survey are not unlike those found in other studies of the homeless; such diverse profiles led Joel Blau to conclude that "the homeless population encompasses so many subgroups—unaccompanied men, female-headed families, children, substance abusers, the mentally ill, veterans and the employed" (1992, 30; see also Snow and Anderson's excellent 1993 ethnographic account of homeless street people). All the identified social types could be found coming for shelter in the Sanctuary and enjoying meals at Sobre La Mesa.

In addition to these basic demographic differences, the survey reflects important dissonant beliefs and experiences on core BnF values between family members and those served by the family business. For example, the Sanctuary residents were *less* likely than the BnF members to report that walking in the supernatural was important to them (r=.28), although both groups were likely to share the opinion that the "gifts of the Spirit" were signs of the coming Kingdom of God. They were also *more* likely to perceive God as a conditional lover who may "abandon and condemn" them (r=-.28) and to be *less* satisfied with their relationship with God (r=-.17) than were family members. Although there was no statistically significant differences between the two groups reported on the charismata scale that tapped experiences of the "gifts of the Spirit," the Sanctuary residents were much *less* likely to be glossolalic (r=.-48) and *more* likely to experience divine healing for themselves (r=-.18) and when praying for others (=-.18). They also scored significantly *higher* on the mysticism scale (r=.31). Unlike the charismata scale, which sets to measure specific Pentecostal-based experience, Hood's mysticism scale (2001) has sought to identify the "common core" of mystical experiences. Using Hood's measure the Sanctuary respondents appear to be more "generically spiritual" than were their providers (who scored lower on mysticism). In other words, our data suggest that the Sanctuary respondents may have experienced forms of general mysticism on which were overlaid (especially since coming to BnF) the charismatic experiences included in the charismata index. There were important nuances in spirituality and spiritual transformation that will become more apparent in the interview data between the poor and their providers, even for the poor who identified with BnF.

We found some additional differences in the way the two groups perceived the coming Kingdom of God that we did not include in the statistics found in the appendixes. For example, the Sanctuary respondents more likely to describe the coming Kingdom "as a perfect world" (r=.37), while BnF family members, on the other hand, were more likely to describe it more abstractly as "righteousness, peace, and joy" (r=.25) and "justice for the poor" (r=.24). Both shared the view that the Kingdom of God was marked by "walking in the supernatural gifts of the Spirit," of "personally growing closer to God," and of "living out my personal destiny." Consistent with much of what social science knows about poverty, the poor at BnF are more likely than are their "caretakers" to be less educated, to think in concrete terms, and to expect immediate gratification of physical needs. If the BnF family seeks "righteousness," the poor seek its direct physical expression, including the satisfying spiritual experiences that are central to neo-Pentecostal spirituality.

Finally (and somewhat to our surprise), the Sanctuary respondents tended to render harsher judgment of the poor (r=-.33) in that they were *more* likely to regard them as being "undeserving of help" and "reaping what they have sown" than were the BnF providers. Despite such negative assessment, there were no differences evident in empathy or altruism scores for the two groups, nor were there any significant differences in satisfaction with relationships within BnF or with their "sense of personal destiny."

As we will demonstrate in this chapter, there was a double divide in the BnF ministry. Not only are there differences in the acceptance of the BnF vision, values, and mission between the providers and the homeless, but there is also a divide between those homeless who accept a modified version of David's vision and those who do not. Even the homeless who do accept David's relational Christianity are in some ways like the BnF family and in others, miles apart.

The statistical findings suggest that the BnF family has gone beyond its middle-class suburban roots to reach out to others who are different from themselves (reflecting some degree of what Sorokin has called extensity). But these statistics also suggest the possibility that the Sanctuary residents and Warehouse trainees, like the residents of Goffman's total institutions, are not only demographically different but may have developed an underlife that both reflects BnF values and opposes them. The underlife at BnF can be described as the poor seeking their own destinies within the context of BnF that are more immediate and concrete than the abstract visions of David. Thus the poor are a means to allow the BnF family to explore in abstract terms the realities of the Kingdom while simultaneously providing a place for the poor to seek more concrete goals. The poor may hear David preach of the divine Kingdom, but most simply go about existing in an underlife that is often invisible and unnoticed by even the most caring of the BnF family. In sum, the statistics support an observation we reported in our discussion of BnF family life. BnF is composed largely of white Christians ministering to African American homeless who identify with BnF's practical mission but not its vision.

The statistics stop here as we return to interviews to tell our story— this time based on the forty-nine open-ended interviews conducted with men and women who were residents of the Sanctuary and/or enrolled in the Warehouse Training Program at some point during the beginning of 2003 and the end of 2004. These forty men and nine women will provide voices from the poor that can breathe life into our provisional theories and statistics.

Love, the BnF Family, and the Poor

The anecdote of David's encounter with Willie that we told in chapter 3 is not only about Willie but also about many Sanctuary residents who freely came and left, only to return again, and often again and again, without embracing the vision and mission of BnF. In the above-mentioned account, David asked Willie what it was that BnF did. Willie replied, "We speak in tongues and we do Twelve," neither of which Willie himself experienced. Willie becomes a prototype of one category of BnF that we will refer to as *instrumental clients*. These men and women come to BnF for a material commodity offered by the family business but show little interest in the community's vision. They may know how to give the right answers to questions when asked, but they effectively refrain from any deeper commitment.

Although we did not interview Willie, we did interview Greg, a divorced African American male, who first encountered BnF as members were passing out groceries in Capitol Homes, the since-demolished housing project across the street from the warehouse. Greg, a vivacious and charming man in his early forties, has always lived in the area and provides a colorful picture of BnF's earlier days: "I was born in this city, just around the corner. I was hatched right up the street, so I always knew the warehouse was here. I first noticed them in 1995 or 1996 when they were sleepin' on the dock. The building had holes in the roof; no bathrooms; no kitchen. They cooked on this one burner, you know. But it kept going on. David had a vision."

While Greg gave ample verbal assent to David's vision, he lost count of the times he came to BnF and then drifted away "for drugs and pimping." Greg, who was in the Training Program at the time of the interview (but left shortly after, only to return again and to leave again), gave the following short account of his dynamic interaction with BnF over the years:

But I kept comin' back to this place. There was something drawin' me back. Revelation, I guess. I was supposed to be here; I have a purpose here. There ain't too many black leaders in this church, and I supposed to be one in my appointed time. I busted out windows from here. I been banished from here. I been barred from here. I cussed out the pastor and his wife. I used to call 'em the white side of money here. But they still let me come back! I come in the Program and stay six days and leave. I in relationship with a girl, talking to her through the Portal. One day I said, "I better go . . ." I left. They let me come back. They ask me, "What's gonna be different this time, Greg?" I don't know. I gonna try it again. I still come here to get something to eat, to get a shower, to get some clothes or stay in the Sanctuary. They let me stay over there even though I do dope. But I tired of livin' like this. I tired of doin' the dope. I tired of sleepin' outside. It killin' me. So you see, God got a plan. He let all these things to happen. But I just see the bad part; I just feel the pain.

Despite his desire for change, Greg was never able to make the commitment that would take him beyond his instrumental client status. The last time one of the authors inquired he was on the street, faring badly with his drug problem but still unable to commit to the relational norms of the BnF community.

A second category of poor/homeless we will refer to as *relational clients*. They too came for some level of goods and services, but the relational clients also (at least in part and on some level) grasped David's vision of the Kingdom as loving God and one another. If they were men, they were likely to have entered the Training Program in one of its evolving forms—at least for a time. It was not unusual for relational clients to first come to BnF for "a hot and a cot"—for a good meal at night and a bed in which to sleep—but then were drawn to the love they experienced. They tended to regard BnF as "home" (they would likely correct anyone who called it a "shelter"). Some would eventually ride through the schism, first with David as leader, then Chris, and finally David again, professing biblical allegiance to whomever "God had put in authority."

The third category that provides a voice for the homeless is composed of the very small minority of Sanctuary residents who have become or who see themselves as full members of the BnF family. Most are men who have recently completed or have nearly completed the Training Program. The women are represented by those who have come seeking shelter and found a place where they could nurture and serve others (without pay) through the BnF family business. A handful of them remained even after the closing of the ministry to serve as caretakers and to protect the property from vandalism until it can be sold.

Each of these sociological ideal types serves the heuristic purpose of providing a frame for the voices of the poor we encountered in our interviews. They are not fixed categories; a very few respondents may have moved through all three of the categories and others appear to be on the margins between two of the types. Those in the latter two categories appear to be more critical of the poor and homeless who remain steadfast instrumental clients, those who show little or no interest in the spiritual and relational facets of the BnF ministry. As we shall see, those who refuse or cannot move beyond the instrumental client status were seen as the primary cause for dissatisfaction among the poor who called BnF "home."

Voice to the Instrumental Clients

BnF had hundreds if not thousands of instrumental clients who came primarily for food and shelter, and occasionally for personal growth. BnF is usually but one of many places that they frequent to have their needs met. Many, if not most, of our interviewees first came to the Sanctuary or Sobre La Mesa as clients in search of food, shelter, or clothing, although some happily reported to have found something more. A minority came through a referral from clergy or director of another shelter who felt that the client's needs could best be met at BnF. The majority learned about BnF through word of mouth on the streets.

It would be difficult to retain the status of an instrumental client indefinitely at BnF. The Sanctuary was defined as more than a shelter (it was regarded as "home") and the feeding program became known as Sobre La Mesa (or "hands around the table"). These labels, of course, reflect David's vision of BnF's being more about relationships than about food or shelter. Those who could not or would not at least verbally move beyond seeking instrumental services would be asked to move on, sooner if they were residents of the Sanctuary (where a general thirty-day residency limit applied). More grace was given to those frequenting the public meals at Sobre La Mesa; but even here, lines were drawn as resources became scarce.

The voice of the instrumental client could be heard when interviewees (even those who had moved into the relational client category) were asked questions about how they heard about BnF, its appeal, and major sources of satisfaction and dissatisfaction. Many echoed the voice of Leonard, who stated simply, "Oh, actually when I first come to BnF—the true story—is that I was looking for a way to get out of the weather. It was cold—real cold—outside." But then Leonard added, "Evidently God had other plans; that's been over two years ago." Leonard, a forty-seven-year-old black male with a ninth-grade education and separated from his wife, then went on to describe his journey from an instrumental client to a relational one. This journey led him into the Training Program and then into "getting lost again" and returning to drug use before coming back to the Program for another go-around. Leonard began to use drugs (as he did after being served by other ministries before BnF) and was asked to leave but was welcomed back when he sought to return. Leonard described himself as "so wacked out; I was like the prodigal son and they welcomed me back with open arms." (We noted that almost all who were to articulate self-censure as they sought to return were quickly "forgiven" and "welcomed home.") Leonard was completing the Restoration phase of the Program at the time of the interview. He was filled with gratitude for the family's forgiving spirit, but also filled with guilt and shame over his relapse. He then added: "To sum it all up—it's a real short story—I got back to where God moved me back into the Spirit. God knows the way. I was fighting a battle that I couldn't win unless I moved into the Spirit. Now I still feel kind of bad for the situation that I allowed myself to get in, but if it wasn't for that situation, I wouldn't be as close to the Spirit as I am now."

Leonard's reported greatest satisfaction with BnF is that it gives him a place "where you come to serve God and God's people." He echoes David's criticism of churches and religions that are God's "weekend brides." As Leonard sees it, "He [God] don't want like a weekend bride, you know. It's what you do on Monday, Tuesday, Wednesday, Thursday, Friday, Saturday—what are you doing those six days?" Then he added, "I'm only just now getting into real love. We weren't grown up with a whole lot of compassion, and we grew up with no passion. Love means loving your brother, loving your neighbor, and loving everyone as you would yourself—you know treating them accordingly and sharing your time. You know, just being relationship; just building a relationship."

Most of the interviewees first came to BnF because they needed a place to stay, were tired of the way they were living their lives, and were drawn in by the love they perceived from those who worked in the family business and the God they served. As Miles, who was in the Restoration phase of the Training Program and directed the maintenance of the building at the time of the interview, reported: "I came to check out BnF when I lived on the streets. I just liked what I saw. I liked the love that they gave to me. It was awesome, and I just fell in love with it."

This sense of being loved by God and others at BnF and a development of a sense of divine destiny seemed to be the reason for the reports
of high satisfaction and little dissatisfaction by Sanctuary residents, many
of whom sought and found meaningful relationships and were provided
with an opportunity to care for others. They were reluctant to voice any
serious dissatisfaction with the ministry and were quick to voice their appreciation for the good meals and safe shelter. Gary, a fifty-three-year-old
black male in the New Beginnings phase of the Training Program, spoke
for many others when he said:

> I came here to try to get a focus on me, and to get a relationship with God.
> Why would I come over to your house and try to change the way you live
> in your house? Why that is just stupid. I am happy here because I am not
> looking for anything back. There is a lot of love here; a lot of genuine love
> here. If you can look through the people who bicker all the time, you can
> see the love and the camaraderie. There is just a peace. I found peace here.
> I didn't have any peace at all before I came. I was in a lot of turmoil; I was a
> walking threat. At any time before I came here, somebody could have said
> the wrong thing, and something was going to happen! I have a lot of peace
> here. I don't feel like I am being pulled in four different directions. I am
> finding out who I am and what I am going to do.

Leonard, Gary, and Miles are among the interviewees who tended to
see God's hand in their learning about BnF's ministry and hearing His
voice in their decision to visit and then to stay with the community. Being
part of BnF has given them relationships and a homelike environment in
which to pursue their divinely given destiny. When asked about any dissatisfaction with BnF, those like Leonard, Gary, and Miles, who are moving away from the instrumental client status, tend to be critical of those
who are not embracing David's vision for the Sanctuary. Gary sees among
BnF's clientele "those factions that would dismantle everything here.
Wherever there is anything of God, somebody's going to come against it."

During the time that they were "running from God," they, and others
like them, had known lives shattered by addiction. BnF pointed to a path
toward God that they wanted to follow. Anthony represents a common
voice as he expressed his fatigue and disdain for his former way of life:

> Well, basically, I knew that for me I had been running from the will of
> the Lord all my life. And I was tired of running from the Lord, and tired

of living the way I had been living. The last few months of my life on the streets—on drugs and on alcohol—I was just tired of that. Period. I pretty much lost everything that I had as far as my family, cars, home, you know. I made a decision that I was going to turn my life around and give it to God. I knew that at an early age, and I should have been doing it all along. I can now do His will and do the things that He called me to do. But I've been running from that most of my life.

Instrumental clients may seek out the services of BnF off-and-on for years—sometimes for food, sometimes for shelter, and at times for personal and spiritual growth—without catching much of David's vision. In fact, it is likely that many never even heard David's vision because most Sanctuary residents did not stay for Sunday church services, even though attending the service gave them priority seating for the famous chicken dinner that followed the time of worship. Will, a Sanctuary resident for just two weeks at the time of the interview, first heard about BnF over two years earlier and was a frequent guest at the public meals. When asked what attracted him to BnF, Will replied:

> Something I was confused about, I had to learn. I thought by coming to BnF it would teach me discipline, but discipline is the wrong word to use. It teaches you structure. Discipline is basically like the military; structure are different phases you go through to better yourself and better your life. If you want to better yourself and better your life, that is not something that is forced upon you. It is something you have to want. So it's a big difference. They give you that opportunity—that choice—you can stay or you can walk. But they are there to help you. The decision is yours. What do you want to do? What you feel is in your heart, and I felt like I needed structure. I have been receiving it ever since.

Like Will, many of our interviewees (but most certainly only a minority of all BnF clients) did report a move from a purely instrumental use of BnF to a relational one. It is difficult, however, to tease the genuine response within each case from the underlife that at times is discernable in the interview tapes. Occasionally an outspoken male client would give us a glimpse into the underlife as he experienced it, only to quickly return to defining BnF as a "blessing" that saved his life. Aaron, a twenty-six-year-old black single male, admittedly came to BnF primarily to eat—and then to play drums with the worship band. He said that he came into the

Training Program, "was kicked out," and then returned once again to enter the drug rehabilitation program:

> I first came here to eat. The thing I remember most about my first visit is that it was so peaceful here; there was just this calmness. Then I met Autumn [a member of the family] and she prayed for me one day. I began to ask God to show me what was real. I had all this religious background and all this study I had done. One night I sat here outside on the steps and just cried. I said, "OK, God, here I am. Either kill me right now or help me. I can't do it any more; I am so screwed up."

Aaron acknowledged that BnF made a huge difference in his life, especially in his conception of God, which was intimately related to his sense of self-perception and destiny: "Knowing God is being honest about who I am and fulfilling my own destiny. God told me to understand who I am and my gifts and I will understand my destiny." For Aaron his gift was music—especially being an artist and playing the drums. He regards BnF and the Program as a "place where I can work on me"—not unlike when he was "a kid and got to live in my parents' house." There was little BnF rhetoric or vision to be found in Aaron's account of his satisfaction and dissatisfaction with life in the Warehouse and in the Training Program.

Instrumental clients are more likely to express dissatisfaction with specific aspects of the BnF culture than were those who emphasized the relational qualities of their attachment. Aaron, for example, confessed that he did not always like the house rules: "It's a systematic program, and I'm not into somebody else's program. . . . It's a good place but, as I see things, controlling." He was willing to put up with the Program in exchange for the time and space to pursue what he saw as his personal growth. He believed his role at BnF was to be a blessing with the artistic gifts he was using. As the interview progressed, Aaron confessed that he was "angry and hurt" because he had been asked recently to quit playing his drums with the worship band. He then began talking about getting an apartment but soon shifted the interview to musing about the problems he had with drugs. When asked whether his time at BnF had affected his relationship with God, Aaron replied, "Yes. Period. God made me realize that I have to rely on him and nobody else. He uses men and women on this earth, but I need to understand that it is a personal relationship with him that counts. That's what He's taught me in this place. It's impacted me good." We have no way of knowing whether BnF actually affected Aaron in any significant way; he left a few weeks later. We do know his interview had a different ring, consistent with our profile of an instrumental client. Life was to be on Aaron's terms and according to his vision; he was moving to the beat of his own drums, not those of David. At times this vision was being shaped more by use of illicit spirits still used by some in the under-life culture than by the Spirit of God.

Women told stories similar to those of some of the men about their first coming to BnF—being somehow "led by God" to a place they soon came to regard as home. At first they might not have liked what they saw, but they began to experience an environment where they could grow personally and in their relationship with God. As far as we can tell, very few stayed long enough to become part of the BnF family, reflecting a dissonance that comes through from careful listening to the interviews. Renee, an African American woman with an eleventh-grade education and Pentecostal background, said she had come to BnF three or four years earlier, left for reasons she attributes to not wanting God in her life, and returned about four months before the interview. She shares the following about her initial visit to BnF: "Well, I was here at BnF three or four years ago—I can't quite remember. It was a long time ago when I first was here. I didn't like it. I didn't have no plans of having God in my life at that time. Now I came back this time, and it seemed like God had a plan for me here. I work with Him. I help serve the food and everything."

Whether Renee had actually had a change of heart about BnF as expressed in the interview is difficult to know. She, like others from the Sanctuary and Warehouse, expressed the belief that she had been divinely led "home" to a place where she was loved and could love others. As had happened with countless others before her, within two months Renee was gone and her address unknown.

Phil Ward is the oldest resident of the Sanctuary, having been brought there from the streets at Easter time of 1994 by a former Atlanta BnF pastor who would later establish BnF Cape Town in South Africa. Phil is an astute white man of fifty-nine years who can be always be found in the BnF Sanctuary, usually reading his Bible or in quiet prayer ("speaking in tongues," he claims). He continues to experience firsthand the difficulties of moving from the Sanctuary into relationships with the BnF family. It is not, as Phil explains it, that there is a deliberate segregation between the two sectors of ministry but rather that there is a "gray area" that seems to keep them divided. The staff employed in the family business, as we have already noted, is largely white; the Sanctuary reflects the racial demographic of Atlanta, where the homeless poor are 90 percent black. But the gray area is deeper than any racial differences. In Phil's estimation, "99.9 percent of the people that come in here [Sanctuary] come off the streets, and 100 percent of the people over there [BnF family] have never been on the streets." Moreover, it is common for Sanctuary residents to have served time in jail; Phil noted, "I know of no one who has been behind bars there." Despite the goodwill of BnF providers and the gratitude of clients, there is a lack of understanding that feeds the underlife.

Although Phil is a deeply spiritual man who credits BnF for his intimate relationship with God, he does note that the quest for the spiritual is not the prime reason that most come to BnF. Phil claims that "there is only a small portion that is really going after God." There is also a division between those like Phil, who call the Sanctuary "home," and those who come only to get out of the rain. Some semblance of a "relational family" operates in the Sanctuary during the summer months when the warm climate weans away the less committed. During the cold winter nights when there is commonly an influx of a couple hundred strangers seeking refuge from the elements, the summer home is quickly turned into a shelter. As Phil succinctly describes it, "We go from relationship in family mode to shelter load each winter."

To the extent that the Sanctuary and the Training Program are both revolving doors, familial relationships at BnF are more of a pipe dream than a reality. Others also noted similar observations during their interviews, including Miles who said: "I see people walk in here on Sunday for the meal that have been through the Program four or five times." Changes do take place in some clients, as suggested by some of the interviews already reported, as they move from viewing BnF as a place to meet their instrumental needs toward seeking meaningful and loving relations with God and with others. But it is not easy. Phil once again points to the crux of the problem: "It's really difficult in here to establish intimate relations because there is so many people coming and going at one time. I can't develop a relationship with anyone unless I've known them six months to a year, and if you are here for three months, I will know you to say 'hello' and 'goodbye.'"

Voice of Relational Clients

Those clients who do stay with BnF long enough will begin, as Willie suggested in his response to David noted earlier, "to speak in tongues" and "to do Twelve"—but they are more likely to speak of the transformation in their own terms rather than David's. Instead of talking about speaking in tongues (which they are somewhat less likely to practice than family members), they would speak about learning to hear from God and of experiencing God's providence and provisions. Instead of talking about the Twelve, there were more likely to speak of learning to love and their struggles to relate to others with whom they were sharing their lives. In general, they spoke freely of the love they felt from select members of the BnF family and about their new and more intimate relationships with God.

Daryl, a thirty-six-year-old black male with a high school education in the middle of the Training Program, called BnF "the most blessed ministry in Atlanta—of all these type of ministries, BnF is the best one. It provides the best opportunity of getting on your feet than anywhere else in Atlanta." He was lavish with his praise of a place that provided him the opportunity to grow in his relationship with God and to learn to love others. According to Daryl, "You will hear the word *love* here more than any other." He reported that "people really care about your having a relationship with Christ and they really care about helping people to reach your goal." He acknowledged that learning to be "relational" was not easy, but he felt it was worth the cost. Daryl believed it was preparing him to learn to relate positively "in the world":

> We have our problems just like they do in the world. But here we can learn to get over these problems. Being out in the world, you don't have to deal with them. You can pick and choose who you want to deal with. But here, man, you learn that you are just going to have to learn to love— and move on. Being here lets me know where I am strong and where I am weak at. I get the opportunity to find out and learn where God is dealing with me in my life. I never realized how many problems I had relating to others until now; I've been working on them.

Unlike Phil, who lives in the Sanctuary, Daryl has the opportunity of forging deeper relationships with the men in the Training Program (although these relationships generally prove to be of relatively short duration once the man leaves the Program). But in both the Sanctuary and the Training Program we found people of prayer like Phil and Daryl who are learning to trust in a God of love to whom they were introduced through the BnF family. Although many self-identified with a denomination (primarily Baptist), they claimed to be "nonreligious" and preferred to be designated as "spiritual." At BnF they learned about the love of God and eagerly embraced a dynamic relationship with the God of love they were coming to know through prayer.

Although this group of clients valued the relationships they had within the BnF community, sometimes mentioning specific individuals who had touched their lives, their approach to family and relationships seemed well seasoned with life experience. Like Phil, their grounding in living with the poor and their being poor left them less idealistic than many family members. This may be one of the reasons why the Sanctuary residents scored higher than BnF family members on the survey items measuring a negative assessment of the poor ("judgmental perception" scale), an issue that we noted earlier in our statistical presentation. Gary, now in the BnF Training Program but who formerly helped manage another rural program for drug addicts, expressed his frustration with his fellow clients in the following down-to-earth manner:

> I get pissed off sometimes when these guys don't want to grow up. Sometimes we got only a handful of guys and they just can't come in one accord. There is always some bickering going on somewhere, and I have a hard time with that. It causes me to want to lash out because I am talking about grown men bickering. They should be happy and rejoicing and praising God, "Hey, I'm alive and I'm not there out on the streets; I'm not drunk; I'm not drugged up; I'm not in jail; I'm not in the hospital." Their bickering and lack of gratitude—it pisses me off—it really pisses me off.

If some respondents were critical of the homeless poor with whom they were fellow travelers, they were also wary of members of the BnF family who had little or no firsthand experience with or genuine understanding of their problems. What many did find renewed (or discovered for the first time) was a strong faith in God and fresh personal experiences of Him—a faith that was strengthened by an intimacy with the divine fostered through BnF teachings and times of worship in both the Sanctuary and the Warehouse. It was in God that the relational clients professed to place their hope for the future. Few were taken with the BnF family rhetoric, but many were delighted with the fresh awakening they experienced at BnF to the power of love, especially God's love. (This observation may help explain why the Sanctuary residents were more likely to score higher on perceiving God as a "conditional lover" who could forsake and abandon them. Many professed to be still new to the conception of the divine being a loving God.)

The Sanctuary survey included both those we are calling instrumental clients as well as relational clients. For relational clients, this love of God was reflected, albeit imperfectly, in the BnF community. Leonard described his experience as a rationale for calling BnF a "loving environment" as follows: "Like I said, everyone has their problems; everyone has their issues. We try to serve and walk in a godly manner, but we're not God; we're flesh. We make mistakes, but we are willing to listen. Most of the people here are willing to listen, and they have a heart for each other. Oh sure, we have our disagreements, but we get past them." This "loving environment" with its warts and wrinkles was often seen as lifesaving for interviewees.

Michael, a white, thirty-three-year-old single man with about fourteen years of education, believes that God worked through a stranger to bring him to BnF and to the Training Program. He was in the library considering his desperate life situation when a man he had never seen before or since approached, talked with him, and then gave him a packet of information about BnF. According to Michael, "For the first time ever it felt right. I came, and BnF was exactly what the person said it was and more. He wasn't really able to describe it in fifteen minutes." He then added:

> I never had any interest in anything like this before. I actually had been completely turned off to it, but this one just slammed me. I knew God wanted me here. I know he did. Since I have been here, there are things that come to me and things that I have learned and things that I felt about God. The relationship that I am developing with God is coming at such a rapid rate! It is almost overwhelming! At this point I may just completely turn my time over and everything I have to BnF. It's beautiful, very beautiful. It is amazing! There is no doubt that they were involved in saving my life.

Michael had sought and received help from Christian rescue missions before—ones he reported that he used simply to gratify his immediate needs: "I had no intent in seeking Jesus. I just kept showing up and getting food from these guys, and they were willing to help me. God must have worn me down enough to where I would open my mind, like a child, to accept and learn from what He has to teach me." Reports similar to Michael's conversion experience were shared in many interviews, an experience of loving and being loved by God that began when Michael first walked through the doors of BnF. As he shared with the interviewer:

It's like, man, this is brand new. I haven't been to the Catholic Church since I was ten years old, and I know nothing. I knew absolutely nothing until stuff just came on me. I'm overwhelmed with it. I was very cautious and suspicious with everything and my defenses were completely dropped. It's amazing! If that can happen to me (I know it's an old phrase) but if it can happen to me, I'm sure it can happen to anybody. I mean, everyday it feels more real. I mean, I realized today that I am truer than I was yesterday. So I don't feel extremely bad about the things I am going through today because I know I am going to grow tomorrow. I am going to be more than I am, which is even better. [short pause] I'm actually somewhat blown away by it really. I have never had a relationship with God that I know of. If He was speaking to me, I was ignoring him. And now I am not. I am looking for a deeper relationship with a passion, and He's speaking. He is talking to me. It's amazing. I know He guides me. . . . What I am getting now is beautiful. It is not like religion or something. It is just very beautiful having a relationship with God. There is no way to describe it—there is nothing more beautiful.

This newly found love of God appears to strengthen love for others, although it does not necessarily feed a desire to become part of the BnF family. Religious love is not unlike romantic love, beginning with colorful fireworks against a darkened sky of emotional experience. Once the fireworks are over and darkness settles in, the real test begins. More often than not BnF family members seemed to lack the experience, the skills, the training, or the time to walk with clients on this difficult phase of the journey.

Raymond, a fifty-three-year-old divorced former minister who was in the final weeks of the Training Program and planning to leave soon thereafter, shared invaluable insights not only about himself but also about the strengths and weaknesses of the BnF ministry. Having entered the Program on the advice of his pastor after a divorce from an alcoholic wife that left his life in shambles and his psyche in acute depression, Raymond describes BnF as the catalyst in his "return to life." Although he was not addicted to alcohol or drugs ("the only thing I did was take anti-depressants," he said), Raymond came into the Program at a time when he was totally "burned out, and it got to the point where it was just so overwhelming that I didn't hear from God anymore." He was initially skeptical about the Program but said he found it "helped me to reconnect and get back on my feet so that my relationship with God could function again." His general evaluation was that "BnF was an excellent ministry."

But as a twenty-five-year veteran of the neo-Pentecostal movement and a former minister who has seen "a lot of programs come and go," Raymond was able to name problems that others were reluctant or unable to see. When asked about sources of dissatisfaction, Raymond responded, without hesitation, "Spiritual pride and arrogance." He described how "irked" he gets with the common remark made by the BnF staff, "I'm just hanging out doing Kingdom stuff," which embodied the arrogance he perceived. He claims to have seen missionaries who gave so much more and yet did not have an "attitude." Raymond went on to elaborate on his frustration:

> You have to realize that you are not better than anybody else, even if you are right in the middle of an exciting move of God. I've been there before. Many good things happen here—especially emotional and inner healings, not so much physical healing—but it is nothing compared to what I saw in Ecuador and Honduras where we did medical missions. Man, I saw things there that would knock your teeth out. I mean what I saw here is nothing compared to what I saw in the field down there. I mean literally I had friends that raised the dead! So I was really excited to be here, but in another way, it's almost like children going through teething process. For me it was a little frustrating—but that's alright. You know, you have to learn how to eat the chicken and spit out the bones. They are a good bunch of people but they need to grow up and mature in the things of God.

He also noted problems that he termed "codependency" in both the Sanctuary and the Warehouse, in which those who "need" to serve are coupled with those who "need" to be cared for. Raymond went on to explain:

> There are a lot of very codependent people over at the Sanctuary with a lot of problems that are being enabled. They pop up, and they go around and around. You know what I mean. In a sense, the Sanctuary can enable people. It can enable their addictions—you know, let them continue on. You know, they come and they go. There is an ongoing conflict over authority. It's a little different here, I would say, because people who come to the Program make such a commitment in giving up their rights and so forth. It is quite a commitment to make allowing everything to be stripped away. I mean it is not easy. I mean the Lord told me to humble

myself under His almighty hand—God tells us to do that and then "I will exalt you in time." It wasn't very nice for me to come in here, and I didn't enjoy it.

When asked whether he found BnF to be a loving environment, Raymond replied, "That is a tough question." He said he could not speak for what was going on in the Sanctuary, but he does know that there were many difficulties at the Warehouse. He was particularly concerned about what he perceived to be a misuse of authority, including the emphasis on the Twelve and father-son relationships: "I've seen it tried before, and they are courting disaster." He concluded by saying, "I think they try—the staff tries as much as they can with their own limitations. I mean they try, let's put it that way."

The Poor as Family Members

By any outside account, Phil, who came to BnF within a year of its founding and diligently served in preparing meals, bagging groceries, and now self-describes as "in charge of this entire building," would be a family member. Yet, despite his commitment and service, it is doubtful that he was ever regarded as a full-fledged member of the BnF family. According to one report from a former leader, even though Phil was not an addict ("I left my love affair with alcohol long before I came to BnF," he reports) and had worked with the family for years, Phil submitted to the Training Program as some in leadership demanded. (The director of the Program who reported this story said she felt very "uncomfortable" with this demand, believing that Phil knew more about running the Program than she did. She then asked him to help her teach the men.)

As we saw earlier, Phil described himself as being in a "gray area"— not really an insider but not an outsider to the community either. He has served alongside BnF members since nearly the beginning of the ministry, but he was not likely to be found in David's Twelve, in family gatherings, or among the Starbucks coffee crowd. It was only after the schism and only as David was trying to regroup the remnants that some in the "gray area" were invited to the other side of the BnF divide. Men in the Restoration (final) phase of the Training Program were invited (much to their delight) and began to show up at family parties and barbecues. During the heyday of BnF's ministry, however, the gray area was very gray and very much in place. No serious or persistent complaints were heard at the time from those who had acclimated to the seismic fault in the family. When interviewers would raise questions about the distant status of the poor in the community, the faithful would generally reply, "That's just the way it is," "They don't want to make a commitment," or "None of us is perfect." And when someone like Starla, who asked when Sanctuary residents would be invited to the homes of family members, would innocently (or not so innocently) question the status quo, the response was one of immediate silence or perhaps even reflection, but little or no action.

It is within this background that we explore those poor and homeless interviewees who regarded themselves as active members of the BnF family. All the men went through the Training Program, a requirement (as we have just seen in the case of Phil) of addicts and nonaddicts alike. Because there was no similar program for women, the path to family for them was exemplary service. Fonda, who first came to the Sanctuary at the onset of the schism and now serves as director of the Program until it closed its doors, serves as one exemplar.

Strictly speaking, Fonda, a Caucasian woman in her early fifties, was never homeless, although she did find herself in need of a shelter when she left a man she described as her "boyfriend." She owns a home in rural Georgia, but she accompanied her friend (with whom she had been living for about three years) to Atlanta. "When I got here with him," she says, "things didn't really work out well." After leaving him, she had nowhere to go but the park. While she was sitting on a park bench, a man, whom she did not know and has never seen again, came up to her and handed her a piece of paper. On it was BnF's phone number. She called the number, was immediately given a bed in the Sanctuary, and "I've been here ever since."

What gives Fonda the greatest satisfaction in living and working with BnF is "love" and the relationships she sees there, particularly among the permanent residents. As Fonda describes her feelings for BnF: "It's the relationship with the people. You just can feel the caring and the love here between the people that are permanent residents here. I mean, right now we have a lot of, you know, overnight people and thirty-day people and stuff. But the rest of the people that's here, there is a lot of camaraderie and it seems like family."

Several other women interviewees from the Sanctuary named Fonda as the reason that they were at BnF. They spoke of the compassion she had for them in their difficulties and the lengths to which she would go to help them. In her first interview, six months after her arrival, Fonda was already leaving her mark on the Sanctuary, both in carrying out the hard work as director and adding a feminine touch to her bit of space in the old Sanctuary. As her tenure increased at BnF, Fonda was given more authority to make house rules to the point that she says in a later interview, "I have freedom to make any decisions that affect this work. I'm sure if I did something crazy it would be brought into line, but I am free to make decisions."

Fonda never had any experience with the homeless before she sought shelter at BnF: "I'm from south Georgia; in small towns people take care of their own," she explained. At a church revival about a decade earlier, however, the pastor said that he "had a word for me." The pastor then gave her the prophecy predicting that "in future years you will be working with homeless people." Fonda adds, "I never thought that would come to be, but here I am." She has even been the recipient of the community's "extravagant giving"—one sign of her acceptance into the family. One BnF International leader gave her a car (for which deed the giver was awarded a luxury car from another "extravagant giver"). Other family members have worked to provide a simple apartment unit on the fringes of the large, one-room Sanctuary.

While women were able to take a direct route from the Sanctuary into the margins of the BnF family, men—even married men—were expected to enter through the residential program at the warehouse. Some entered the Program, only to drop out within the first few weeks; others move through it to completion; it is difficult to find someone who has gone through the Program to become a bona fide family member. John, a forty-year-old African American male, was completing the Program for the second time when he was interviewed. Both the Warehouse and the Program have changed since the late 1990s: "It's more structured now, so we are able to build family," says John. John's attitude toward becoming part of the BnF community has changed as well:

When I was here the first time, I was just concerned about getting off drugs and going back into society. Now I got to the place where I don't even want to go back. I like what I am doing here now. I am in the last phase of the Program, which is Restoration, where I work here in the kitchen. Once this is all over with, I am thinking about turning around and volunteering. I like what I am doing, and the Lord has laid on my heart so heavy to come back and do it as a volunteer.

John appears grateful for what he has received through BnF and he wants "to give back that service." He reportedly gets much happiness out of "giving back"—"Just to speak life into people and allow them to speak life into me." He noted that when he was in the Program the first time, there was no Twelve: "Everything was so fresh and brand new. It was just going out to the streets and winning souls. Back then we would go out with a band and food and just worship. But now it's about building Twelves. A couple of months from now it will be about building Twelves and going back out onto the streets and doing what they did a long time ago."

John completed the Program around the time of the schism and became engaged to one of the newer BnF family members who supported David during what David called his "exile." The couple married and undoubtedly could have become part of the inner core, but they slowly fell into the shadows as have scores of former family members of the past, often grateful for what they have received from BnF but unwilling or unable to commit their lives to the community.

Social Boundaries and the Art of Loving

Although in theory love can permeate socially constructed walls, it often stumbles when attempting to cross racial, religious, gender, age, and economic divides. Often new boundaries develop to make the task of loving more manageable, as it has in the Sanctuary: relational clients express their dissatisfaction with instrumental ones and a gray area appears to separate the BnF family from the family that develops among the poor. If we are to assess love by looking at interaction patterns, we see (in accord with Sorokin's thesis) that intense love is constrained by a short leash (extensity, says Sorokin). We would like to suggest that another way of considering the love at BnF is to look at the family and client in relationship to the BnF vision.

The BnF community (David's "family" as well as the Sanctuary/Warehouse clients) in some ways share a common vision. Ralph once told David that if he wanted to see his vision of the Kingdom in operation, he should "hang out" with the residents of the Sanctuary. In some ways the Sanctuary respondents seemed to understand even better than David's followers that the Kingdom was not about "religion" or about "Twelves" or even about "tongues." The Kingdom, according to David's vision, is about living out a life of godly love.

If a word count were to be done on the word *love* in each of the interviews, it would be found far more frequently in those used in this chapter than in the previous one. It is as if the homeless respondents had caught a new vision and were excited with the God of love whom they were coming to know and the possibility of loving former strangers with whom they were now sharing their lives. In a sense the Sanctuary residents and Program trainees had the harder test, being forced to live with others who were poor, mentally ill, or chemically dependent. As we saw from Daryl's testimony, one couldn't just "walk away" from relational difficulties as one could do "in the world."

This is not to say that the poor loved better than their providers; we don't know that from our data. We only know that the situation and mode of expression were different for the two groups. We also know from events that have transpired that the familial relations that did evolve among the homeless were dependent on the social situation provided by BnF. The schism would drastically alter life for the homeless at BnF, where even those committed to the family were subject to diaspora.

Some residents of the Sanctuary/Warehouse, like the BnF family members, had spiritually transformed and were trying to live out their respective versions of David's vision to serve the poor. Both groups reflect a deep spirituality that enabled them to put flesh on their beliefs about the Kingdom. Members of both groups were touched by love and sought to share this love with others. The love found in both groups, however, had its own respective limitations in what Sorokin called extensity and intensity. As members moved away from their inner circle, the love demonstrated seemed to be less intense. The gray area noted by Phil, which divided the Sanctuary from the family business in the Warehouse, was one way to denote the social barrier that existed to limit interaction between the two groups. Most Sanctuary residents appeared to accept this gray area as a given in the ministry, working around it to get what they needed. Their relationships were primarily with others who were homeless and poor rather than with those on the other side of the unstated divide.

Within the Sanctuary family there was another divide—between those who sought and accepted relational commitments and those who did not. Love was freely extended to others who were trying to move beyond a simple instrumental exchange, but its givers were critical of (and seemingly less loving toward) those who rejected the relational path. Sometimes interviewees would distinguish between the poor and addicts in talking about this divide—the poor, we were informed, are always grateful; the addicts are perpetually dissatisfied and always wanting more. A "family" member was always grateful and sought to be an "extravagant giver." The giving and receiving had social parameters that drew a line between the instrumental and relational clients.

This observation offers another take on our survey finding that the poor were more critical of the homeless than were the BnF family members. It may well be that the poor were better aware of the relational problems they had with the "addicts" than the BnF family members who had comparatively little intimate ongoing contact with the poor and homeless. As we saw, Raymond was wary of the codependency that he observed in the Training Program and joined others in questioning the revolving door that continually brought in new people without having seen lasting changes in the ones who were leaving. Several other interviewees expressed their opinion that the addicts needed a "kick in the butt" rather than the coddling that BnF family often offered in the name of forgiveness.

Despite the finding that Sanctuary respondents were less likely to report that walking in the supernatural, spirituality was important to them. The poor, most of whom were from black Baptist backgrounds— "Bapticostals," they have been called—seemed to have worldview of God actively involved in their lives not unlike BnF's neo-Pentecostals. They score lower on the particular Pentecostal distinctive trait of speaking in tongues; yet, as we have seen in this chapter, nearly all the men and women interviewed had a sense of God's leading and speaking to them and they were even more likely to experience physical healing. Perhaps because they were older and financially destitute, the homeless were more likely to pray for spiritual healing for others and to receive spiritual healings themselves. Researchers have found that the homeless have much less access to medical assistance and hospital services than do other sectors of American society (Snow and Anderson 1993; Blau 1992), and thus it is not surprising that they would be more likely to employ religious alternatives (especially prayer) than were elite family members who still had access to conventional medicine.

Numerous narratives of divine healing were told in the interviews with the homeless. We will take time to share only one here. Our choice is the story told by Phil, the Sanctuary respondent who has been with BnF for the longest period of time:

> Like I said, in 98 I had a heart attack. My heart is fixed, and every doctor I talked to wanted to do a triple bypass at the time. I was willing to undergo, but they made the mistake of giving me two weeks before the

operation was scheduled. During that two weeks I changed my mind. I said if God wanted me to live, he will heal me. If he don't, I'm going to die. I am ready either way. So I had no way of knowing myself, when I went back in 2000 for something else and they did some more tests on my heart, it was practically sound. There was nothing wrong with my heart. I said, "Thank you, Jesus."

More on Faces of Godly Love

The *L*(ove) model of godly love reflected in the BnF vision seems to assume different faces. For David, community members, and clients alike, there was much love talk during the interviews, in which accounts were told about experiencing God's love and how this divine love fueled a deeper love for others. Despite the common feature of a link between experiences of divine love and human love, there were differing portraits—faces of love, if you will—mirrored in the narratives. The differences become more striking in comparing stories and responses of the BnF community with those of their beneficiaries, differences that reflect Rolf Johnson's typology on the meanings of love developed in chapter 4.

The seeming incongruities mirrored in the qualitative data find quantitative support from the survey findings for Sanctuary residents and BnF members reported in appendix C. As we have already noted, no differences in care-love were found between the two groups. BnF's homeless beneficiaries were just as likely to report similar scores on altruism and empathy as were the benefactors. The data suggest, however, that the objects of the care-love differed for the two caste-like groups. Sanctuary residents formed relationships with other homeless men and women while the BnF community developed strong bonds with other family members. David's vision of a single integrated family in which love was extensive as well as intense and of long duration simply did not materialize.

Using Sorokin's dimensions of love to guide our qualitative assessment, we observed how the intensity of love is paralleled by extensity as long as it is within the parameter of BnF family. When love is extended to the truly homeless, it seems to falter and operates on a minimum level of intensity. At the same time, stories told in this chapter suggest that homeless respondents often knew little about love—within the parameters or family or without—before coming to BnF. They claim in various ways that they have learned to be more loving as they came to know the love of God and to experience the love of others.

This observation raises questions about the role of vision—Johnson's appreciation-love—in assessing godly love. As we have suggested earlier, the object of love for David and perhaps some of his followers may have centered more on appreciation-love or the vision of the coming Kingdom of God than lived-out relationships. Appreciation-love, however, seemed to have little direct meaning for the poor and homeless, who were more concerned with concrete goals and needs rather than with abstract vision. We noted this earlier in the chapter when we reported differences between the two groups in the meanings attached to the Kingdom of God. These differences are also reflected in the survey finding that Sanctuary residents were much less likely than BnF family (r=.28) to say that walking in the supernatural was important to them. It could be said that appreciation-love is the point at which experiences of divine love and human love intersected for David's middle-class followers. For the poor, however, abstract vision was less important than the expressed care-love many found in the BnF household.

Union-love is represented by the vertical line in the L model. It was reported to fuel David's experiences of God speaking to him as it was in the transformation accounts of David's followers. Similar transformation accounts can be found in the narratives of the Sanctuary residents and recovering addicts found in this chapter. Significant differences in the conceptualization of union-love, however, can be observed for the beneficiaries and the benefactors in survey findings found in appendix C-1. We know, for example, that the Sanctuary residents were significantly less likely to report speaking in tongues (r=-.28) and significantly more likely to report having experienced a divine healing (r=.18). Sanctuary residents were also more likely to report higher scores on Hood's mysticism scale (r=-.31), a general index that is not religiously specific, than were family members. While we have no way of knowing whether the experiences of the divine were actually dissimilar between the two groups or whether they preferred different ways of articulating their experiences, we do know that the reported experiences of the divine on select questionnaire items were quantitatively different.

Based on both qualitative and quantitative measures, it is clear that union-love—love that reflects encounters with divine love—was a significant factor for both groups in accounting for differences in reported care-love (altruism). It appears, however, that union love may operate differently for BnF family than for the Sanctuary members. The general mysticism scale was found to be a better predictor of altruism and empathy for

Sanctuary residents while the Pentecostal charismata scale was a better predictor for BnF family members. What is perhaps most important here are not the differences found for the two groups in measures of union-love used in the survey as much as the significant role that union-love plays in accounting for care-love in both groups. We heard it in the narratives provided through qualitative data and found supportive evidence reflected in the quantitative statistical findings. Experiencing the divine is in synergistic interaction with loving others, providing what Collins has called emotional energy (EE) that community members and many homeless sought and valued. This EE empowered family members and many homeless residents who were affected by BnF to acts of caring and compassion.

The one-shot statistical survey provided a limited profile of godly love in the BnF community. This picture has been fleshed out by our longitudinal observations and interviews. Based on our extended fieldwork, we noted that despite BnF's reputation of being one of the most unique attempts to serve the poor of Atlanta, its achievements reflected a godly love of less duration and intensity than proposed. BnF was a revolving door for the poor, failing to draw them into the familial relationships proposed in David's vision. It is fair to say that despite its once-impressive success as a ministry, BnF failed the homeless by the visionary criteria that VanCronkhite himself established. We saw little evidence that it genuinely served to transform the lives of the homeless. It appeared to us more likely that the poor were the means by which David mediated his beloved vision of the Kingdom to his closer family members and to benefactors who financially supported him. If the Kingdom is about Atlanta and if the poor are central to that vision, despite the sincerity and genuine love that exists at BnF, that love is far from adequate in actually transforming either the lives of the poor or a large metropolitan area.

7

Ideology and Tradition in Conflict

We may distinguish a continuum of cultural embeddedness ranging from ideology to tradition to common sense. Ideology, tradition, and common sense vary in how explicit and self-conscious versus implicit and taken for granted their meanings are. . . . Ideology is more explicit, less embedded, and more open to challenge. . . . [It is] "an articulated system of meanings, values, and beliefs of a kind that can be abstracted as [the] 'worldview' of a social group." . . . Traditions, on the other hand, are articulated cultural beliefs and practices, but ones that present themselves as fixed, expected parts of life. . . . Common sense, finally, consists in assumptions so unselfconscious as to seem a natural, transparent part of the structure of the world, objectively real and needing no explicit support or elaboration to be true.

—Swidler 2001, 94–96

Interaction rituals (IRs) are often Janus-faced, and this is true for godly love as it is for experienced inter-human encounters. On the one side, they may produce positive EE (emotional energy) that binds together like-minded devotees in interaction ritual (IR) chains that empower them for greater care-love, a phenomenon found in many of our reported narratives. It could be said that IRs are often the glue that bind groups together. As Collins notes, "In its Durkheimian formulation, successful rituals produce group solidarity. Teasing apart the mechanisms and fine-grained processes of an IR, we could say instead that successful IRs produce heightened mutual focus and bodily emotional entrainment" (2004, 125).

But not all IR rituals are successful in generating positive EE that is the nucleus of social solidarity. Negative EE, reflected in anger, anxiety, depression, and fear, also has an impact on ritual interactions. Such forces produce disruptive dissention and conflict, as can be gleaned from some of the interviews presented in earlier chapters. Collins has long been known for his significant contribution to an integrated sociological theory of conflict (Collins 1975; Ritzer 1992). Although his discussion of conflict is not fully developed in *Interaction Ritual Chains*, as it is in other works, Collins (2004, 121-24) does remind his readers of the relationship between conflict and IRs that are reflected in power, dominance, and social stratification. While still using Collins's general theory to frame our study, the conflict-ridden schism that developed at BnF is better described by cultural forces than by the stratification and structure featured in IR theory. We retain Collins's basic theoretical approach, but we supplement it in this chapter with Ann Swidler's theory of love and culture (2001) to better understand the conflict that engulfed the BnF ministry. As we see it, part of the conflict at BnF was over privileged social positions insofar as David's vision could not be challenged. A greater share of the conflict, however, was due to differing assessments of the adequacy of the lived-out BnF vision of godly love for the poor.

Godly Love, Vision, and the BnF Culture of Love

BnF is a culture of love—union-love relationships with God that are said to empower care-love relationships among family members and the poor and homeless—that is wrapped in a vision of walking in the supernatural to usher in the coming Kingdom of God. David and his faithful followers believe that the BnF vision is given by God. Seeming supernatural experiences of both the collective community and individual members—family and many homeless alike—reinforced its authenticity. This visionary wrapping of "cultural embeddedness" challenged the commonly accepted vision of the American dream with a call to usher in the Kingdom of God through godly love for the poor and homeless. BnF's radical supernatural vision (a type ideology, as Swidler would put it) proved in fact to be "more explicit, less embedded, and more open to challenge" than the beliefs and practices represented in the larger culture; this was especially the case of the traditional business community represented in the BnF board of directors, despite the fact that most were evangelical Christians.

While none at BnF would label David's vision as ideology, it is a type of appreciative-love that is an object of love. Ideology or vision can be conceptualized as a linchpin between divine union-love and human care-love. We suggested that in Swidler's sense, David's vision is an ideology—a "face of love" that can be assessed using Pitirim Sorokin's dimensions, just as care-love can be assessed through Sorokin's theory.

Most family members at BnF tried to put its ideology into practice, and some lived it out in remarkable ways. They sold their possessions and moved into inner-city Atlanta in exchange for a vision and a dream, fueled by a sense of divine calling and a love for the community they saw at BnF. The ever-changing details of David's vision, however, fed the unsettledness of the community, an unsettledness reflected in the disciples and potential disciples who came, listened, and left through BnF's welcoming but revolving door. The pivot for that revolving door was always the acceptance of David's vision and the particulars on what he demanded for the vision to be lived out.

The homeless who were committed to the BnF family (familial clients) tended to adopt David's ideology with little questioning—at least until the schism. The recovering addicts and homeless poor, on the other hand, were more likely to accommodate and acclimate to BnF's required principles and promises in return for goods and services (instrumental clients). Others who were poor and found themselves spiritually transformed by BnF might adapt and modify the ideology to meet their needs (as did relational clients and most familial clients).

Ideology in Situational Context

Ideologies—even ideologies about love—do not exist in a vacuum. They can be appraised only in cultural situations and the interactions that occur within those situations. BnF is, as are all emerging churches by implicit definition, what Swidler calls an "unsettled situation" (2001, 94). Emerging churches seek to remain in "unsettled situations" characteristic of post-modernity, situations in which "people use culture to organize new strategies of action and model new ways of thinking and feeling" (Swidler 2001, 94). Unsettled lives demand a strong coupling between ideology and action, and it was David's ideology that has guided the church and ministry as it defined its boundaries. Those who were unable to accept David's authority, whether "family" or beneficiaries, either drifted away or were encouraged to leave in search of another "home."

The new ideological patterns of thought and behavior that David believed were required for bringing in the Kingdom were in tension with dominant traditional modes of American business practices. The tension came to a head when the new board of trustees, savvy and proved effi-cient in the ways of the traditional business community, tried to align BnF's finances with norms and practices that are legally required of both profit and nonprofit institutions. Most of the board members respected the tangible ministry that they observed at BnF. Gaps between the ideol-ogy of an unsettled BnF and the tradition of the settled business com-munity could be accepted by board members—as long as these "gaps" did not threaten the financial stability of the ministry they felt David called them to oversee.

The narratives we have presented in earlier chapters reflect both a co-herence and incoherence in BnF's ideology with a tension common to un-settled situations. We have told the stories primarily with an ear for the coherent, not only to help the reader to make sense out of a world that may seem very strange, but also to present the voices of the community as we heard the accounts early in our research. As new situations unfolded other voices were heard and dissonant sounds were amplified. In this chapter we bring the voices already introduced together with new voices to explore what can happen when ideology and tradition collide. The task we set for ourselves and for the reader, however, goes beyond noting the consistency and inconsistency in the narratives. The issue is rather, as Swidler suggests, "not whether the glass is half empty or half full, but what creates cultural coherence and in what places, and what accounts for the extent and shape of cultural incoherence" (2001, 182). The schism that developed at BnF represented a war between two cultures, both using the language of love with heartfelt sincerity.

From New Paradigm to Emerging Church

John Wimber, the founder of the Association of Vineyard Churches, paid a visit to BnF the month before he died. As the story goes (it was a com-mon narrative, retold during BnF tours, conferences, and conversations with visitors), Wimber came to BnF in October 1997 to hold what would be the last conference of his life. David says that he arrived "as a grumpy old man," but his countenance began to change as he was given the cus-tomary tour of the facilities. By the time he got to the second building, Wimber's spirits had lifted and he was "prophesying and moving in the supernatural." He then turned to David and urged him never to abandon this mission and vision. Wimber, whose churches were model new-para-digm congregations in which there were ministries *for* the poor but not *of* the poor, reportedly said, "This was the only thing I ever wanted to do. I'm going down as a man who 'changed worship,' but all I ever wanted to do was to work with the poor. Don't get distracted." John Wimber died a month later and the following year BnF withdrew from the Association of Vineyard Churches to pursue what we see as its journey as an emerging church.

It was also during 1997 that BnF moved away from using the metaphor of being an "army" to that of a "family," thus changing its emphasis to the type of relationship that has been identified as one of the three "core practices" for emerging churches. (Although "emerging churches" were in fact developing autonomously and anonymously in the late 1980s and early 1990s, it was not until 1998 that Brian McLaren challenged ministers to reinvent their churches and 2003 that Dan Kimball developed a blueprint for emerging churches.) Eric, an African American in his late thirties who would for a short time be named BnF's pastor, described the change in relational models that occurred shortly after he joined the community: "When I first got here, the vision for this place was an army—an army of men going out to take the city. And now we are not an army anymore; we are a family. And that's two totally different—totally different ways of taking the city. One is by force; the other is by love. And I really believe—*I know*—the love part is the strongest of them all. It's how God wants it—to love people into the Kingdom, not to force them in."

Together with the relational change away from being God's army toward being His family came another history-of-ministry marker, namely, the call to "go take Atlanta." This vision, increasingly important in David's ideology, was supported by a modified passage from the book of Habakkuk: "Look at *Atlanta* and watch and be utterly amazed. For I am going to do something in your days that you would not believe, even if you were told" (1:5). (One former leader commented on this strange biblical base for David's belief that God was telling him to take Atlanta—a modified passage that David often cites to this day. As she pointed out, the "promise" in Habakkuk is one of doom and destruction for Israel and of unleashing the powerful Babylonian enemies to execute justice.) As we shall see, David's vision for taking Atlanta is an issue that would come up repeatedly in the board minutes given to us by its president, Cissy Watson, particularly as it related to purchasing additional properties to expand BnF's presence in the city.

We have already noted the importance of the story of the acquisition of the warehouse property, from David's hearing a divine call to the purchase of the buildings to the miraculous final mortgage payment. The myth became a central symbol for challenging the American dream with an unwavering trust in the supernatural. It wasn't until the dark days of the schism that a frustrated member of the board of trustees told us in the midst of other interesting disclosures that there was more to the story of the warehouse: "I am one (with two or three others) who raised the money to pay off the mortgage of three hundred fifty thousand dollars. I could have gone to the bank and gotten the note renewed just like that. But I didn't do it. I told David, 'Don't renew it; pay it off.' And so he and I met with others, imposed on friends, and begged, borrowed, and pleaded until we raised three hundred fifty thousand dollars."

And as we write this in 2007, it appears that David's account contains another devilish detail. As far as all reports go, David owns the warehouse. It remains unclear what, if any, constraints apply to what David can do with the money from the sale of the dismantled artifacts and from the sale of this prime property in downtown Atlanta.

God Gives BnF a Board of Directors

In a succinct report we were handed by VanCronkhite during our preliminary site visit of June 2002 appeared the following statement: "Throughout the years, the Lord has been faithful to bring many people alongside Blood-n-Fire to support us. More recently, we have begun to realize the importance of having a strong Board of Trustees in place. This year we solidified our Board and are truly in awe of the men and women the Lord has brought. These are men and women who are nationally recognized for their contributions to the areas of expertise which they represent."

Although BnF had a couple of other loosely structured boards before 2002, this one had a special narrative as being something given and ordained by God. As best we can judge, the earlier boards (no one is certain exactly where one left off and another began) were informal arrangements in which David would casually ask someone to be part of "the board." The person would walk with David in this fluid arrangement and then move on when it became apparent that David really didn't need or want his services or counsel. This new board was different with its list of members, formal procedures, and recorded minutes. Among the basic responsibilities that could be found listed on three occasions in the minutes of the board (2002-4) were to support the executive director and assess his or her performance, to ensure adequate resources and help manage them effectively, and to ensure legal and ethical integrity and maintain accountability. These agreed-on responsibilities—and David's sense of the divine—would be challenged during the schism.

David had often been critical of the corporate business world that he left behind to begin his work with BnF. When asked in an interview with us (June 28, 2004), knowing what he did about corporate American, why he brought together such a high-powered group of people to be his board of directors, David (referring to his sense of God's leading) replied, "It wasn't *my* plan." He then began his story about the plan's divine serendipity:

> There was a man called Abner, a man who said he had been looking for me for twenty years. He found a VanCronkhite in Denton, Texas, and called the number; he got my mother. Abner said to her, "There's this guy called David—he did a great favor for me twenty-five years ago. He's the only person who's done me this great a favor, and I want to repay him. Do you know David?" A month later he comes to the warehouse in Atlanta and says, "I don't understand it all, but you helped me tremendously and now I want to help you. How can I help? I don't know how to help." I told him to hang around and look and see how he could help. Then Abner says, "I got some friends. What if I introduce you to them?

Abner then introduced David to Dan Cathy, Chick-fil-A's chief operating officer, who in turn introduced him to other Atlanta entrepreneurs who then got their friends involved—each asking, "What can I do to help?" This board was to play a significant role in altering the history of BnF, as we will see as our narrative continues.

The seeds of dissension were sown as David began to mix two models that could not easily function together—one ideological and visionary, the other traditional and business oriented. The ideological model was home for David's prophetic stance and his willingness to walk in faith with his ever-changing vision. Having secured the warehouse, David's faith was now centered on securing additional real estate holdings for which a debt-ridden BnF did not have funds. The other model was a corporate one that demanded keeping the ministry within proper fiscal guidelines and expected ethical responsibilities to be met. While David's corporate friends on the board were mostly Christian believers, their fiscal policies were far from prophetically based. The board demanded that he live within a budget, regardless of whether the funds were ultimately provided by God.

The Year Was 2002

In the spring of 2002, Margaret approached David to discuss a possible research project. David replied, "Come on, Margaret, we are ready for you." What we didn't know was that the newly established board was pressing David for facts about the ministry and recommended evaluation studies that needed to be conducted on the various programs. Here again, the board reasonably used their corporate sensitivities to determine the cost at which services were being delivered to the poor. When the topic came up again at the August 13, 2002, executive committee meeting (a six-person subgroup of the board of trustees, including David), David reported that "Margaret Poloma was conducting research." (At this point we had explored the possibility of writing a proposal; the project had not yet been approved or funded.) A site visit by both of us in June did in fact convince us that BnF was ripe for systematic study. Its mission and vision was defined, and its organizational structure was set in place, including the new board and the "family business" with its Sanctuary "home"/ shelter, the nightly public meals, the Training Program, and an intern program. Names on the mailboxes suggested even more promising ministries, most of which we could only note during this preliminary site visit before applying for research funding. We were soon to learn that some of our initial observations were less than reliable. One problem that haunted us throughout our study was the inability to get any hard numbers about anything. If the board lacked fiscal figures, we lacked even simple figures about the number of persons who were in a program and the number who had graduated.

During our pre-research site visit we observed a Sunday morning worship gathering of "the family," newly restored after having been dismantled for some two years (reported in chapter 2). In the place of a largely white suburban congregation coming together in an old downtown warehouse was an integrated gathering of blacks and whites, young and old, homeless and housed, who gathered to worship, a congregation that is every emerging church leader's dream. The service was basically neo-Pentecostal in the Vineyard style for which John Wimber, founder of the Association of Vineyard Churches, is remembered. The music favors David's innermost circle but is far from accommodating to his largely African American homeless constituency.

The faithful gathered in the Sanctuary surrounded by beds for the homeless; no longer was it a refuge for middle-class suburbanites who merely wanted a different kind of church experience on Sunday mornings. With the killing of the cash cow, BnF had moved closer to the ideal type that Gibbs and Bolger (2005) would later construct of emerging churches. Yet one could not help but notice that the homeless African Americans for the most part sat passively on their chairs while the white worshipers performed the music, responded in dance in the front of the Sanctuary, managed the expensive sound system, led the service, and did the preaching/teaching. BnF would also host conferences in the Sanctuary from time to time, where friends and other interested persons could come to hear name neo-Pentecostal speakers, all white and most males. They talked about the poor and the gifts of the Spirit, especially the gift of prophecy, but again most black residents sat along the sidelines as conference attendees used their "home." The guests flew in, stayed in hotels, and ate meals at Atlanta's trendy restaurants. Never did we see any poor invited to dine with conference participants. Furthermore, conference guests preached to but seldom interacted with or talked one-on-one to the Sanctuary poor.

Prior to this initial site visit, we had learned on the BnF Web site of another interesting endeavor that proved to be more of a promise than a program (http://www.bloodnfire.com; accessed March 22, 2002). "One Way Companies" was described as follows: "One significant role of the church is to ensure that 'there are no needy persons among them' (Acts 4:34). It is the church's responsibility vs the government's responsibility to care for the needy of the community. To do our part, Blood 'N Fire is incorporating businesses with community based leadership to train and lead men, women, and their children out of the cycle of poverty into providing for their own family needs."

As with other business plans that we saw rise and fall during the subsequent years of our study, One Way Companies promised businesses and jobs for the recovering addicts and the homeless but was little more than an unfulfilled dream. There is no hard data that BnF has a success rate either for achieving success in alcohol or drug rehabilitation or in providing jobs for the homeless aside from the unpaid work at BnF (which includes extensive work on David's lake house). We had come with hope that we were to study a truly remarkable ministry that was transforming the lives of the addicted poor. This we did not observe. If BnF is credited with transforming lives, it is only in the inner circles of volunteers who share David's vision that such transformations can be documented.

We were invited on a tour of the neighborhoods emanating in four different directions from the Capitol Building and the BnF Warehouse (an area known as Capitol Corridor) to see the additional properties owned by BnF and those whose purchase was anticipated. These properties were to be of immense concern to David's board. How could they be financed and refurbished? On what fiscal authority was David operating? We walked the Fourth Ward to Edgewood by Grady Memorial Hospital and the site of a then-vacant building where Café Ruach was scheduled to open in October 2002. The building was to pay for itself from the renting of proposed loft apartments on the second floor. It sat empty and vandalized, however, until the property was sold during the height of the schism and its attendant financial crunch.

At the time of the tour we were unaware of the role the board was playing in David's vision for Atlanta. In the board of trustee folder for March 11, 2002, we found a memo from David to the executive committee, thanking them "for gently but firmly demanding that Blood N Fire begin defining basic values, purpose and vision. . . . and for gently demanding that I establish criteria for measuring our effectiveness and accomplishing our goals." The executive committee meeting minutes from April 10 made note of recommendations for "annual audit and the legal process of financial-clean-up." David was no longer a businessman willing to abide by traditional business regulations. The board seemed to recognize the problems spawned by a committed visionary running the day-to-day operations of a nonprofit ministry; they acknowledged that "a transition was happening with BnF." Despite the ripples of dissent that we would later find in the board minutes, the visionary and his board still seemed to be on a honeymoon at the time of our original site visit. As one trustee noted of the unsettled situation, "I am not disturbed by what is happening; I rather enjoy it."

The minutes for April 2002 indicate that David had finally responded to a request for a detailed strategy, including a description of operations and needed warehouse renovation. Central to David's report was his description of a BnF "core value" that he termed "presence." He again told the stories of how God called him in 1992 to purchase the warehouse properties and the call ten years later to "go get Atlanta." The document then described Capitol Corridor neighborhoods where David wanted to establish a presence by owning property: Fourth Ward, the "historic and spiritually significant area known as known as 'Sweet Auburn'"; Simpson and Ashby, "one of the most drug infested, violent areas of inner city Atlanta"; Broad

Street, "a one-block area just south of the critical Five Points Station"; and West End. The executive board responded by unanimously approving the purchase of the Edgewood property where Café Ruach would be housed and rental incomes upstairs would pay for this facet of the "family business." As David noted in his report on "Presence" that he submitted to the April board meeting: "Housing is a tremendous strategies and financial decision for us. The Edgewood Building will help some but we need housing for staff family and 'graduates' of the rebuilding process to build community. Our plan is to work with investors who are willing to purchase houses in the 'right areas' for us and let us rent from them."

The community and ministry that we saw at BnF during our initial site visit was innovative, creative, and seemingly effective. In the winter months, hundreds of homeless would find a safe haven in the Sanctuary while they and other poor would be fed meals each evening worthy of a good family-style restaurant. The thirty or so men in the Training Program consistently testified to changed lives brought about by the ministry, even though we eventually learned that some were gone the following month and others had been involved in a second or third go-around in the Program. In reading the minutes from board of trustee meetings for this period, it appeared that we were not alone in our mixed evaluation of BnF's unique vision and ministry, aware of the weeds but also of the wheat. David appeared to be at the center of it all—a man with a vision for developing what he called "a Christianity worth propagating." David is a masterful speaker whose charismatic personality resonated during his "talks" as it did with his hugs.

From Abeyance to Abundance

The BnF International "tribal gathering" (as the annual meeting was called that year) in January 2003 marked the beginning of our formal research project. In retrospect, it was a watershed for the BnF community. After years of struggle ("abeyance," Papa Jack Taylor would say) it appeared that BnF had reached a new peak ("abundance," said Papa Jack). Finances, ever a problem but always a source of stories of divine serendipity, were in better shape than ever thanks to the new board of trustees. Although it was another year before we learned the details of the "miracle," the near euphoria over the good fortune experienced by the community over the payment of a $436,000 debt to various creditors (with an additional $100,000 to begin the new year) was evident. David joyfully reported to the gathered community, "I think we are going to have a fantastic year—feasting and fasting and praying, always."

Although the properties were paid off in 2001, BnF had fallen into debt, some of it internal to the BnF family but much of it owed to outside creditors. Cissy Watson, the board president, reported being concerned about the payables due with no money to cover them. She believed, however, that up until now nobody seemed willing "to take the time and energy to raise money." Watson noted that to get by each month they were borrowing money from one account to pay another and told of the times that she personally would drive downtown with her checkbook to keep the water running and the lights on. The executive board then decided to sponsor a fund-raising party to pay off the debt BnF owed to its creditors by December 31, 2002. David's version minimized or even concealed the central role of the board in fundraising as he had done earlier in the warehouse story, shrouding the account in a serendipitous process in which "one foundation guy called and gave fifty thousand dollars; Chris gave one hundred fifty thousand dollars; another guy gave one hundred twenty-five thousand dollars, and so on." Money seemed to be the new manna from heaven as the last donation came in by December 31, which put the board's fund-raising efforts over the top.

Even the board was surprised by the success of their venture, held as it was during the holiday season. The board of trustees meeting minutes from January 7, 2003, noted how president Cissy Watson "talked about God's provision and her excitement about the money that God brought in to take care of our accounts payables—that it was a huge kiss and squeeze from God." Watson's account in her interview of January 6, 2004, contained more details:

> There weren't many people at our party, but money kept coming in. I went skiing the weekend after Christmas for a week, and this was like so God to me—such a confirmation. When I left for the skiing trip, we were one hundred fifty thousand dollars short of meeting our goal of paying off the four hundred thirty-six thousand dollars, but we were thrilled with the amount we had raised. When Chris called me on Monday and said we were only forty-six thousand dollars short with one more business day to the year, we all started praying. That afternoon, I sensed God saying, "You keep thinking it's you that brings the money in. Will you quit thinking that it is you?" So here we are in this warming hut drinking hot chocolate, and I got a call: "We've gotten all our checks in today.

Guess how much money we got?" I guessed, thirty thousand dollars. No. Forty thousand dollars. No. Fifty thousand dollars. No. We had gotten one hundred fifty thousand dollars that day. I started crying. God delivered us from the debt, and we have over one hundred thousand dollars in the bank.

While jubilation sounded in the first board meeting of the New Year, more somber sounds were also in the air. Words of fiscal responsibility were spoken by at least one trustee about God's "wanting us on a cash basis."

There was another word of caution spoken at the conference, which was held, along with the tribal gathering, by Jack Taylor, David's "spiritual papa." It was a word that proved to be prophetic, but one that was largely ignored. At the Wednesday evening gathering of the BnF family after hearing the narrative about the retired debt, Papa Jack said, "Your greatest challenge is about to come. You have proved you can do it when abased, but what about when in abundance?" The response David gave was, "The key is, can we give?" David then proceeded to take up a collection for Ned and Susan Hill, founders of BnF Cape Town, as he challenged each person to "give extravagantly, give what you do not have." The small group of some seventy people, nearly all of whom belonged to BnF, reportedly gave $40,643. Whether this amount was actually collected from those gathered is something we will never know. We later learned that such collections, praised by David as examples of "extravagant giving," were sometimes quietly supplemented with BnF funds.

It was during the days of the 2003 family gathering and conference that we began interviewing members of the BnF family, a project that continued throughout the year. Margaret returned in March and again in early April to visit the site and to conduct new interviews. During this time LeAnn Pearson was commissioned to oversee the entire Training Center and Warehouse while Chris Franklin was named chief of staff. Unlike other times when David seemed to be around for coffee and conversation, we talked with him only a few times and briefly. He and Janice were spending most of their time at their lake house an hour and a half away from downtown Atlanta and doing some speaking engagements and traveling.

When Margaret returned to Atlanta at the end of April, Eric seemed to be playing a larger role in the Sunday services. Eric, a middle-class African American, never had any contact with the homeless until he came to BnF in 1997. His wife, Debbie, is a white woman who remembers the old

Capitol Homes from her childhood as she visited her grandmother who lived there. Eric and Debbie Stagg were the only members of BnF Atlanta who had purchased property in what Eric described ("using a worldly term") as "a 'bad neighborhood.'" They shared in their interviews the spiritual journey that directed them away from buying in a gentrified area where others in the community had purchased restored or new homes to a section of west-end Atlanta called Capitol View, a part of the Capitol Corridor. Eric recalled that he was reluctant to move his family into an area filled with crack addicts and prostitutes: "I had issues of security—do I really want to bring my family here? And God showed me a picture of a house in the vision, and the entire neighborhood was dark but there was light shining from this house. And God said, 'This light is your security; no darkness will enter because I have the light on your home, and you have nothing to worry about.' So I have never had anything to worry about" [laughs].

Eric and Debbie personified both David's vision for the poor and his vision to "take cities," especially Atlanta. Eric spoke of his and Debbie's commitment to David during his interview: "Our vision is to take neighborhoods; to take cities. And our neighborhood is the neighborhood God has called us to take. So it will be an integral part of taking the city of Atlanta that God has given David. God showed me that the only way for us to take the city of Atlanta is for us to take our neighborhoods first. This will pull the city; all the forces will then come together."

When Eric spoke over the microphone in a Sunday service, his voice and message sounded much like David's. On one Sunday he shared the story of buying the house and praying over the land. He told of the dreams, visions, and revelations that he and Debbie received to confirm the move and to guide their actions. As God led, they began to make friends with the broken people—the prostitutes, the pimps, the alcoholics, the drug addicts—in their neighborhood, simply seeking neighborly relationships with them. It seemed somewhat strange to us (and to them) that David had never visited his protégé's home or personally toured the nearby neighborhood that Eric and Debbie called their home. Eric and Debbie were in David's oversized Twelve and had a Twelve of their own with others who shared their desire to be with the poor. For some reason, however, their attempt to live out David's vision seemed to us to be paradoxically marginal to David's world of relationships.

During this site visit in April 2003, David did tell Margaret that he was planning to make Eric the pastor of the BnF church. David then elaborated, "I have had to repent; I had a bad attitude toward the term. But God has clearly told me that Eric is to be the pastor of BnF." (David preferred to have family call him "Dad" and to list himself as president and founder of BnF rather than "pastor.") Although Eric had little in common with the black homeless men that dominated the BnF clientele, he clearly had developed a genuine concern for them. He noted the difficulty at first of "getting used to the smells, getting used to the looks, getting used to the language." But he said a change came over him "when the Spirit started to move in me and showed me what God was doing with everyone involved with BnF, including the homeless people. At the time it seemed that under the pastorate of Eric and the administrative leadership of LeAnn and Chris, the stage was set for David to pass the baton of direct ministry to others as he took a more limited role of guiding BnF as a visionary and prophet. As the baton was passed, the board could anticipate greater fiscal responsibility in the practical management of BnF. Eric's pastorate, however, proved to be of short duration.

The Gathering Storm

It is only in retrospect that we can see the clouds that were gathering at BnF between David the prophet and members of the corporate board of trustees who sought to exercise their fiscal responsibilities. Despite the favorable impression that David and the ministry made on the star-studded board of entrepreneurs who had come together on the board, they represented, in Ann Swidler's terms, a "tradition" of norms and values from the business community rather than the ideology of BnF. Having once been a leader in the corporate world himself, David knew the norms of the corporate culture. For a while he was able to navigate between his seemingly fragile ideology and the tested tradition of the business world. Repeatedly in the board minutes, however, we noted the board asking for business strategies, budgets, and measures of outcome while David simply requested more money to support his prophetic visions. How was this visionary, a prophet bent on "taking Atlanta for the poor" to compete for the increasingly valued property at the heart of the New South's greatest city? The task was daunting. As one board member reported in a statement that echoed others in interviews and in the board minutes, "So here we are without the financials or any accountability measures, and David spends the first thirty or thirty-five minutes talking about vision. And the vision changes, by the way, monthly."

The budget seemed to be a volatile issue at the March 29, 2003, board meeting. David presented his perceived need for more money to hire staff while the board was concerned about the need for fact gathering in order to approach foundations for help. One board member said, "I will not vote on bringing on more staff for a couple of more months until we're sure we can back it financially." Jack Taylor spoke in support of his spiritual son's faith-filled vision, which brought a retort from another board member, "We have to come out of the wilderness. Let's get a realistic budget together then addresses the staff need." Another responded, "We need to model responsibility," to which David responded, "We need to take a risk." David took a risk in purchasing the warehouse, and he repeatedly used it as the rationale for not being concerned about audits, budgets, or good credit. The storm was to gather momentum at the next meeting.

A discussion draft prepared by VanCronkhite for the March 29 meeting began with the following "budgeting overview" to challenge the board to provide for full-time staff:

> Blood & [*sic*] Fire Ministries—Atlanta has operated based upon people of vision sacrificing time, energy and dollars to walk out the beginning aspects of a movement or vision. This has blessed the organization with strong visionaries willing to sacrifice salaries, housing security and resources needed to accomplish the very best results. These "prophets" need to make way for a group of leaders more intent on building the vision versus establishing the vision. We must begin bringing in the implementers of the vision by whatever name we call these wonderfully talented and gifted individuals. In terms of the Bible we have been operating on the foundation of the "prophets" and the "apostles" and need now the evangelists, teachers and pastors. In other terminology the explorers must make way for the settlers, the prophets for the barbarians, etc. As is the case in any start up this requires securing a people more interested in security than those that have come before them. Our budget thinking must factor in this need.

The "need" in dollars and cents that David presented was for an increase of $41,500 per month for salaries to cover administration, communication, the Training Center, the Sanctuary, and leadership.

There was no record of a meeting in May, but the one on June 2 witnessed more confrontation, and David was losing the battle. He started out by asking for assistance in establishing companies like One Way, mentioned above, now specifically billed as a "merchandising company." Other prospective businesses included in the proposal were Matrix Construction (a short-lived company that failed to get off the ground), Café Ruach (the Edgewood property that was vandalized and never developed before being sold again), and a Jehu Customs (a custom motorcycle shop to be run by Chris Franklin and to continue David's infatuation with Harleys). One board member noted the potential "conflict of interest" in such proposals and spoke to the need to keep BnF "focused." David replied: "Back to the presentation. Our number-one priority is relationship, the poor, and justice, from when we get up to when we go to bed. Our desire is to provide affordable housing and employment; it is not about starting businesses." Again, while the prophet speaks, the message in profit terms is lost. How can one provide "affordable housing" (for the poor) on inner-city land whose value sounds high even when assessed by the square inch?

More objections were raised from members who were dissatisfied with David's failure to respond to questions about detailed information the board had been seeking for months. David replied, "I have an issue—you are missing the heart of what I have to present. It is not about numbers." One board member, reflecting the time-tested tradition of the business community, seemed to cut to the chase with the following observation:

My perception of what is going on here is that we are here to oversee and to guide. You [DvC] are the visionary, but you have more vision than resources. It is a fantastic vision, but unless we can keep this place open, your visions are useless. People who give serious money want to see serious figures. We have a few months before we will be in a deficit again. When I hear discussion about buying and building—we don't even have income to keep things running here. You look to us to bring in the money. We are not focused on the right things as far as I am concerned. We need to know how we are doing with what we've got and need reports to show it. We need better operational reports. Are we making progress? We need measurable reports.

A discussion ensued about who might prepare which report until another member commented, "David has a heart for ministry but is the worst detail manager I've seen. Is David in submission to the board or is the board in submission to David? It is time for legitimacy."

David responded, "I have one hundred twenty hours in this document, and we will never get to it because you wanted numbers. There are no secrets about what we are doing. Do I work for you? I guess it's not going well if I didn't give you what you want. I love you guys. I spent time preparing what I thought you wanted." A review of David's report for the meeting would show new positions, new businesses, new names; and while a differently detailed document, it provided little of the factual information the board was seeking. It seemed apparent to the board that David was fixated on detailing his God-given vision while the board wanted detailed numbers that could be reported in audits and used to attract prospective donors. Although the battle was made to seem like David wanted to talk about love and the things of the Spirit while the board was concerned only about the mundane details, at least one trustee emphasized the spiritual importance of paying one's debts:

> We are not taking the spiritual side out of this; we have never wanted to do that. You can do that spiritual stuff all day long—speaking in tongues, healing, the whole nine yards. But look at your creditors. They didn't say they wanted to give their income to BnF. They can't feed their children because we owe them fifteen thousand dollars for electrical work. You tell me where there is justice. You tell me what is godly about what you are doing. For every person we are saving in the Sanctuary, in the business world we are turning against God. They look and say, "They're Christians—and they don't pay their bills." We are turning off more people than we are turning on.

Another meeting was held a week later on June 9, and there was some excitement that "healing has occurred since the last meeting" as apologies were made and forgiveness extended. Papa Jack Taylor used his vocation as a preacher to teach the board: "The word has come again and again—supernatural. The last part of the word is natural. The first part is super. Super always transcends the natural. The work of God must be business like but not run as a business at the level you run your businesses. There will always be angst between business and spiritual priorities. Natural elements must be brought into play but not be run by them." He assured the naysayers that God "has support out there; God will open up areas of darkness to bring in the money." Here the clash between the profit sense of the corporate world and the prophet sense of BnF is absolute. To us it seemed as if Papa Jack Taylor tried to take the supernatural with him to a tax audit for BnF!

A few capitulated to the supernatural talk, but one trustee insisted that he was concerned about prioritization of things, asking, "When we borrow money, is that supernatural? I want to get your opinion on that. If we are frustrated, we may be taking responsibility that is not ours. We are asked to be on the board (and David says he was led by God to bring us on); we have to be responsible. We have to be prudent." Another trustee would later note, "There is a natural tension in what we do. The board really wants to hear about how the asset is doing, our accounts payable, how's our fund-raising, and all that. David doesn't care about that. He just wants to talk about the vision of taking Atlanta." Still another trustee reported, "Success for David is to be able to retain his vision; for him to continue to be able to not only touch the lives of those he loves but so many more. We need the warehouse on a firm footing so that the fire marshal wouldn't shut them down. We want a place that can pay its operating expenses, so they wouldn't have to turn people away saying 'We can't feed you tonight because there's no food.'" Although there were affirmations of God being present and the devil being defeated at that June meeting, all was not well.

Jack Taylor had saved the meeting, but the storm would not pass by that easily. Papa Jack made the announcement that he was going to recommend that David and Janice "get away and rest"—a sabbatical the family would call it. A motion was made and seconded that David be granted a ninety-day leave of absence. Devoted followers would come to see the June meetings as the catalyst that broke David's spirit and caused him to sink into clinical depression. The storms would grow more intense, however, before David would emerge from what he called his "exile" to actively lead BnF once more.

Meanwhile, Chris Franklin and LeAnn Pearson worked with the board to assure that the family business would proceed well in David's absence, and we continued our research without undue interruption. In fact, as we will see, some claimed things were going better than ever, which would pose a problem when David sought to return. One trustee described the David's tumultuous return to BnF several months later as follows:

> David comes back from sabbatical and things are hunky dory for a little while, and he is seeing how well the warehouse is doing. We are feeding more people; it's orderly; people are happy; there is just a peace in the

house; the board is thrilled. And this just freaked him out because there is not a place for him in his mind—not in ours, but in his mind. I could just see it happening. He's wondering, "Where do I fit in now?" Everybody's doing a better job. The board is so thrilled that Chris is giving us the accountability measures and all that. We are happy because we are not expending more money than is coming in. We are on solid footing, and we are all happy about this. And he just—he gets paranoid about it.

Although Margaret had regular contact with Katina (David's sister, who always was gracious in returning phone calls), her reports about David's sabbatical were always upbeat but vague. In mid-August, two months after David left for his sabbatical at the lake house, Katina told Margaret that David was now "getting new revelation," but that he was not yet ready to return. It took another week or so and a visit to Atlanta to realize that David was not with the poor of Atlanta. He was at his lake home battling severe depression. The psychologist among us does not care to wonder at the cause for this depression but does remember David's firm antidrug stance, not simply for drugs that come from the streets, but those from the pharmacist as well. But David would now accept the fact that his depression was an illness, treatable by prescription drugs. At the end of September 2003, David sent a couple of e-mails to the BnF family listserv, the first thanking the recipients "for loving us and being dear to us in our 'redux' moment with the Lord." The second came a few days later, announcing that the annual family gathering had been booked for January 4–8, 2004. David also shared a word Janice and he received from a British friend, John Keating, two weeks earlier: "I felt a wave of love flow over me, and it was not just my feeling for you, but God's love for you. Be expectant of his love pouring down on you. The picture I got was of a misty morning how the dew clings to everything and nothing escapes it. So I think God is saying this fall he will be soaking you and all your people with his love. You will be overwhelmed by his love; it will be bursting out of you."

Ideology's Unsettling Dilemma

The warehouse properties are important for BnF for both symbolic and instrumental reasons. Everyone involved knew the story of God's telling David that the warehouse was David's to "go and get"—that story was perhaps BnF's single most important and enduring narrative. A number of significant capital improvements had been made on the properties, including the new industrial kitchen that was dedicated in September 2002, enabling BnF to feed hundreds nightly. Additional monies and volunteer labor brought about the development of living space for more volunteers, recovering addicts, and some family members. The interior appearance of the warehouse buildings improved dramatically from when Margaret made her first visit in 1997. After having paid off the mortgage and debt and having brought order out of the financial chaos during David's absence, board members were eager to ensure that David would not run finances into the ground yet another time or sell the property for personal gain. The following is an excerpt from an e-mail from Cissy Watson to members of the executive board of directors, dated September 9, 2003, which reflects the storm's growing momentum:

> I had a lengthy conversation with W [a board member] on Tuesday, and he gave me an update regarding the formation of a trust vehicle that could hold the title to the warehouse. As you are all aware this was an attempt to make sure that the warehouse would not be sold for profit but rather all of the value of the building would continue to be used for the poor even if it were sold at some point. Anyway as I understand it from W, this task has been next to impossible. We have all experienced similar situations throughout our tenure as the Executive Committee of the Board of Trustees for Blood-n-Fire. So we are at a crossroads. David Kula cannot get comfortable with any scenario that would hamper of limit the ownership of the asset in a trust.

David Kula, a former successful Chicago attorney and a labor negotiator, has known David since 1990. It was Kula who had built and once owned David's beautiful lake house. David and Val Kula and David and Janice van Cronkhite met in Australia, where the two couples had gone on a mission trip sponsored by their respective Vineyard churches. They continued to run into each other at church conferences, but it was the neo-Pentecostal prophet Jim Goll who stirred Kula's interest in BnF. Goll told him "about this place called Blood-n-Fire—and as he was telling me about it (inner city, warehouse kind of thing), my heart kind of exploded." Kula had already been doing some inner-city work of his own in Chicago, working part-time on his law practice while pastoring a little church in Valparaiso. On their way to a Florida vacation in December 1994, the Kulas paid their first visit to BnF—to a warehouse that was "trashed," with "more rain coming in than there was being kept out." These were the early days of BnF—days that one respondent referred to as BnF's "charismatic moment." Kula reported, "I just came in and started to weep. We spent fifty minutes to an hour in there, and then went down to Florida. But I was definitely impacted by what I saw."

The Kulas remained in touch with the VanCronkhites, and some two years later David called and said: "I've called to ruin your life. We want you to come down and partner with us. We want you to come down and come on staff." Kula felt the time was right, so within two months after receiving the call, he and his wife moved to the Atlanta area. It was 1995; for the next six years they were part of BnF Atlanta.

Although they reportedly moved to Asheville in 2001 to work with young homeless teens who had settled for a time in western North Carolina, their narrative revealed other significant push-and-pull factors. The Kulas had a daughter who left home at the age of seventeen and became a "traveler" or "gutter punk" (as these teens were commonly known); continuing their relationship with her while she was on the road brought them into contact with her subculture. As Kula put it, "She got off the road a few times and would settle down; she settled from three to six months in Asheville. We went to Asheville to visit her, and basically just fell in love—had our hearts broken over the kids that traveled with her."

Kula also reported a push factor from Atlanta that he described as "God setting up the flow or momentum in certain directions." He elaborated on the decision to move from Atlanta, acknowledging that there was a growing tension between the two Davids that made the move to Asheville appealing: "Things here got pretty difficult for a couple of years. It was all difficult and wonderful at the same time. I think that David and I had a different approach to some of the things we were doing, but we always tried to honor each other and respect each other. I mean the reason he asked me to come down originally is that it was clear that our gift sets were different. He said, 'We need what you have in our leadership—we need pastoral gifting.'"

At the end, personal differences trumped community need. Although the two Davids met weekly or more often when David Kula was at BnF Atlanta, once Kula left to launch BnF Asheville they "were out of contact for a few years" until the time of David's episode of depression. "The people who left were marginalized, and David had such a high value for loyalty," Kula explained. There were probably several reasons for the estrangement, but two came through clearly in the interview: first, ministering to the "gutter punk" was not in accord with David's vision of ministry to the poor; and second, Kula seemed to perceive that VanCronkhite's focus was on the success of the family business and not on any personal relationship with him. At one point during the interview Margaret noted the emphasis on "father-son" relationships at BnF as she says to Kula, "But David was not your father." To which Kula responded:

> No, and that is part of where we parted. He was approaching that, and I said, "Hey, look David, it's just not going to work for me. You are my captain, my pastor, and I honor you as if you were my spiritual dad. That's the dynamic that I am submitted to. But your focus is on the corporate ministry—the movement agenda of BnF. If it came between BnF and me, a dad would choose me over his family business. I don't want you to have to make that choice. Frankly, I don't think you can make that choice in my favor. I don't want to put you in the place of having to choose between the vision God has given you and my best interests. So, no, I am not your son."

The Asheville BnF was listed among the Internationals, but David would openly question whether it really had the BnF "DNA."

Despite Kula's own personal difficulties with David, he indicated that he remained loyal to David and David's vision of the Kingdom of God. Kula elaborated:

> Do you understand? (I don't mean to be patronizing, so forgive me if I do.) It's a Scripture that everyone has up on their refrigerators—Isaiah 51—"No weapon formed against me will prosper." I had a revelation about that a few years ago. God was saying, "I am the blacksmith that has formed the weapon against you. I am the one originating, orchestrating and strategizing your personal disaster/trial." I'm not going to give you a theology that God causes all our problems. We live in a corrupt and fallen existence. When people get hurt, the question isn't about authoritative, overcontrolling pastors; the test is, "What is my response?" What is my response? How am I going to deal with it? How faithful am I to walk out a biblical response. That is not excusing at all what the overcontrolling, manipulative pastor did. But the response is our choice—we can do it biblically, or we can do it the way the world does it. The real issue is how am I going to respond in the Holy Spirit realm—rather than the natural realm—with biblical principles.

For David Kula, as for the other leaders of BnF International, the godly and biblical thing to do was to support David's "ideology" of the Spirit world over the "tradition" of sound business practices. He acknowledged that David had "screwed up" ("but which of us hasn't?" he interjects rhetorically). But David has "confessed" many times, asserts Kula, that "there was a perversion—a missing it in the walking out of this father-son dynamic." That was sufficient reason to extend mercy and grace. Kula then added: "If you think the normal biblical way of walking out organic church life is a democratic governing board, then I think you are as wrong as wrong can be. Yet that is the way the American church primarily functions, at least the Evangelical wing of it. I do not buy it. It is the source of the sickness and lethargy in the American church. There is no model for it in Scripture."

Ironically, despite Kula's support of David against the actions of the board that sought to guard BnF against David's potentially damaging interference, he and his wife shut down Asheville BnF in July 2004 in response to the opposition of his followers to its ideologically driven vision: "It was something like what happened here at BnF," says Kula, "and I don't want to make it seem like I got it figured out, but I chose the integrity of our relationships and taking the common tasks out of those relationships. It's all really in our relationships." His wife, Val, concurred and added, "Instead of running off the relationships we wanted to nurture them. They didn't want to do the vision any more. So we just said, 'Be free, be free.'"

Support for David over the board and the schismatic BnF family members who were then running the day-to-day operation of the family business began to mount. At one point early in the storm, it appeared that David was going to release the warehouse properties and the ministry to the board and thus to those who were running it so effectively in his absence. Sounding much like the birth mother of the baby in the famous biblical story of Solomon, David said he would rather step back from the ministry that he had birthed than see it destroyed. He sent out an e-mail to his family members telling them that he was giving the warehouse away to the new Compassion Center that was then directed by Chris and LeAnn. But he quickly rescinded on the offer and began to negotiate terms to gain the deed to the BnF property.

Tradition, Ideology, and Godly Love

The voices of the executive committee of the BnF board of trustees and those of the BnF International represent dissonant voices heard in the larger schism—voices that Swidler has called "tradition" and "ideology." Although it is perhaps inevitable that there be tension between traditional and ideological values, such tension has the potential of being constructive. It can also be destructive, however, as it was in the case of BnF.

As the chasm between the two forces widened, David continued his struggle with the aftermath of clinically diagnosed depression at his lake house outside Atlanta. One might expect an almost Job-like scenario, a suffering that cries out to God and awaits response. Surely God's love is sufficient. This has been David's claim for others with clinical or psychiatric illnesses, for which even the taking of legitimately prescribed drugs was denied to Sanctuary and Warehouse residents. To speak of God's love healing David's depression would be a story worth telling. We cannot say God's hand was not outstretched, but David's use of prescription medication for his own ailment is one that he denied to others. To our knowledge he did not seek help from those in spiritual healing centers commonly used by other BnF family members. Armed with his prescription, David returned to BnF in an almost diachronic mode. First he would give away BnF, a remarkable gesture by any criteria. Just as quickly, however, David would challenge the board and demand that BnF be his and his alone. The reader may fairly ask, "What's love got to do with this?"

Love, as we have already seen, has many faces. Specifying the object of love is difficult. Is it God, David, the vision, the BnF family, or the homeless? The personal love objects behind the label of "Atlanta's poor" were increasingly vague. Soon the ministry would be torn apart by a conflict between David and his followers and vocal dissenters. The tension that we have reported in this chapter involves the pragmatics of doing charity in America and the ideology and vision of the founder. With fiduciary responsibility commonly understood as a norm for doing the business of charity, leaders of the business community—even committed Evangelical Christians who composed nearly the entire BnF board—knew their primary responsibility as one of assuring fiscal soundness and accountability. Within this tradition of the business community and in accord with Swidler's thesis, there is room for diverse ideologies that are loosely coupled with action. The board did not have to accept David's visions to appreciate the ministry. The board could function to fulfill its responsibilities regardless of whether they accepted David's vision. What seemed to matter most to the board was that this seemingly unique and effective ministry for the poor would be able to continue to do its work without being mired in debt.

David's ideology, however, seemingly could not afford the luxury of the "loose coupling" of traditional business practices with BnF's norms and practices. The supernatural was the heart of David's vision, and walking in the supernatural required taking risks in the name of God. David would decry that "his faith had been stolen" by a board who could not or would not accept the workings of the supernatural world of his vision. Moreover, David seemed to intuit that there was a tenuous link between ideology and unsettled situations. Both ideology and social situations changed frequently at BnF with David, who repeatedly professed his love for taking risks and for change. With each change in David's vision there was a realignment of faithful followers whose voice would profess the change, even if the appropriate behavior was not immediately forthcoming.

8

Smoke, Mirrors, and Holy Madness

> Adepts—masters of spirituality—come in all magnitudes of spiritual accomplishments. Many are authentic, but some are not. Many teach in a legitimate way, but some do not. Most adepts present themselves in a manner that, though inevitably in opposition to consensus reality, is sufficiently familiar as not to alienate us. A few, however, use their life as a symbol for what, from a conventional point of view, is the upside-down world of spirituality.
>
> —Feuerstein 1990, 254

In his extended discussion of holy madness, or crazy wisdom, Georg Feuerstein explores the varying approaches of masters, sages, saints, and holy people—those eccentric individuals who typically "use their eccentricity to communicate an alternative vision to that [vision] which governs ordinary life" (xvi). According to Feuerstein, these adepts, who share much in common with the traditional figures of the tricksters and clowns, are "masters of inversion, proficient breakers of taboos, and lovers of surprise, contradiction, and ambiguity" (1990, xvi). Feuerstein's insightful analysis provides another grid for understanding the dissonance found in the voices we bring together in this chapter. In presenting the cacophony heard during the schism, we hear accounts from David VanCronkhite and his faithful supporters, some voices of dissent found in both the ministry and the board of directors, and reports from graduate research assistants who observed at the BnF site and gathered interview data during the first eighteen months of the project.

Leadership in Crisis

In January 2004 at the annual gathering for BnF Internationals and their friends, VanCronkhite was in a self-described "exile" as he emerged from the solitude of his sabbatical. The exact details of David's sabbatical are unknown, but it did include a mixture of spiritual soul seeking and medical assistance for his depression. The daily operations of BnF's ministry were carried out by dissident members of the BnF family under the leadership of Chris Franklin and LeAnn Pearson with the financial support of the board of directors that David himself had established and was now trying to disband. From an administrative perspective all was going smoothly under the direction of the interim leaders of the family business—now renamed the Compassion Center. Not only were physical needs of the poor being met through the programs and the budget balanced each month, but also staff members told us how they were relieved to be spared David's erratic outbursts and the roller-coaster ride fueled by his often-unpredictable innovations. It was agreed by the leaders of the new Compassion Center and the board of directors that David had claim to the name Blood-n-Fire to use for the church congregation and to carry out any personal itinerant ministry. The details of this agreement for the Compassion Center and the BnF church turned out to be devilish and daunting.

It was in January 2004 that both Chris and LeAnn began to speak openly with us about how their eyes had been opened to the problems David's leadership posed for the continued operation of the ministry. LeAnn, whom David only a year earlier made chief operating officer of the Warehouse, shared in an interview (January 10, 2004) about how she and Chris (then BnF's chief executive officer) began to talk with each other about difficulties each was seeing. As LeAnn described the situation:

At first we didn't talk much together about problems we both saw. The "not attacking God's anointed" thing can be a strong inhibitor against asking hard questions. Then things came to a head for me when Chris was gone for a month this summer to care for his [bed-fast pregnant] wife and David took some time off from his sabbatical [to take over Chris's work]. This is when David told me he was going "to mess things up for Chris and let him fix it." David proceeded to spend money that BnF could not afford to spend, without records or receipts. He simply refused to adhere to the procedures and guidelines set up by the board after they retired the huge debt last January.

The board was aware of David's erratic behavior and what some perceived as his anger management problem, but they still had hopes at this time of resolving the growing tension between Chris and David. It would be a mistake, however, to present the voice of the board as one of unified dissent. There were those (especially the members of the executive board) who called for fiscal responsibility over abstract vision while there were others who felt that David had founded the ministry and had the right to run it his way. Names were added to this sector of the board as the schism brewed—people whom David claimed had always been board members but who were not on the official list of the newest board that David said God had told him to establish. As with other numbers in this faith-based church/ministry, it was difficult to ascertain who was a bona fide board member and who was a shadow voice from a past board now ready to come forward to support David's cause.

In seeking to resolve the management problems of BnF, the executive committee proposed a plan for Chris to continue as CEO of the Compassion Center and for David to function as the visionary, prophet, and leader of the BnF church. A distinction already existed between the "church family" and the "family business," but this newest proposal aimed at making the division between the two components much less permeable. Chris had proven himself to be an exceptional maintenance leader in managing the Compassion Center in David's absence, and he was to continue with that position. He took the focus off David's charismatic leadership and put it on the maintenance of the organization. During his brief tenure as the head of BnF, Chris not only balanced the budget but also seemed to give more voice to the poor blacks, establish norms for paying staff to replace favoritism, and consistently enforce house rules rather than the selective "Spirit-led" enforcement that was so much a part of the old leadership. David, on the other hand, built the ministry that had attracted the new leaders and the board of directors in the first place. He was undoubtedly the visionary behind BnF. The proposal sought to use the strengths of both David and Chris. In leadership literature David is an *innovative leader* while Chris is a *maintenance leader* (Trice and Beyer 1993). The board made an effort to encourage David and Chris to cooperate for the greater good of BnF.

David, however, denies that such a proposal to secure his role as prophet and visionary was ever made. He contends that the board was never willing to listen to his vision but only wanted "numbers." In response to questions about the proposal, David accused the board of trying to reduce him to a fundraiser as they "stole" his ministry to give to Chris. From Chris's perspective, there was no way anyone could "steal" David's ministry; it was God's ministry and God would do with it as He pleased. What Chris did know is that he could no longer work with David. The question of whom God chose remained implicit as other believers began to challenge David's leadership of BnF.

In an interview with Margaret only a year earlier, Chris had demonstrated unwavering filial devotion to David and professed unreserved trust in his spiritual "dad." Now he insisted that the relationship was impossible to restore; the trust he had in David had been destroyed. As Chris shared details about the collapse of their relationship, he noted how weary he was of David's erratic behavior, providing incident after incident of what he called "broken promises and twisted truth." Chris insisted that he wanted only what God wanted for BnF, denying that he was in rebellion or wanted the ministry for himself. In fact, he said that he was eager to move on with his own perceived calling to work with the poor in another setting. He believed that God was instructing him to stay in the middle of a situation that he would have preferred to abandon. In an interview with Margaret on January 8, 2004, Chris explained his dilemma with David:

> David accuses me of being an Absalom and being in rebellion. I am not in rebellion. I am in alignment with the authority that God set over this Warehouse, and that authority is the board. I have been submissive to them. *You know, I am tired of what I call R & R from David—revelation and repentance.* [emphasis in interview] When you come to me and say, "Can I share the revelation that God's given me," I say, "Sure." When two or three days later there is another revelation—and it is totally contrary to what was given earlier; and two weeks later there is another one totally contrary to the other two things—what is going on? That is the way David operates. It's like his practice of repentance. He always does it—I can't tell you how often he "repented" at Twelve meetings. But there was never a change. If you want to repent, that's great. But let's change.
>
> I don't trust David, and I cannot follow him. I told David that. And what did he do? He sent this e-mail out to everyone saying, "Trust is from God, not from man." He totally dismisses the fact that his actions were why I can no longer trust him. Yeah, God did give the trust, but David defiled it.

Chris was not alone in having lost trust in David's visions. While the battle was heating up with the largely middle-class service providers and upper-class benefactors, for the poor it was life as usual. The Sanctuary continued to provide them a place of refuge, the Training Program was available for help with drug addiction, and public nightly meals were served to anyone in need. These are all aspects of maintaining the vision that were less central to David than they were to the lives of those who sought help in the Sanctuary and Warehouse. Although we lack precise statistics, based on the field observations of both authors and our graduate student research assistants, few of the poor and homeless left or stayed away from BnF at this time because of the tension and conflict. BnF continued to function effectively as safe heaven providing food and shelter to the homeless.

Observations of a Graduate Student Observer

Ralph's graduate student, Christopher F. Silver, was involved in our project beginning in January 2003 when we came to the BnF International gathering to formally begin our research. In response to our request, Chris submitted a summary report at the end of his work with BnF. In it he described being "impressed by the warmness of the members," but as someone who had no previous contact with the homeless in a big city, he felt "a bit apprehensive about doing interviews in the Sanctuary and the Training Program." Chris proved to be more than adequate for the task of navigating the two cultures found at BnF, and his apprehension about interacting with the urban poor gave way to facile interaction that produced rich and informative interviews. Chris went on to describe his initial experience at the January gathering:

> I initially was impressed by the compassion of the BnF staff and those attending the services. I also was impressed by the number of middle-class individuals who attended the services. It appeared from the outside that there was a strong interaction between the staff and the homeless. It appeared to me that everyone was aspiring to be like Jesus Christ and were directed by the Holy Spirit. As time passed and I had more interaction with the staff and homeless, I began to discover that outside experiences can be deceiving. Through discussions with the staff and some of the leaders of the Sanctuary, I began to hear some of the problems occurring between David and others of BnF. While I would consistently hear about these problems, I did not give them a second thought because of my own experience in nonprofits. There always seem to be disagreements between leadership and staff.

But Chris recalled the complaints he had heard after the transition that occurred during David's sabbatical leave. In his summary statement he offered an evaluation of the changes that he observed within weeks after Chris Franklin and LeAnn Pearson took over as BnF leaders:

> Within weeks of David's temporary exit, I began to notice that BnF took a turn for the better. There appeared to be less stress among the staff and the homeless became more empowered to take on projects themselves to make the complex better. Staff members appeared to be more engaged spiritually with the homeless and those in the training program. Most striking was how the homeless became more engaged in worship and were using their spiritual language (glossolalia) more. I also noticed much more Bible reading and discussion within the Sanctuary. Whereas before the residents were being prodded into participation, by the summer/fall of 2003 there was a more engaged participation by residents. I also noted that the staff-Sanctuary interaction increased, and that there appeared to be closer personalized relationships. All around things appeared more efficient in the feeding and care of the homeless. By this point, the financial problems appeared to have been resolved, and staff members were not as concerned about the financial support for the feeding programs and religious ministry.

Interviews with the homeless and addicts, both before and during the schism, did confirm that many of them perceived a divine calling to BnF, a place where they found hope and a sense of personal destiny. What seemed to cause concern and apprehension within the Sanctuary was the unrest that soon developed with David's attempt to return to BnF in the fall of 2004. It is doubtful that most residents actually cared whether David or Chris was in charge. Given the turnover that appears to be part of BnF's history, by this time few residents knew David. The apprehension that developed among the homeless was spawned by uncertainty—uncertainty about exactly what was really happening and whether BnF would survive. As Chris Silver noted: "The Training Program had one of its largest drops in participants. Many of those in the Program left and the staff did not know why. I would theorize it was due to the power struggle between David and the staff of the Compassion Center. . . . As time progressed, rumors began to permeate the Sanctuary. Some rumors would be close to the truth while others would be seemingly bizarre—like LeAnn having a fistfight with David or that David was going to close BnF for a Hispanic ministry."

What Chris was observing about residents of both the Sanctuary and the Warehouse not being informed about developments was nothing new. Communication breakdown was a common complaint among family members, even during BnF's best of times, but the poor were rarely in the loop at all. For example, in one interview with a twenty-eight-year-old Sanctuary resident during this transition, the interviewee compared the BnF he experienced briefly under David's leadership with that of Chris Franklin's. Nathan noted how "upset" he was when David's team left: "It kind of really upset me 'cause worship is one of the things that drew me here. Like when Joel and Rachel and everybody was up there—and they prayed and they sang—you could really feel the Holy Spirit come down and fill the room. It is not the same as before David left. Love is still here, but it doesn't seem like the same kind of love." As the interviewer probed for more details, it became increasingly apparent that Nathan was concerned not so much about the waters that had already gone over the dam as about the uncertainty he experienced at the time of the interview:

> This could all be just inside myself—uncertainty of not knowing whether or not David VanCronkhite left this building. Not knowing if he just left because he is starting another BnF down here, or because he is moving elsewhere or because he was forced out for whatever reason. I don't know what is really going on—and neither does anybody else really. But the feeling that, yeah, they really do know what's going on—something is going on, you know. Something has to be going on. But nobody will talk about it. It's the "hush hush" that raises all the questions.

When asked by the interviewer what he thought was really happening, Nathan responded:

> I personally think David was pushed out. But . . . well, overall, I don't really know. It's just wanting to know because there is a lot of murmuring going on and nothing's been settled. I really don't care if David was pushed out. I never really knew him. He did a couple of services a couple of times, but I am more familiar with Chris Franklin, Charles, Nate, and Nicki and all of them. It is just that you hear all these murmurs or rumors or whatever you want to call them, and they just go around and around. It gets on my nerves. It makes you uneasy, and uneasiness isn't good for a restless soul who is struggling to achieve a better spirituality and better his life, you know.

A Caveat on the Voice of the Poor

The poor were not only uninformed, but they were as voiceless at BnF as they are in most outreach programs, whether faith based or secular. Staff changes were a normal occurrence at BnF. The poor, particularly the instrumental clients, remained oblivious to the internal politics of the BnF family during the schism. BnF effectively functioned as a shelter to house and feed the homeless, and staff changes had little effect on the general operation of the ministry. Chris Franklin concurred with a related observation, namely, that the poor had little contact with David. Chris commented, "The truth is, they don't know anything else but us. Except when David would show up on Sundays, David is never here. And the only reason they have an affinity to David of late is so they can manipulate something. That's how they have learned to survive. And I am not offended at that."

LeAnn shared this perspective and offered the following account of David's behavior at the Training Center, which resonates with our evaluation: "The 'family' is the group that has been shaken up by David's erratic behavior—not the Sanctuary and not the Training Center. You know, David sometimes comes by the Training Center when I am not there, and he will single out a man, saying, 'You are my son.' They have no clue who David is! They will tell me about the man with the white hair, want to know who he is, and what is it that he wants. [laughs] David has not been around on a regular basis for a very long time."

The theme of the graduate student's exit report of June 25, 2004, centered on how impressed Chris Silver was with the changes he saw at BnF during David's absence and the setbacks he observed when David returned. Under Chris Franklin and LeAnn Pearson's leadership, Chris described a passionate and caring staff who tried to empower the poor, which contrasted with the anomic milieu that he attributed to David's personality:

> The staff had a deep spiritual dedication, almost a glow that one can feel from them when they talk about their belief in Jesus and their mission for the world. While I am the skeptical Buddhist, I came to know individuals who were dedicated to compassion (action) and wisdom (the Bible) and would implement the two everyday. I felt that this glow was beginning to be shared by those in the Sanctuary.
>
> Now (with David's return) there is less authority. It appears that ego (in the Buddhist sense of the word) is the problem. While I cannot comment on Dr. Poloma's exchanges with David (because I am not there),

I can say from what I have observed that David is an individual ruled by his emotion and causes havoc within the organization. From my perspective, David is looking for interpretation within his own emotions that he perceives as the Holy Spirit moving on him. If he were truly unstable emotionally, then this would explain the erratic changes in how he deals with people and the organization.

The leaders of the interim Compassion Center, inspired by their interpretation of David's vision, tried to listen to the voices of the poor. Not unlike our experience as researchers trying to follow up on our subjects, however, LeAnn and Chris encountered numerous problems. The poor who seek shelter at BnF are a large and diverse population and they come and go at will. It is difficult to establish ongoing links with them. Most of our contacts with the poor were one-shot deals; few of the interviewees stayed around for the duration of our study. Likewise, LeAnn and Chris found the transient nature of Sanctuary residents a barrier to establishing caring relationships of intensity and duration. At the onset of this study, we hoped that perhaps BnF had found a way to, as David often said, "be family to those who have none." But insofar as family entails relationships of intensity and duration, the poor never became family at BnF.

A Wedding as a Watershed

By early January 2004 most BnF family members, the leaders of BnF communities outside of Atlanta, some religious leaders in Atlanta, and the members of the expanded board of trustees found themselves on one side of the schismatic divide or the other. While ideological differences as discussed by Swidler do provide some insight into the tension between David's vision and the board's requirement of fiscal responsibility, there is more to be understood. An account that features discrepant narratives surrounding the wedding immediately preceding the family gathering of 2004 allows for a richer interpretation of the schism based on Collins's interaction ritual chains (2004).

What was to be a happy event for the BnF family—the wedding of Kathryn, David's niece, gifted disciple, and much-favored "daughter," to Christopher, a young man from Norway—became a time and place etched in many minds as when the fault line broke wide open. In the words of one respondent, "It was at Kathryn's wedding that the battle lines were drawn." Different interviewees offered different perspectives on what transpired.

One recurring theme voiced by David's dissident "daughters" centered on what they perceived to be a subtle manipulative power that David had over young single female followers. They noted how anyone who became involved in a relationship not approved of by David would incur his open criticism. In order to mitigate the tension one respondent felt over David's critical eye toward any potential suitor, Liza made a personal vow never to marry anyone of whom David did not approve—a promise she soon disavowed after Kathryn's wedding. We do not know whether Kathryn's experience was similar to Liza's, but we do know that we heard many reports from family members about David's reservations about the upcoming marriage.

Commonly circulated was the story of David publicly saying that the recent wedding of a favored BnF "son" to a "daughter" in the community meant more to him than Kathryn's wedding. Kathryn reportedly then confronted her uncle, telling him that he did not have to officiate at her wedding. According to the story, Kathryn asked David Kula to perform the ceremony, which was held at the Warehouse just prior to the 2004 annual international gathering. While faithful followers of David would recount how beautiful the wedding was, the dissident wedding guests focused on the tension that filled the air. The gist of the comments read something like, "We were family; I loved everyone there, but it was difficult to know who I could approach without being rebuffed. I wasn't sure who was on what side. It was awful! I felt so sorry for Kathryn and Christopher." David disputed this account, saying that he was the one who asked Kula to officiate so that he could enjoy the wedding with his family. Whatever the actual nature of the event, the discrepancies in the accounts are notable. Even if some were oblivious to the tension, most of those who told us about it felt as if a cloud had darkened what was to have been a joyous occasion. Interpersonal relationships, consistently reported as one of the greatest sources of satisfaction by BnF family members during interviews conducted just a year earlier, were in jeopardy. Clear lines of demarcation had begun to separate David's loyal followers from those who had lost trust in their charismatic leader. The lines became more pronounced at the annual BnF International gathering held two days after the wedding.

BnF International 2004 Gathering

With the dissidents in charge of the Compassion Center and David still perceiving himself to be in "exile," the 2004 family gathering was held at the Atlanta Vineyard in nearby Norcross rather than at the Warehouse. There was a good deal of love talk at the conference; there were few concrete suggestions, however, for repairing the relational rifts in this time of fragmented fellowship. Few of the workers in the Compassion Center chose to attend the gathering hosted in the suburbs and miles away from their daily responsibilities of housing the homeless, feeding those who came for nightly meals, and staffing the program for addicts in downtown Atlanta. The conference was attended by David's loyal local followers, others who were still trying to discern what was transpiring, and representatives from all but one of the International BnFs.

One of the exercises repeated at the gathering involved having one of the women, at David's request, read 1 Corinthians 13—the apostle Paul's famous discourse on love. Each ritual enactment would involve the slow deliberate reading of this familiar Scripture and David asking that it again be repeated. The attendees, some of whom fell to their knees or lay prostrate on the floor, seemed to be responding emotionally to the call to let the words of the Scripture penetrate their spirits. The sound of silence would overtake the normally loud and exuberant group of worshipers as Becket, one of David's "daughters," read:

> If I speak in the tongues of men and angels, but have not love, I am only a resounding gong or a clanging cymbal. If I have the gift of prophecy and can fathom all mysteries and all knowledge, and if I have a faith that can move mountains, but have not love, I am nothing. If I give all I possess to the poor and surrender my body to the flames, but have not love, I gain nothing. Love is patient, love is kind. It does not envy, it does not boast, it is not proud. It is not rude, it is not self-seeking, it is not easily angered, it keeps no record of wrongs. Love does not delight in evil but rejoices with the truth. It always protects, always trusts, always hopes, always perseveres. (1 Corinthians 13 [NIV])

Using a common distinction found in charismatic teachings between the Bible as *logos* or the written word and the Bible as *rhema* or the word taking root within the hearer, David shared (in between readings, revelations, and repentance) how his understanding of 1 Corinthians 13 had changed from *logos* to *rhema*. It was an exercise seemingly designed to make room for the spirit of the Scripture to take flesh in the hearts of family members who were experiencing the pain of perceived betrayal and the fracture of family. At least on two occasions, someone spoke aloud other Scriptures dealing with forgiveness rather than love—"Forgive us our trespasses as we forgive those who trespass against us," says the Lord's Prayer—but no move was made by David (who was in control of the service) to take the prayer in the direction of forgiving present injuries or past hurts. This was David's gathering with David's agenda. While love for the in-group was being stirred, love for the out-group was not mentioned. Unknown to the out-of-town guests, the ritualistic reading had been going on at BnF Sunday gatherings led by VanCronkhite for several weeks prior to the January gathering. When Margaret shared her observation about the fervor of the worshipers during the extended time of this Scripture reading and prayer with Chris Franklin, his response was less than enthusiastic:

> That's good—if anything is really happening—but that passage has been so twisted and used by David. He says this thing that "love always trusts"—if you love me, you have to trust me. That is twisted. He has been preaching it over here at the Warehouse as well as in the Sanctuary for four weeks in a row! I am tired of being pitted against each other. And that's what David does. It's happened over and over—until I am done with it. Do I love him? Yeah. But am I going to walk with him? Hell, no! So how do you redeem the relationship? I forgive him, but would I walk where he is in authority here again? Not at all. God has released me from that.

David skillfully manipulated the conference to garner the support of his disciples to return him to a position of absolute leadership. As we see it, David was engaged in what Collins refers to as an "emotion contest" (2004, 121) through which he sought a restoration of his previously uncontested authority. As David often did through a mix of teaching, preaching, and personal sharing, he used this religious interaction ritual to generate emotional energy (EE). He demonstrated little interest in trying to reconcile the two feuding groups; instead he focused on interaction rituals that would replenish his own emotional energy and that of his loyal followers—EE that would affect the direction of BnF's interaction ritual chains. In the emotion-laden context of religious services held during the annual meeting, David confessed sins of decades back (without mentioning allegations of the present), assuring his audience that he had repented and was forgiven, asking them to remember his namesake, the fallen but restored King David of old. Were they still willing to follow him? It seemed that they were. David also used his "exile" and his struggle to regain his ministry to identify with the poor and the broken. On more than one occasion he stated, "Now I know what it means to be voiceless just as the poor are voiceless—to speak but to find that no one is listening." But if one listened carefully, one could hear other voices speaking on David's behalf—voices that condemned the alleged injustice done to David by the dissidents and the board. Many would proclaim once more heaven's favor on God's anointed one. Judging from our interactions with those who attended the conference, David was still a charismatic figure who was able to generate emotional energy in a select group of followers.

Hearing the Voice of the Prophets

As we have seen earlier in the BnF narrative, prophecy played an important role in its key myths and narratives, from the naming of the ministry, to David and Janice's receiving of the Catherine and William Booth anointing, to the securing of the warehouse, to the purchase of the lake house, and even to the establishment of the board of directors. Prophecy continued coming in different forms and packages to support David and his vision. One such prophetic word was carried back from South Africa by Rose Bigelow, one of David's earliest remaining disciples, who replaced Kathryn as a "favored daughter" and who at the time of this writing directs what is left of BnF Atlanta. The prophecy, shared by Rose in an e-mail of February 10, 2004, was given by a Tasmanian "right before my return to Atlanta—around mid-October [2003]." Parts of it read:

> The nations are your inheritance
> Atlanta is a base—the headquarters of your ministry
> From there you will keep being launched to different nations . . .
> There is an enormous step completely in front of you, like walking at the
>   base of a cliff . . . Just keep taking steps as God reveals.
> This enormous step is not the nations—it's something in the next three
>   months . . . God will encourage you to understand
> He has made a way; He will show you step by step
> Keep trusting and taking His direction and guidance; He will lead you.
> When you get back to the core of what He has, you will know it is God
> He will take you to higher levels each time.
> The core will take you even higher.
> There is a team of people coming around you and you will send them out.
> Lots of youth. You are doing something new . . .

This prophetic word was one of many signs that we would see over the next couple of years that would be used to move the center of BnF's vision away from the more tangible creation of a "church of the poor" toward "taking Atlanta" first and then "the nations" for the Kingdom of God. The focus would move away from the poor and toward empowering youth for the task of receiving this divine "inheritance."

David frequently would give prophecies to others—generally in a moderated tone and never with the old Pentecostal closure of "thus saith the Lord." Walking in the supernatural, including the giving and receiving of prophetic words, was commonplace and part of everyday reality. Perhaps even more effective as a tool for training disciples was David's preaching/teaching that wore a prophetic mantle. It has always been David's voice and vision that is central for BnF prophecy. Other prophets might speak and have their words heard if they were in line with David's, but most prophetic words (as in most charismatic gatherings) are forgotten as quickly as they are heard. During the dark days of the early schism, David's prophetic voice seemed lost in the fog that engulfed the family. David and his disciples would begin traveling around Atlanta and the South to prophetic conferences where they could hear from God. Slowly, David began to get fresh revelations that, together with the voices of other prophets, would provide support and a new sense of direction. BnF would change as David's vision focused on new instructions that he felt God was giving to him.

Upon his return from his sabbatical, David described himself as vulnerable and broken. During the 2004 family gathering, David confessed and repented of specific sins of thirty years ago; repentance regarding concrete issues that were currently troubling the dissenters, however, was much less specific. As an example, answers to questions about improper relationships with his "daughters" were veiled as David simply repented of "perverting the Twelve." His repentance touched the hearts of his followers but not the hearts of the dissenters. They claimed to have seen David's "repentance without change" before. David acknowledged that he had "made a mess of things" and was asking for "mercy and grace." He consistently refrained, however, from dealing with any specific allegations.

Most other leaders, both in BnF International and in the larger community, were more willing to grant mercy and grace than were the dissidents who labored in the Compassion Center and the executive board of directors who were confronted with problems that David continued to cause. Many of his followers recognized VanCronkhite's role in the schism, as when Papa Jack Taylor said publicly to David, "You have created quite a mess for yourself, son, and you are just going to have to clean it up." Yet they continued to reaffirm the anointing that God had on David's life and ministry. Both Papa Jack and David frequently used the biblical story of King David—David's "namesake"—to support the position that David had not lost his throne or his inheritance. King David was a murderer and an adulterer, yet he was also God's chosen.

Similar support came through prophecies given by itinerate prophets, some well-known in the neo-Pentecostal prophetic circles and others less so, to affirm David with words from God about the great future in store for his ministry. Prophecy at BnF was generally taken to be positive and affirming, but it also took a dark side in the midst of what became the war over the warehouse. Women dissidents were visited by BnF family members, weeping as they told how they "saw" the punishment that they would suffer for their disloyalty to David. Prophecy was used at varying times, publicly and privately, to threaten dissenters with the wrath of God for opposing "God's anointed one." At other times it was employed to discredit a dissenter, as noted earlier in the word given by a local prophet that Chris Franklin was an "Absalom," the rebellious and deceitful son of King David. For her role in working with Chris to save the ministry, LeAnn was pronounced a "witch" with a "Jezebel spirit." Whether the prophecy was positive or negative—uplifting David and BnF or attempting to silence a dissident voice—little was done at BnF to sort through or "discern" the many prophetic voices that spoke.

For David the turmoil that engulfed BnF was due to a conflict between "vision" and "fiscal" as he sought to gain the support of other prophets and religious leaders. He could be observed trying to rebuild bridges he had burned, especially with the religious leaders he once critiqued for their spiritual mediocrity or their lack of "BnF DNA". Meanwhile, the board of directors still supported Chris as the executive officer for the new Compassion Center, hoping that David would step back from his personal claim to the warehouse property and that Chris and David would work out their differences. Working together was not an option, as we have seen, that Chris would accept. For his part, David would have Chris and the board involved only on his terms—namely, a subservient board and a submissive Chris. As David would insist, "BnF is organic relationship, and it cannot have two heads."

The crux of the schism may have stemmed from "vision versus fiscal" and fueled by disputes over legitimate spiritual authority, as David and others suggested, but a bigger battle was soon to develop over the valuable warehouse property. David was not about to relinquish the warehouse or allow for any restrictions to be placed on that which he believed God had given to him. Nor was any reconciliation likely between the workers in the Compassion Center and David's remnant group that would allow for the continued use of the facilities in the old "family business" for the poor. All seemed to be at a standoff in the early months of 2004.

A Dissident Provides His Account

An unexpected match was dropped on the combustible tension between the two family sectors in the spring of 2004. It came in the form of a letter from a former addict, Steve Ruff, who had successfully completed the yearlong Training Program and had been working with LeAnn in the program designed to rehabilitate addicts. Like LeAnn, Steve stayed on with the staff that Chris led during David's sabbatical and into the self-described "exile." Steve's letter was first sent to Cissy Watson, president of the board of directors (from whom we first learned of its contents), but then was circulated on both sides of the divide. With Steve's permission, we choose to use sections his lengthy letter of May 5, 2005, to Cissy Watson as a credible voice of dissent. He admits to being helped by the BnF ministry, and he also worked for the ministry after he completed the Program. Steve writes to Cissy and to whomever she chose to share the detailed and informing letter, which began with an account of changes he personally observed at BnF:

> I want to tell you about the huge difference here at the ministry since the change in leadership, and I attribute it to one thing—today we are encouraged to seek, teach and promote Jesus Christ. Not "Twelve," not "spiritual authority" and not "fathers and sons"—just Jesus. Today it is all about, "Lord, come, and Your will be done here today."
>
> I have been here for two and a half years, and I have the unique perspective of going through the program, and then going on staff and helping run the program. The change is drastic. Although I was never in David's "Twelve," I was called into a "Twelve" by someone who was, and this is what I know to be true. Blood-n-Fire was run by David and his "sons and daughters"—and the atmosphere here on any day was hectic and uncertain, and for several reasons. People were put into positions that they openly said they did not want. There was absolutely no accountability

with David or his "Twelve." Example: While I was in The Portal, New Beginnings and Transition, the first, second and third phases of the program, one of David's "sons" ran the program. He routinely disappeared for two or three days at a time to smoke crack and pursue the lifestyle that those of us in the program were trying to get away from. And this was the guy who was leading us! He stole money and equipment from the ministry to fuel his drug habit, and then he would return, sleep for two days, and we would wait a couple of weeks until he did it again. When he would return, the issue was never addressed, discussed or explained. We were not allowed to question it either, because he was one of David's "sons." So the addiction program was run by an active crack smoker who was beyond question because he was only accountable to David. As was evident in many things, David did not really hold anyone accountable to anything. His main concern, as I have heard him say many times, was "Are you following me? Are you doing what I do?" . . . We were told that our destiny and inheritance was dependent upon how hard we chased after our spiritual fathers and what they said and did. To question or disagree was to be in rebellion, and we were told that rebellion as "as the sin of witchcraft." I am going to say this—the ministry was a cult, and there is nothing else to call it.

The structure here at the ministry was a hierarchy determined by who was closer to David, and closer to David was determined by how much you chased after him. He encouraged the entourage that followed him everywhere. He routinely changed the guidelines set in place. There was nothing to stand firm on, because nothing stayed the same. We broke commitments, we lost relationships, and the poor and the vision of Blood-n-Fire took backseat to David and his "Twelve." Church on Sundays became a vain attempt to communicate new revelation that only furthered "Twelve." The meals at night became a quest for larger number, and then it became a quest to do it bigger and better than other ministries downtown. (I specifically heard Task Force mentioned often.) It became competition, outdoing everyone else, and the poor lost out every day; the staff was frustrated and run into the ground because David changed rules and formats daily due to his "new revelation."

There was no voice for the staff because the people David had put in place were there to see his vision furthered. There was no voice for the poor because they took backseat to "Twelve." The scripture was misused and conformed to fit whatever was important at the moment. We were told to just submit and obey—not to question. We were told that people who had left the ministry and those who didn't agree with David were his enemies. And why would we want to be in relationship with his enemies? We were told to be careful around anyone who wasn't in the immediate "family." The other Blood-n-Fires were not all in the family; they didn't all follow David, we were told. When the board stood up to David, it was communicated that they were wrong, they didn't understand, and they impeded the vision.

Lives are being changed here (at the new Compassion Center) with lasting results. The meals at night are peaceful and orderly. The staff are not frustrated and running around crazy, so we have time to focus on relationship with the poor. The food is good; the meals are big; and the poor are being served. The Program is in excellent shape. It is full right now, and we have more people wanting in then we have room for. I haven't seen that during the warm months since I have been here. The success, the peace and the changed lives are a testimony to the difference between how David ran the ministry, and how now Chris and LeAnn run the ministry. You don't hear me talk a lot about Chris and LeAnn because they don't make it about themselves. They facilitate and encourage what God is doing, and I see firsthand how they daily seek God for his will. Chris has NEVER mandated anything about how things must be done. He knows that God called different people to facilitate different areas, and he supports and encourages us in what God is telling us to do. He has NEVER said to follow him, but he has told me (more than once) that he is here to support me as I go after what God called me to do. That is what Chris and LeAnn do—they support the staff and there are here for us. They are always easily accessible, and they give God free reign in this place. . . . The staff here are daily encouraged, supported and loved. Today this house is a house of peace and a house of God.

These are things that I know firsthand, not through or because of someone else. I write this to you, and I hope I have communicated the difference between then and now. I feel very strongly about this because I have lived it, and I know first hand the lives affected. If David ever came back here, in any leadership role, the poor would lose, the addicts would lose, and the staff would lose.

David did return to power, and his return ushered in dramatic changes. The dissidents who lived in the Warehouse were immediately ordered out. In quick succession the Warehouse with its Training Center was closed; the public meal program was discontinued; and BnF offices were moved into the Sanctuary, where a remnant of homeless poor were permitted to stay in order to avoid vandalism of the property.

Steve's "open letter" began to circulate among board members and then David's disciples. Archie Crenshaw, one of the members of the executive board, checked with "seven other persons who were involved in the Warehouse" to see if the letter was a "reasonably accurate portrayal of happenings." Archie reported, "All seven said they agreed with the characterizations of this e-mail, and further offered their telephone numbers and their willingness to discuss these or any other matters which might be of interest to you." The accusations made in the Steve Ruff letter soon brought responses from David's followers.

The Disciples Respond

E-mails would soon be circulated from several key disciples in support of David. One example is Jerome's succinct response to Steve's e-mail that David forwarded to the board (Jerome is the leader of the Training Program who Steve alleges "routinely disappeared for two or three days at a time to smoke crack and pursue the lifestyle that those of us in the program were trying to get away from"):

> Thank you for that wonderful reminder about how David allowed one of his sons to go out and get high, and to return to Blood-n-Fire. I am so thankful that there is such a thing as grace, because without it, where would you be today? It seems to me that you have forgotten, when you were in New Life, you took some money from one of your brothers and left to go get high. There was David, with grace, welcoming you back. Also, there was a time when you went downtown in the back of a restaurant with a needle in your arm and you overdosed. Aren't you glad that David was there with his heart full of grace. So you see, Steve, because of God in him, he had grace for both you and I. And we should thank you, David, for being so gracious to us.

Another letter of support for David came from John and Beckett Richardson, a young couple from Texas interviewed during the pilot study visit as they were preparing to leave for BnF Cape Town. John and Beckett wrote a three-page letter to David that was forwarded by David to one of the authors as a "response to Steve Ruff's open letter." Part of the response read:

It is interesting as you reread the story of Steve's early days at BnF, that all the things he loves about Chris and LeAnn would have assured him that he would not have made it more than once at BnF. But instead, people fought for him and "walked by the Spirit," meaning each and every person who comes to the Sanctuary or the Training Center is an individual. And if you aren't hearing by the Spirit, only by the rules, you end up destroying people. That was the biggest change that we saw in the eight months Chris was in charge is that rules and structure became the driving force versus love and Spirit.

Rose Bigelow, a "daughter" who has walked with David since the beginning of BnF is now serving as CEO of what is left of BnF. She too would respond in defense of David. Rose had been a member of the Atlanta Vineyard that birthed BnF when she befriended David's niece Kathryn, who encouraged her to visit the emerging BnF church. Rose soon became involved in the downtown outreach:

> I was put in charge of doing this Saturday outreach at an old high rise. Now I didn't know what tongues were; I didn't know what healing was. I didn't know what any of this stuff was. I started doing this high-rise thing—would fill up my car with groceries and would begin knocking on doors. It was there that I saw my first healing. I prayed for a man who had emphysema—he had the, you know, tanks and could barely talk. (His name was Lionel.) I prayed for him to be healed, and the next Saturday his oxygen tanks were gone, and he was healed. So it was one of those things where I started learning that God really does show up. I prayed for a guy in a cast—I prayed for him. And the next week I came back, and it was gone. So these were the things I was learning about. One day I was praying over this lady in this apartment, and all of a sudden tongues came out. I just got tongues. They just came on me, and from then on, I spoke in tongues.

Rose's commitment to BnF grew steadily if slowly. There were things in her life that she felt needed to be "cleaned up" before she could make a full-fledged commitment. In 1999 Rose walked away from her job in management to work full-time with BnF. She began the women's and children's ministry, while also managing the books. In time became the chief of staff who trained Chris in the family business. In 2002 Rose left Atlanta for Cape Town where she planned to launch an orphanage, and she was in South

Africa when the schism developed. Before her work with women and children could take any structural form, she "felt the prompting of the Lord" to cut short their time in Cape Town and to return to Atlanta. Rose called David and Janice, who were somewhat surprised by her asking to return. Nonetheless, they told her that "if that's what God said, then that's what He said." Rose returned to find BnF in the midst of a serious church split.

Rose's two-page reply to Steve's "open letter" began with how saddened she was that those who had worked at BnF over the years were "portrayed so poorly" by those who had come into the ministry only relatively recently. She questioned why Steve got involved with BnF if they were "so screwed up all this time." As to BnF's being a "cult," Rose responded: "Steve was not crying 'cult' when he was coming out from the gutter and sleeping on the couch in my home. We had to be doing something right!" At the time of her e-mail, Rose, who had always been known for her compassion for other family members as well as the poor, was still hoping for reconciliation among all parties, and she ended the letter with a question, a call for reconciliation, and a request for forgiveness: "When are we going to be Christians about this? Ghandi [*sic*] once said that if all Christians lived according to their faith, there wouldn't be a Hindu left in India. How true that is . . . IT'S TIME TO STOP POINTING FINGERS AT ONE ANOTHER AND START POINTING UPWARD! I HAVE SAID BEFORE AND I WILL SAY IT AGAIN: PLEASE FORGIVE ME FOR ANYTHING I HAVE DONE TO CAUSE SUCH A GREVIOUS SITUATION" (emphasis in original).

None of the letters of support denied that mistakes had been made; instead they noted that David had repented of the "perversions" reflected in Steve's allegations. David did not attempt to answer the charges in any of the e-mails we received from him. At one point in an interview with us (June 27, 2004), David mused, half seriously but tinged with irony, "Everything is so flawed. Whose fault is it that BnF is where it is at. Well, it's mine. But it is not all mine. Chris played a part. And Jack [Papa Jack Taylor, who was present during the interview] played a part, thank you. And the poor played a part. So where else do we want to cast blame? Well, it's Abner's fault. It Abner had not called me and said, 'I want to do something for you,' we wouldn't have the problem. So it has to be his fault."

Voices from the Community

The voices from greater Atlanta—including the BnF board of trustees, the involved business community, and representatives from the church community—reflected the chasm between David and Chris that was mirrored in the divide between David and the board of directors. Their primary languages of discourse represented the differences between the two cultures of "corporate" and "visionary church," reflecting again Swidler's cultural distinctives of tradition and ideology. One of the board members, Edward "Woody" White, shared with Margaret a personal experience he had that taught him the difficulty in combining charismatic leadership with maintenance or institutional leadership. It was a story he had told the larger board, and it was one of the reasons he was regarded as a voice of support for Chris and LeAnn.

White told the story of coming to Days Inn of America (where he is now president of the foundation) during the 1970s. The gifted charismatic founder told him, "If I stay with Day's Inn, I'll kill it." The man wisely stepped back so that Woody White could step in with necessary maintenance skills. That incident, White says, immediately came to mind when he came to the BnF board meeting in January 2004: "I just knew that was exactly what was happening. David is saying 'I have a vision, help me.' The Board is saying, 'We just got out of debt!'" Ministers who served on the board resisted this sociological thesis of "charismatic" and "maintenance" cultures having different leadership needs. They were more likely, as we will see, to "spiritualize" both the problems and the solutions.

Clergy—both from inside BnF International and outside BnF in greater Atlanta—did rally around David in his hour of need. Ministers from other churches whom David came to know over the years were coming to his support even if the relationship had been suspended. They seemed to share the position we found represented among the BnF International that David was the legitimate authority and was responsible only to God for his actions, not to a corporate board.

One such supporter whom we interviewed was Johnny Crist, the Vineyard pastor who launched BnF from his congregation. When tension developed between him and David about the intensity with which to pursue inner-city ministry, Crist (June 2003 interview) gave VanCronkhite the following alternatives:

> We basically have three choices here. One, you become an associate pastor, full-time on staff for me, and downtown is an outreach of our church. It is funded by the Atlanta Vineyard. You are the one in charge of it, but it is under our authority. Two, we could split you off as a church plant and you just go out—and God bless you. Three, we could have an alternate

campus model whereby we would have two churches still under the Atlanta Vineyard—you could pastor over one church and I the other. I gave pros and cons to each one.

David chose to become an independent Vineyard that allowed him to pursue his own vision without outside oversight.

Crist reported feeling some hurt about the way the break took place, but he was eager to "bless ministries" that had spun off from his congregation. The costs were high, however, in terms of the number of people who left with David to found BnF. Crist believed that David was "working under a different radar screen": "Though he was in the Vineyard, he didn't look to me for direction or help or any of that stuff. So it became sort of an independent Vineyard. It had a different kind of model—a different DNA."

Relations between David and Johnny Crist were strained for a few years. Crist replied to Margaret's questions about the tension by assuming the blame for the difficulties: "We probably were out of joint for two years. We still had contact but it wasn't that wonderful—I am a pretty broken guy—I use the term wounded. I felt he was rejecting me. So I was insecure." Crist reported that he was asked to be on a BnF board of directors (David had at least three over the years), but that was short-lived. Eventually he said to David: "David, I don't want to do this anymore. I've given a lot of time and I've got my own church to pastor. I don't see that I am making any difference."

But when David called for help during the impending schism, Crist was quick to answer. As he put it

There is an invisible connection between pastors and spiritual leaders. There are pastors who are going to be voted in and voted out at leaders— and that is going to happen until Jesus comes again. But there is another breed of pastors who move to a city whose purpose is to spend their lives in that city and to transform that city—caring deeply what happens there. That's kind of the cloth from which we are cut. And that relationship of what God has done with our hearts, knitting them together, really goes beyond whether your church is successful or whether I am jealous of you. There is a sense in which we are the pilot fighters and we are bound together. So there is a cadre of guys in this city that David has put his hands on—we all care about the poor—we are all deeply involved with BnF with our churches at one period of time or another. For whatever reason, everyone dropped off for a time—but when we have events, we all just show up. And so when David was going through his quandary, he wanted the wisdom of that team to help him sort out in his own mind, relationships. If there is anything I am good at, I am good at that. I would be an emergency room doc as opposed to a GP. I wouldn't go to the oncology floor day after day and that kind of work.

While Crist recognized that in many ways David was responsible for his own problems—"problems that were started with a good heart, by the way"—he saw the underlying difficulty stemming from the fact that the board comprised people with two conflicting visions. He summarized his position on the board as follows: "We had gathered here people with two completely different visions. And we thought this tent was pretty big, but it was not." For Crist the conflict was more due to a class of cultural values (spiritual versus worldly) rather than leadership styles and gifting (charismatic versus maintenance).

A similar defense of the pastoral support given to David comes from comments heard from pastors who had experiences similar to David's struggle with the board. Although we did not interview Robert Lupton, he had been a member of one of David's earlier boards; and, like Johnny Crist, Lupton returned to a newly expanded board to support his colleague. Lupton, the founder and president of FCS Urban Ministries in Atlanta, wrote a version of what had transpired at BnF (although he was far from the day-to-day activities) in one of his books, *Renewing the City: Reflections on Community Development and Urban Renewal* (2005). Before presenting his account, Lupton shared a story from his past that cast light on his decision to support David.

Lupton wrote of a personal struggle that occurred within his ministry that was similar to David's—his burnout, sabbatical, and learning more about his own temperament. In a self-description that could have easily been David's, Lupton reports: "Some things energize me, such as vision casting and plotting new community development strategies. I would rush back to them tomorrow. But the day-to-day management of an organization depletes my energies" (2005, 115). The CEO, who took over for Lupton during his sabbatical, "did a good deal of reading" while Lupton was gone, concluding "that the founders of organizations were seldom the best suited to manage their companies in the long term" (2005, 116). The CEO's conclusion was that both he and Lupton should leave for the good of the ministry—with which, not surprisingly, Lupton strongly disagreed. His CEO lost the battle, but the skirmish resembled what David was encountering at BnF. In discussing the case of David and Chris, Lupton described David as one who "had always been free to move with the promptings of the Spirit," while Chris had "a heart for hands on ministry" (2005, 181). Perhaps while reminiscing about his own administrative struggles of a time back, he spoke of David's return from his sabbatical as someone returning with "batteries fully charged" and with an "enthusiasm [that] was contagious." His "new revelations" were met by Chris and the board "immediately applying the brakes."

Lupton's abridged history of the struggle at BnF (2005, 179–84), while representing one perspective, reflected his belief in the absolute legitimacy of spiritual authority—albeit with a caveat. His concluding statement is worth repeating here:

> For better or for worse, divine visions seem to be entrusted to individuals, not committees. Board, bean counters and benefactors, though essential to the life of a movement, are not the source of its spiritual fire. Visionary leaders, while certainly needing a level of accountability, must be free to roll out their visions as the Spirit reveals it to them. It is, however, a risky business. No one hears the voice of God with absolute accuracy. But clip the wings of the visionary and the vision will never get off the ground, let alone soar. (2005, 115)

The unanswered question for this needed "level of accountability" was never adequately dealt with in David's case. As with other things at BnF, it shifted with the wind. For a time David would contend that he was accountable to his spiritual mentor, Papa Jack Taylor. In fact, however, Taylor was rarely around to observe the day-to-day issues reported by the board and those who operated the Compassion Center. By most insider accounts, Taylor knew only what David told him. As the schism unfolded, the leadership of BnF International promised to provide David with a spiritual covering to replace the board of directors. In the end, David would emerge unshackled by accountability and fully in control of BnF.

Funeral and New Birth

After months of struggle David finally won the battle, regaining control over BnF and the warehouse properties without restrictions. Lupton, as part of the expanded board of trustees, was an eyewitness to events that occurred. He described the scenario as follows:

It was the desire of everyone involved to resolve the matter in a just and godly manner. During weeks of earnest discussion, the expanded board, which now included former members, wrestled with various scenarios for holding on to both David and fiscal accountability. But again and again the debate returned to an underlying theological impasse: with whom does the final authority for a God-given vision lie? Some argued that the board had both legal and ethical responsibility. Others held that the visionary had primary authority, confirmed by and accountable only to the movement leadership.

It would take a miracle to resolve this stalemate. But no miracle came. Fractures only widened along philosophical fault lines. It degenerated into power plays between current and former board members, legal saber rattling and the squeezing of the cash flow from the board and its deep-pocketed allies. It was not a pretty process. In the end David was reinstated by a margin of a single vote. (2005, 183)

In a ritual ceremony held early in June, a funeral was held for BnF1 and there was celebration over the birth of BnF2. During the site visit we made during the last week of June, a death certificate for BnF could be seen hanging in David's office. "1990–June 2, 2004; BnF died—after 14 years it died; the Lord said it was time to start another." Next to it hung a birth certificate for BnF2: "God is moving fresh and new; He didn't like what we were doing; we didn't like it either."

9

Epilogue

A Social Scientific Assessment of Godly Love

A few weeks before Christmas 2006 in response to an earlier draft of this manuscript, David VanCronkhite e-mailed Margaret:

> It is a humbling reality to suddenly grasp that a small band of people chose to leave, even to some small degree, their comfort zone; that they attempted to move into more meaningful relationships with one another and attempted to include the poor in those relationships while seeking the supernatural reality of a Kingdom of God on earth as it is in heaven; that they attempted to experience the reality of signs and wonders as a part of everyday life among the poor; that they attempted to integrate the extreme rich with the extreme poor of one city—Atlanta; that they attempted to do something so full of personal risk that it would impel well known researchers to spend four years researching the dreams, visions, and practices under the label of Blood n Fire.

He continued,

> Our prayer continues that our personal journey of life will progress in such a way as to cause many to recognize the greatest gift, our greatest need, is for the King and His Kingdom to reign in every area of life: "Do not be afraid, little flock, for your Father has been pleased to give you the Kingdom" (Luke 12:32). Our faith and message causes us to believe that the stories of our journey will continue to be noted by academia and the world as we receive the grace needed as broken, yet supernaturally empowered people, walking out "loving Him with all and loving neighbor as self." (Matthew 22:34-40)

David VanCronkhite's experiences of divine love and the interaction rituals embodying these experiences—both divine-human and human-human—played a vital role in BnF's vision to transform American culture. David not only held the keys to this dynamic vision that energized the community; but, as BnF's charismatic founder, he also controlled much of the emotion energy (EE) that motivated and rewarded his followers. Collins has noted the primal role that charismatic leaders play in what he calls "long-term feedbacks," that is, "when the outcomes of one IR feed back into the conditions that make it possible to carry out a subsequent IR" (2004, 146). Charismatic leaders are persons with high emotional energy (EE) who have "the enthusiasm to set off new *emotional stimulus* and pump up other people" into what becomes an "interaction ritual chain" (2004, 146). David is clearly such a leader.

David's interaction rituals were prime transmitters of his prophetic visions, retold again and again in family gatherings and conferences, in personal prophecies and prayer with recruits, in newspaper accounts and on the BnF Web site. Although David's IRs were sources of EE, the radical modification of his vision reflected in BnF2 interaction rituals can be conceptualized as a social gamble. Many gambles—like BnF's early separation from the Atlanta Vineyard, David's purchasing the warehouse properties, and his sacrificing the sacred cow of a thriving inner-city church *of* the poor—paid off, generating more EE and more followers. The schism and subsequent funeral for BnF1, however, seemed to cost far more in EE than David and his small band of followers were able to produce. Most long-term devotees eventually sought emotional rewards outside their once-beloved BnF family. David's ability to produce EE spiraled downward during and in the aftermath of the schism. His energy was restricted to a smaller number of dedicated followers after the break.

Assessing the Changing Vision

The expressed mission for BnF1 was to transform the lives of the poor. During the years of BnF1, David spoke specifically of providing for the poor—"providing for their daily needs [the command of Isaiah 58]." It also included working with the youth as BnF sought to "equip [them] in kingdom values to go to the poor." Finally it proposed to "equip teams to go into the nations with the proclamation and the evidence of the Kingdom of God" (http://www.bloodnfire.com; accessed October 13, 2004). It was not immediately clear to us, despite repeatedly questioning of BnF2 leaders and members, exactly how the mission and ministry to the homeless would differ in BnF2 from that of BnF1. It soon would become apparent that the centrality of a concrete expression of godly love for the poor was being displaced by the message of "taking Atlanta for the Kingdom of God." The transformation of the mission from concrete goals to more prophetic abstractions over the next two years was more than a mental exercise; it was a process fueled by a drastic decrease in revenue. As ministries were shut down, services for the poor were curtailed and David and his dedicated followers interacted with the poor less and less.

Margaret noted the decided shift in emphasis from tangible service to spiritual abstractions during her visit to the Warehouse on June 30, 2004, in a pre-prayer talk given by one of David's daughters (Autumn) to the one hundred or so people who gathered for a public meal. We often observed during the two years of our most intense fieldwork how Autumn exuded godly love and personal charisma when she spoke and prayed with the homeless. She not only was eager to pray for the guests, but she made an attempt to learn their names and to remember something specific about each person. Her warmth, her expressions of concern and her charm were not lost on those who attended the public meals. This night, however, her words seemed to ring hollow as she shared about the immanent changes and the birth of BnF2:

> There has been a lot of change here. Do you know why I am excited about the change? I am excited about BnF1 being buried and BnF2 being birthed. Because we are going from ministering *to* people—ministering *to* the poor—ministering *to* those in need—to becoming a church *of* the poor—a church *of the poor in Spirit* and a church of the poor in the natural as well. We are going to be a church *of*.
>
> Last year—some of you guys were here—I asked you to write it down. I asked, "If you could have anything to eat, what would it be?" And you wrote down all kinds of good food—some foods that we had never even seen here at BnF. Remember that?
>
> Then God showed me another vision. He showed me a picture of a room in heaven—with miracles. He showed me creative miracles. You know, when a person is sick in body, only the One who created that body can provide what is needed. He showed me miracles—the supernatural. I am talking about the blind seeing and limbs growing back out. I saw this happening. There were hundred in this room being healed. You know, we had lines coming here because the food was so good. But we will have

lines coming to this house because of the presence of the power of God. It won't be the food in the natural that draws them but God himself.

Autumn's vision, one that was intertwined with David's own prophetic words in community rituals, was preparing the guests for a cutback that preceded the total elimination of the public meal program. Spiritual food was to replace the chicken, fish, and sometimes steak that once filled the plates of the homeless. The same theme could be heard in David's Sunday-morning sermon a few weeks later (July 18, 2004) on one of the first occasions he preached publicly since his return to BnF. He began by speaking of a vision that Johnny, a self-proclaimed homeless black minister, reported to him:

> Johnny—I can't remember whether he said he had a dream or a vision—but he was walking downtown and this homeless person came up to him. And the homeless person came up to him and looked him flat in the eye and said, "When are you going to start feeding us?" Isn't that amazing? When are you going to start feeding us? As soon as the guy said it, light bulbs went off. Because somewhere along the way we stopped feeding—somewhere along the way we stopped giving what God had given us to give away.
>
> I don't think we missed a day of giving food away out of the kitchen, but we stopped feeding. We stopped giving the food that God gave us to give away. The book says in Isaiah 58 that it is mandatory to give the hungry food, shelter to those without homes, clothing for those without. This is absolutely mandatory if we want the glory of the Lord. But we are also called to give away the Holy Spirit food—signs and wonders—Holy Spirit food. "When are you going to feed us?" Do you know what a difference we can make in the streets of Atlanta if we start giving food away?

David was upbeat in this sermon as he told those gathered how the collection each Sunday had gotten larger and larger. "I think you know," he said, "that we exist on the Sunday offering. The corporate offerings have stopped. That's good by the way. We just got way too dependent on corporate offering." The increase in Sunday offerings may or may not have been real, but the proclamation seemed to offer evidence to followers that the changes underway were God's ordained and that He would continue to provide for them.

Margaret talked with Autumn after the service, asking for more details on the changes she saw between BnF1 and BnF2. Autumn told how the schism ("exile," she called it) was allowed by God "to shaken all that wasn't of God and wasn't of love." She explained: "The mandate of BnF has not changed. God has given us a mandate to the poor—but not solely. We will always have the poor; we will always have family; we will always have relationship. What changed is the way we walk it out. BnF1—even though our hearts wanted to be family oriented first, we wound up being ministry oriented first. There was a lot of focus on performance—on the doing—on the roles (like what we do at the Warehouse). It was very outwardly focused. I hope I am being clear."

Clarity would come for us, but only after two more years of tracking BnF2 from the sidelines. We were to see the ministry to the homeless, the poor, and the addicted abandoned; the Warehouse dismantled to "harvest" the antique bricks and boards; and the vision of ushering in the Kingdom of God with poor and rich partnering together in family-like relations unrealized. It became clear to both of us that insofar as BnF was to be judged by success in transforming the lives of the homeless in Atlanta, its success was minimal.

By October 2006 little if anything remained of BnF ministries; any activity we observed was directed toward reestablishing the BnF church in Atlanta. In January of the same year the Sanctuary had been closed to all but a handful of homeless residents left to guard valuable sound equipment stored in the nearly abandoned building. In April the warehouse had been put up for sale, and the homeless now living there are on borrowed time. When the for-sale sign had been up for longer than anticipated, the delay was reported to be in obedience to the divine command given to David to "go slow." "Go slow" was soon followed by divine direction to completely "dissolve" the ministry.

To us the new vision that marginalized the poor appeared to be riddled with twists and turns through which we watched and waited as David continued to hear his instructions from God. After the divine command first reported in February 2005 "to consolidate," David says he heard God telling them to go to the streets again. As he continued to ponder the instructions of God, another word came: "Then suddenly, another word of action came. Suddenly . . . we were birthed in that fashion and we live in that realm . . . suddenly, the leaders of Blood-n-Fire Atlanta, both the church and the ministry, heard it clearly. And we again have begun to take action. Suddenly, He said to dissolve. Dis-solve: to break up, or break something up, into smaller and more basic parts. It was the advice of fifteen years ago, if you will, and now it filled our spirits with joy and hope."

At first the call to consolidation was interpreted as a call to purchase new, smaller properties as ministry bases to replace the warehouse property that would position them to "take Atlanta." But Atlanta realty had gotten too expensive "to take," as the downtown areas are increasingly gentrified and the poor effectively displaced. By fall 2006 David realized that when God said to "dissolve" he really meant it. On October 10, David sent another message; the subject line read "shifts in the atmosphere":

The Sanctuary of BnF-ATL has, as Rose says, finally been put to rest (RIP). I (David) once more had to repent to the residents of the Sanctuary and our local BnF church and the city for being disobedient to the word of God. As most of you know, we all reported (especially me) some 18 months back that it was time to move away from what we had been doing for the past 15 or so years and that God had a new expression of walking with the youth and the poor for us.

The Property at 188/225 called the Warehouse—David, slow! This continues to be the word. All are willing to move slowly so as not to miss the voice of God. The best we know is what the sign says out front the building complex, it is available. We are waiting and watching as God's purposes unfold.

Margaret visited the warehouse properties in spring 2007 to find a large sign reading "AVAILABLE" in front of the partially demolished buildings enclosed by a new chain-link fence. A couple of family members were involved in demolition work. We soon learned that BnF was trying to salvage what it could and sell it via the Internet before the property was sold. The two old warehouse buildings into which well over a million dollars and countless volunteer hours had been invested by benefactors on behalf of the poor, like the ministries they once housed, were now doomed. We were told that at least one other ministry to the homeless in Atlanta was interested in securing the property, but the asking price of more than ten million dollars was out of the question. When the property is finally sold it will bring a considerable blessing for the faithful remnant. Whether the money is David's to use as he desires is legally unclear, but the old board dissolved without putting any legal restrictions on the profits. Perhaps equally uncertain is David's assessment of what God is telling him to do.

Charismatic Leader, Covenantal Vision, and Contractual Society

David faced a classic dilemma in his vision to usher in the spiritual Kingdom of God through supernatural happenings and the tangible ministry to the poor that had brought BnF widespread recognition. The acclaim given to the ministry by many visitors, beneficiaries, benefactors, and media missed a central fact about BnF: providing "three hots and a cot" for Atlanta's poor was not the heart of David's vision. His vision was one of a relational covenant rooted in a believer's "supernatural walk" that would usher in the Kingdom of God. The BnF church family exemplified this vision through its emphasis on intense, inclusive, and enduring relationships. Although the promise of covenantal relationships drew many middle-class followers, it had less appeal for the poor and homeless, who were more likely to have been drawn to BnF by the tangible rewards of food, shelter, and help with addictions. Thus, BnF ironically provided more spiritual nourishment for those who provided services for the poor than for the poor themselves. Still, David remains a remarkable charismatic leader for those who can accept both his vision and his authority,

Bartkowski and Regis (2004) in their study of "charitable choice" have noted that although covenant and contract are often melded together in faith-based ministry, they are forms of social relationships that are generally at odds with one another. Certainly this became the case at BnF. The covenanted family was responsible for carrying out the contractual social ministries of feeding and housing of the poor. Many family members were drawn to the covenant but had less interest in the daily duties of fulfilling the contract-like responsibilities of the ministry. The tension could be felt in the stories (and the statistics) we reported dealing with the family, the family business, and especially the board of directors. In our survey data, we noted the difference in the expectations between family members and the recipients of BnF services in their acceptance and articulation of the BnF vision. The two groups were clearly seeking different primary rewards. While the BnF family stressed the interpersonal relationships of covenant, promising primarily a deeper relationship with God and with family members, the homeless served by the ministry, preferred contract and the promise of concrete services. David's battle with board members from the business community was largely mirrored in the struggle between covenant and contract. While intrigued by the visionary covenant, the board needed the facts and figures of contract costs and provisions to carry out their fiduciary responsibilities.

It will never be known whether BnF would have reached new heights had David's vision and charisma been merged with the resources of those skilled in the canons of sound business practices as proposed by the board of directors in their efforts to avoid the schism. Perhaps this dual vision of David's prophetic word coupled with sound fiscal management could have done more to transform the lives of the poor. It appeared to us and to others with whom we talked, however, that David was unwilling or unable to take on collaborators who would not uncritically accept his absolute authority. As we watched close collaborators come and go in David's life we observed that he did not seem to sustain intense relationships over time with those he selected for positions of responsibility at BnF. Much like the gurus described by Anthony Storr (1996), David sought the love he spoke of so eloquently, and his disciples gave it to him. But they could remain disciples only as long as they remained submissive and obedient. Followers would find their loyalty questioned and their positions in jeopardy when they disagreed with David. Storr notes, "Almost by definition, charismatic leaders are unpredictable, for they are bound by neither tradition nor rules; they are not answerable to other human beings" (xv). David believes in his divine anointing and believes that God guides his actions. With such a strong prophetic sense and the absence of collaborators who could question and challenge him, there was little to mitigate the tension between the covenantal vision and the realities of social contract from developing into a strong schismatic force.

David's charisma is most evident to us in his undivided attention when interacting with individuals on a one-to-one basis. IRs with the poor captured a picture of intimacy that we found intense and inclusive but lacking in duration. Margaret was at first impressed with his seeming respect for the homeless when she would see him politely interrupt the conversation at hand to engage with a homeless person waiting to speak to him. A poor man might light up as David would put his arm around him, look into his eyes, and make him feel (at least for the moment) that he was the most important person in the world. Encounters such as these left some men and women feeling that they were very special to David—that he truly loved them. While the affect may have been genuine and intense, we came to notice that it was inevitably of short duration and extended only to the handful of homeless who captured David's fancy that day. The passing ritual encounter did not develop into long-term relationships with the power to transform lives—not even for the homeless men found pictured with David in different media presentations of BnF.

We don't know how much interaction David had with the poor during its earliest period when the community could be said to have been in its "charismatic moment." Some who were involved before the warehouse became an icon described these early years of street ministry without a permanent building as BnF's finest hour. The passing of years can bring nostalgia. But what we did observe over the four-year study period is that David spent less and less time at the warehouse. He was much more likely to be found interacting with his core followers (and others whose favors he courts outside the community) than in relating to homeless men and women in the Sanctuary. David speaks passionately about the poor but has little interaction with them, and his new vision reflected this increasing distance from the poor and homeless. In a long conversation we had with David just after he came off his sabbatical leave, he shared his vision with us—one still centered on the poor and the Kingdom of God. He lamented that so few (especially the corporate board of directors) really heard the message to abandon the American dream for the coming Kingdom. Ralph, drawing from our survey data and interviews with Sanctuary residents who aspired to be "family," told David that he was "hanging out with the wrong people"—that if he wanted others who were committed to the vision, he should go to the Sanctuary. David returned to that thought a couple of times during the lengthy interview, which included a lunch break before gathering back together. After the interview was over and as we were saying our goodbyes, we asked David where he was heading now. David replied, "Janice and I are going up to Oklahoma and then to North Carolina to 'hang' with some of the prophets." Perhaps David did at one time "hang" with the poor as well as the prophets; we just don't know. We do know that the homeless were not an intimate part of his life during the years of our study and that they were soon to be removed from any significant role in David's new vision.

We have suggested that the vision of godly love and its interaction rituals (IRs) can be assessed by the traits first identified by Sorokin—intensity, extensity, duration, purity, and adequacy. If we apply these criteria to assess godly love at BnF, the task is complex; the assessment is colored by the use of the lenses of covenant or contract, whether BnF1 or BnF2 is being assessed, and which narrative voice is doing the assessment. From what we can glean from our many hours of interviewing David, his preferred lens is that of divine covenant. He had left the world of contracts and corporate America with its "bottom-line" philosophy. His actions reflect an assessment that BnF's contract ministry was an inadequate expression of godly love in that it failed to bring about covenantal relationships for the poor and homeless. There was to be no compromise; any implicit contracts with the homeless needed to be severed.

The board of directors, on the other hand, while intrigued with David's covenantal vision, wanted an assessment on how well the ministry was fulfilling its contract. Although exact figures were hard to come by throughout our study, we believe that any assessment of BnF1 in contractual terms would provide a mixed report. If approached in terms of a social contract that assesses the outcome of goods and services according to the input made by the benefactors, BnF was perhaps only marginally effective, even in its glory days. The cost of operating the ministry seemed at times to us to be disproportionate to the services provided. This was the problem that the board sought to address—a problem that was temporarily resolved through the interim leadership of Chris and LeAnn with the support of the board of directors.

When we attempted to apply a mix of covenant and contractual outcomes in a single assessment, we recognized how the picture can change. In some ways BnF1 was an exceptional ministry, as suggested by the news articles we used in our early descriptions and reflected in the voices found in our grand narrative. Even if one would prefer not to term the peace and order generally found within the Sanctuary and Warehouse as "the presence of God," there was an ambiance not commonly found in homeless shelters. It is extremely uncommon, for example, for women and children to be safely housed in the same large dormitory room as homeless males, and for there to be only curtains to separate the sleeping arrangements. BnF was often said by residents to be the safest shelter in Atlanta. Nor is the sense of a private space in the midst of the dormitory beds where personal possessions could be left undisturbed a common feature of a homeless shelter. For the most part, the homeless consistently were treated with respect that gave rise to a sense of personal worth and divine destiny. Even some who had vandalized and voiced violence toward BnF were forgiven and welcomed back. The nightly meal program was run effectively; volunteers graciously served hot meals (which were at times billed as the "best in Atlanta") to as many as many as five hundred people or more. It was no small achievement to serve hundreds of homeless in a temporary family atmosphere, seated around large tables, having meals and drinks brought to them.

For those in the BnF family who worked the ministry, the secret of success was prayer—frequent worship services, the prayer walks around the neighborhood and around the grounds, intercession for divine resources to meet financial needs, praying individually for residents and guests, and the all-night prayer sessions that were once in place to support addicts as they detoxified. There were many reports of spiritual blessings by the homeless and addicts. BnF may have been inadequate as the "church of the poor" described in its vision, but it did provide a milieu where many poor and homeless, at least for a season, believed they grew in their love for God and for one another. Others who may not have experienced such growth still benefited in that they had a physically safe sanctuary where they were sheltered and fed. We believe that most family members would agree with the above two-sided assessment based on the premises of covenant and contract.

Although most family members seemed unwilling or unable to critique BnF1 during our original interviews, in follow-up discussions many reported high marks for some aspects of the lived-out vision but are now critical of other aspects. Despite the warts exposed by the schism, the covenantal vision was valued by most middle-class white followers. BnF transformed many of their lives; and even those who would eventually break with David would report that their experience of godly love at BnF was rewarding. They expressed sadness and grief over what had transpired, but few expressed regret over the years they had spent in family and ministry.

Changing the Face of an Emerging Church

Ray Anderson, a theologian who has written on emerging churches, observes that they represent a social movement that "produces a new system and a new way of behaving rather than a new behavior within the same system. It has a high degree of discontinuity through the transition of change" (2006, 21). The changes brought about by the schism from BnF1 to BnF2 were dramatic changes, but they left BnF well within the molten requisites of the emerging church movement. The central practical concern that Dan Kimball (2003) has laid out in his discussion of emerging churches is one that appears to be shared by David's faithful remnant. Kimball recognizes that today's post-Christian generations are not responding the same as generations before them. The big question is how many factors need to change, including preaching, leadership, evangelism, spiritual formation, and, most of all, how church is conceptualized. BnF2 seemingly has changed its focus from the poor to youth; it developed a special emphasis on the arts.

Changes in the church could be seen almost immediately following VanCronkhite's reinstatement as BnF's undisputed CEO in the summer of 2004—changes that were particularly evident in the Sunday morning worship services. Zach Smith (another of Ralph's graduate assistants) provided a report after a visit he had made, demonstrating the effect of the changes on the Sunday community. Zach wrote:

> My initial impressions focused centrally on the service itself and the congregation. The setting was changed, having moved into the dining area as opposed to the sleeping area with which I was accustomed. The emphasis on art was exemplified through the numerous paintings hanging on every inch of the walls in the room (and the artwork was quite good, I might add). A striking difference from my previous encounters with service was the inclusion of a "house band." . . . Coming from a musical upbringing, I was shocked and amazed at the consideration taken into incorporating this level of music into the worship service. I have been to actual musical concerts will less inspiration.

Our young research assistant was exactly the kind of person BnF now seemed to be courting for membership. The simplicity that characterized the surroundings after David dismantled the "cash cow," causing most suburbanite members to leave the fold, was no more. Also gone were the beds of the homeless that surrounded the worship area in the Sanctuary that served as a symbol of the nature of true worship. Zach made some important observations about the people who came to attend the service he visited: "The individuals present at this service also seemed different in comparison with previous encounters. The primary difference was the addition of the numbers of non-homeless. I say this because the individuals did not fit the description of BnF members that I observed in previous Sunday morning worship. They were all young and white, wearing designer clothing, hygienically well-kept, and they drove cars. I would approximate a 60 percent homeless, 40 percent non-homeless split at this particular service."

Zach had come to BnF during the period when the interim leaders were encouraging the homeless to participate actively in religious services, making room for their a cappella singing, simply crafted poems, and heartfelt testimonies. The music band and their expensive instruments and sound equipment left with David and returned when he returned. This change under the leadership of Chris and LeAnn created the space for the homeless to make their unique contributions to the worship service. The ambiance was enhanced with simple drawings that could be seen displayed in the Sanctuary, which was home to some of the homeless. The service described by Zach suggested that the poor who came to Sunday morning service were once again relegated to the role of spectators.

"Creative Combustion" became one of BnF2's core values, one that reflected a "core criteria" of emerging churches as "communities that follow Jesus and the Kingdom into the far reaches of the modern culture" (Gibbs and Bolger 2005, 236)—in this case a young, middle-class post-modern culture. "Creative Combustion isn't just a catchy phrase but a revelation. It's bringing God's Kingdom to earth through the arts," claimed the BnF Web site (http://www.bloodnfire.com; accessed June 10, 2006). Despite some earlier sporadic attempts to develop a sound in worship that would appeal to poor African Americans, BnF music has generally been a better fit for the white middle-class youth than the poor they served. The changes observed by Zach were still another marker for BnF's shift away from a biblical preference for the poor toward the youth of middle-class white America.

The BnF Web site (last accessed on October 11, 2007) has been cleared of the old stories about its history, information about current activities, or visions for the future. Not even a time and place for worship is provided. From all reports we have received over the past months only a small number of followers gather together weekly in Rose's home for worship and fellowship. There is a link for information on "mission," but clicking the link delivers only a promise—"coming soon." What information that does remain on the Web site is largely about the arts. Creative Combustion is described as "preaching the gospel through a painting; setting captives free through a dance; hearing fierce raging worship through the beat of a drum." There is a link to information about BnF Cape Town: "Twelve and the arts bring hope and a future" and "Touching youth through the arts." There is also a link to Janice VanCronkhite's Web site, where there are images of approximately one hundred of her original paintings and a list of conferences where Janice will be appearing as a prophetic painter. Prints of her latest painting, "Love Is the Key," like other paintings, are available for purchase. Significantly it is Janice rather than David who now is being invited to churches and conferences, not to speak about the poor, but to paint as part of a ritual that is increasingly popular in emerging churches that seek to incorporate more of the arts into worship.

A Theoretical Caveat on Prophetic Vision

In many ways, the vision of BnF1 with its focus on the poor was remarkable in its ability to attract evangelical and Pentecostal followers, many of whom had given up on church as usual. They entered a creative emerging church with a special mandate focused on transforming the lives of the poor. Most who were attracted to David's vision were middle class, well educated, and if not already successful were well on their way to being so. The vision that attracted David's followers, as is the nature of visions, was rooted in ideals that measured well against Sorokin's idealistic dimensions of love. There was *purity* in the call to leave behind ego satisfaction proffered by the materialistic and greedy American dream for a Kingdom in which godly love reigned through a life of service to the poor and broken. The call was for a lifelong commitment (*duration*) to the family of God, composed of people of all ages, races, and nations (*inclusive*). It put into a contemporary context Jesus's command to love God with one's whole heart, mind, and soul and to love one's neighbor as oneself that required a high degree of *intensity*, which only could be fueled by the divine Spirit of love. While lofty in its ideals, in final analysis a vision can only be assessed by its capacity to touch the earth without losing its ability to soar. In fact, at the core of our research design was a proposal to assess the adequacy of love as it took form in the BnF church and family business. One of our primary concerns was to document the transformation that BnF promised for the poor of Atlanta. In this sense we too were attracted to David's vision.

Our project began with a challenge put forth in Sorokin's statement of more than a half century ago: "Only a few persons and agencies have purposefully endeavored to improve in their own interactions this process of love production, or have devoted themselves to this task to a considerable degree" (1954/2002, 38). In our preliminary investigations, we were intrigued by the possibility that BnF under David VanCronkhite's leadership and guided by his vision might just be such a place. Our research was not to be about David, but about his vision for the poor and how it was actualized through the work of his collaborators and disciples. This was intended to be more than David's story, which had been told many times in the Atlanta press, Christian magazines, and on Christian television. The diverse stories representing different BnF voices that we have woven together are the building blocks of our BnF grand narrative. We used them to provide content for the theoretical interaction ritual chains that composed the cultural milieu in which "love energy" (emotion energy) was being produced and stored at BnF.

Through the many voices of people we interviewed and through our personal observations we documented David's charismatic effect on others. As a visionary David has the power to create and to destroy through his control of emotion energy. Collaborators that David could hear and trust might have been able to diffuse the negative emotion energy associated with the schism. Resolving the issues between covenant and contract in BnF would have permitted the visionary to soar while the collaborators' feet remained planted in the realities of life. This was not to be. Those who once seemed like potential collaborators were turned into villains, regarded as thieves trying to steal the ministry. As the prophetic leader of BnF, David denies this status to others. This is both a source of strength and of weakness. David shares his visions, but not his power.

Godly Love in Cultural Context

Godly love, as it shines through the many accounts woven together in our narrative, is more than an isolated act. As we have conceptualized it, godly love consists of interaction rituals linked together in what Randall Collins calls interaction ritual chains. Central to the process of godly love are vertical interaction rituals with God that empower loving horizontal relationships with others. The story of BnF is thus more than a series of isolated interaction rituals. It is a way of life that illustrates Sorokin's "active ideationalist culture"—one that is antithetical to the dominant sensate culture of the American dream. It is a culture that strives "to convert others to a vision of God and ultimate reality" (Johnston 2006, 146). BnF's "ideationalist culture" is attractive to those who follow David's vision, which rejects the materialist and sensate American dream in favor of a spiritual walk promising to usher in the Kingdom of God.

The culture of BnF, with its neo-Pentecostal vision and practices, thus provides a milieu in which divine-human interaction is normative. Research on prayer has shown experiences of the divine to be commonplace; surveys have found that a clear majority of respondents say that they "hear from God" in prayer, at least on occasion (Poloma and Gallup 1991; Poloma and Pendleton 1991). Blood-n-Fire provides a milieu in which divine-human interaction is encouraged as part of the lived experience of community life. This was not only true for David, but also for all the major voices in the BnF story.

David's prophetic experiences and teachings created the community and the culture that encouraged followers to listen for the voice of God. Those we interviewed—active followers, board members, as well as homeless addicts—all had stories to share in which they told of hearing from God. Many came to BnF already aware of a God who walked and talked with them; others learned to hear the divine voice through community interaction rituals; but nearly all seemed to find BnF to be a place was God was active in a special way. While it remains outside the parameters of social science to determine whether God was in fact speaking, the narratives do attest to the emotion energy linked with such encounters—EE that energized human interaction rituals and the development of interaction ritual chains—especially for those in the BnF family.

Godly love implies that the vertical relationship with the divine will have effects on daily life. Despite inevitable human frailties, David's vision of a relational family church did take root in his disciples. The BnF members we interviewed during the first year of the study unequivocally cherished the depth of relationships they found at BnF. Although many said that being "family" was not easy, it was highly valued. The poor who identified with the BnF family also valued family-like relationships. Those living in the Sanctuary formed them with each other, as did the men in the Training Program. Any relational ties of the poor and homeless with David and his inner circle, however, were weak at best. As we have demonstrated, despite David's attack on the American dream, BnF culture was largely one that appealed to white middle-class followers and not the poor.

We observed a common disjuncture in the BnF interaction chains between David and his followers, including the homeless. David functions best as a prophet of God; for him, human relationships are always secondary. In David's mind, as he told us on many occasions, it is a matter of choosing "God rather than man." While on the surface it appeared that David had collaborators in his visionary journey, such relationships were judged by us to be of short duration, as can be illustrated the following recent account from a BnF International leader.

Mike, together with his wife, Roxy, had journeyed with David at BnF Atlanta for nearly ten years before leaving (as we began our research in 2003) to establish a BnF in Minneapolis. As our study progressed, we began to see that Mike and other leaders of BnF Internationals were potentially close collaborators who were often perceived by David to be weak links. Despite the solidarity with David that all of the BnF International leaders demonstrated during the schism, a closer examination of David's reports and of their personal accounts raised questions about the intensity and duration of these relationships. The leaders all cherished David's vision, but most seemed to find less intense interaction provided by geographic distance preferable for maintaining a relationship with him. Despite the umbrella of the BnF name, it seemed that international leaders were commonly in the dark about David's latest vision or sometimes-bizarre actions. An example of the distance David kept from these collaborators is found in a recent reported interaction between David and Mike. Debbie, a woman who left BnF with her husband, Eric, during the schism, had photographed the demolition going on at the Warehouse. These photos soon circulated among ex-members via e-mail. One photo was sent to Mike, who in turn contacted Debbie. She reported to Margaret that he was quite upset that David had never told him that the Warehouse was being torn down and the ministry to the poor abandoned. Based on what we have observed, this breakdown in communication with supposed collaborators was not atypical. We believe that a major problem for producing successful interaction ritual chains at BnF is due to David's failure to establish and maintain close relationships with potential collaborators—men and women he could trust to help him discern the prophecies he believes he has been given.

David's relationships with collaborators, disciples, and especially the poor at BnF all proved to be of low-to-moderate intensity and of short duration. We documented numerous replacements as David chose those whom he felt could best aid him in implementing his vision, only to discard the relationship when the vision shifted. He often demonstrated an intensity of love for his closest followers, especially as they joined in his passion for what God was revealing, but it was difficult to remain a close follower of David. Those who left BnF came to doubt that David was in fact a prophet who heard from God. Prophets are scorned by some and accepted by others; such is true at BnF. Some would come to see David as more concerned with self-aggrandizement than with humbly transmitting God's vision for the Kingdom and for the poor

While David's visions of godly love, as we have seen, have often been about the poor, they seldom have attracted followers among the poor. BnF, despite seeking to create a culture that would successfully challenge the American dream with the coming Kingdom of God, failed to make full citizens of the poor, the homeless, and the addicts. For most of the poor, BnF was simply a homeless shelter. Many were nourished and enjoyed a temporary respite, but lives were generally not transformed. Ironically, most of the stories of transformation were reported not by the poor, but by past and present followers of David who heard the call to follow David's vision.

In terms of the adequacy of love, David's vision regarding the poor and their central place in God's plan for taking Atlanta became a means to express a displaced love. The poor could no more receive unconditional love than David could provide it. Our own view is that unconditional love was most approximated at BnF during David's sabbatical leave. If so, there is an irony in that it was the dissidents at BnF who best implemented David's concern for drawing the poor into relationships with the rich. As a prophet in abstentia, David's vision for the poor, often eloquently preached, became most fulfilled for a few months in the Sanctuary at BnF that is no more.

Appendix A

Margaret Poloma's Reflections
on a Research Journey

I had been deep into research on the so-called Toronto Bless-ing, an epicenter for the global revivals that were sweeping through Pen-tecostal and neo-Pentecostal congregations in the mid-1990s, when I first learned about Blood-n-Fire. Churches that received the "blessing" were reporting a resurgence of phenomenal "signs and wonders"—strange physical manifestations, prophecies, healing, and miracles—as the millen-nium was drawing to a close (Poloma 2003). It was at the Toronto Airport Christian Fellowship that I met Jose Ortega-Bettancourt, a Cuban Ameri-can pastor who was weary of middle-class revivals that were oblivious to the social ills plaguing the larger world. Soon after we met he visited BnF and was excited about what he saw. Ortega invited me to meet him in At-lanta to observe for myself what was happening in this "urban church of the poor" that walked in the "supernatural." At first I dismissed his invita-tion, but my curiosity intensified. I finally agreed to make the trip to see for myself what so excited him.

It was about that time I came across an article featuring BnF in *Voice of the Vineyard,* a publication of the Association of Vineyard Churches (the denomination with which BnF was affiliated), that described the founder David VanCronkhite's strategy for and commitment to serving Atlanta's poor: "Our understanding of church is taking it out to where the people are. That's our heart" (Bogart 1997). VanCronkhite was clearly among a small but growing number of church leaders who were challenging con-servative Christians to step out of the safety of suburbia and become in-volved with the poor, the homeless, and the addicted.

My initial encounter with VanCronkhite was through Ortega. We met at a Cuban restaurant in Atlanta together with Gray Temple, an Episcopal priest (the former pastor of one of my graduate students) who was actively involved in gay and lesbian rights as well as with the cause of the homeless in Atlanta. Although I initially felt that inviting Temple to join VanCronkhite and Ortega (both of whom were involved in conservative denominations that were less than sympathetic to anyone advocating gay marriage or ordination) might be a recipe for disaster, the lunch together was memorable and spiritually uplifting. VanCronkhite, a vivacious man who looked younger than his fifty years, took the lead, sharing his vision of the Kingdom of God and the pivotal role of the poor and homeless. Even Temple's volunteering information about his role in the struggle for gay rights in the Episcopal Church could not dampen the contagious enthusiasm that permeated the meeting. Temple indicated that his beliefs resonated with BnF's vision but that it probably would not be wise for VanCronkhite to team up with him; the latter responded, "I am not here to judge anyone. I know that God has brought us together—and we have work to do! How about we pray?" There in a Cuban restaurant we clasped hands around the table as David led us in prayer. The presence of the Spirit seemed palpable. I would later record in my journal, "I felt as if I were on holy ground."

My first meeting with VanCronkhite and Ortega left me impressed with the man and the ministry. In my experience, bringing up the issue of gay rights generally brought about argumentative retorts supported with select Bible passages, not a call to intimately shared prayer. Moreover, the personal spiritual therapeutic focus of much of the middle-class American revival currently under way placed little emphasis on the cause of the poor in North America. While short-term mission trips to developing nations where revival fires were burning was encouraged by some renewal leaders, little was said by most about the plight of the poor in American cities. VanCronkhite was different. His charismatic piety was reflected not only in his sprinkling of glossolalic prayer or "praying in tongues" into seemingly secular conversations, but also in his encouraging others to "walk in the supernatural," expecting to be an instrument of healing and prophetic words. I was intrigued enough with VanCronkhite and his unusual ministry to return to Atlanta for two other events that summer. I attended a general revival conference in August where I again met with Ortega, Temple, and VanCronkhite. My next trip occurred a short month later when I attended a BnF-sponsored conference on the urban poor. VanCronkhite described the gathering in the conference brochure as follows: "Blood-n-Fire invites you to 'If I Have Withheld.' You will hear from gifted men and women leading the restoration of our cities and then be able to put into practice what was heard and imparted. Come prepared to be spiritually 'ruined' for life. Truly a life changing experience. Focus will be on *Compassion* for the *Poor* and the *Father's Heart*."

One of the speakers was Jackie Pullinger, a missionary who for over two decades had worked with the poorest of the poor in Hong Kong. Unlike many charismatic or neo-Pentecostal conference speakers, Pullinger challenged rather than comforted. In the midst of a revival that focused first on "feeling God" through paranormal "signs and wonders" and then on "saving souls," Pullinger combined the belief and practice of the "miraculous" with a biblical perspective, calling for an active involvement in the plight of the poor. Statements like, "How rude to go after people just for their souls! You go on loving people whether they believe in Jesus or not. You love them simply because he died for them just as he died for you," would leave many Evangelicals speechless, convinced that Pullinger was carrying things to an extreme. Others, like VanCronkhite, who called Pullinger his "spiritual father," were refreshed and challenged by her spiritual insight and commitment.

Over the next four years I would return periodically to Atlanta to stay connected with what was happening at BnF. On two occasions Van-Cronkhite came to Akron, Ohio, where I lived and where a minister of a new Vineyard church plant was considering making his church an affiliate of BnF. That never came to be, but VanCronkhite did bring his message and ministry to a conference sponsored by that congregation, and I was able to observe him, the reception of his message, and the "signs and wonders" in action on my home turf. During these early years of contact with BnF, I gave at most only passing thought to doing research on the ministry, regarding it more of an encounter for personal spiritual challenge than a research opportunity.

In 2002 a call went out from the Templeton Foundation, sponsored Institute for Unlimited Love, for research proposals on "unlimited love." I immediately thought of BnF as a potential research site. I proposed to do a systematic study of what we are now calling godly love, exploring the relationship between perceived charismatic encounters with God, sacrificial giving of personal dreams and ambitions, and empowerment for service to the poor and broken. During our ongoing if intermittent contact, VanCronkhite and I had developed a seemingly good relationship, to the point of his insisting that I was part of the BnF family. When I inquired about the possibility of doing systematic research on BnF to study the relationship between the charismatic gifts of the Spirit and love, Van-Cronkhite responded, "We are ready for you, Margaret. Come right on."

After securing a promise of cooperation from VanCronkhite, I approached psychologist of religion Ralph W. Hood Jr. as a possible collaborator. I knew that my involvement at BnF was to this point more that of a pilgrim than a scholar, and I sought a suitable colleague to balance my personal involvement with a more detached perspective. Ralph had been involved in the story of Pentecostals in Appalachia who include in their experience of the signs and wonders the handling of serpents and the drinking of deadly poisons. While Ralph's study of serpent handlers had included participant observation over a period of fifteen years, he also is widely known for measurement-based empirical research in the psychology of religion. Ralph remained less of a participant observer at BnF and more of a detached observer than me, with the costs and benefits that go with each observer role. (Perhaps this is best illustrated by my active involvement in prayer and ritual—singing, dancing, responding to prayer initiatives, receiving prophecies—while Ralph would often stand in the back or stroll around the room observing the religious ritual from different vantage points.) Once a collaborator in this work, he also had designed a longitudinal, quasi-experimental study based on what at that time was a programmatic one-year program at BnF for transforming homeless street addicts into committed Christians and teaching them skills that would assure employment. This methodology, as well as other quantitative and qualitative methods that evolved as we continued to study BnF through its many shifting visions, is presented in Appendix B.

Much of our research involved in-depth taped interviews with active community members, sometimes conducted by myself or in tandem with Ralph but more often conducted alone. I developed an ongoing relation with a number of interviewees, which opened the door for many additional repeat interviews throughout the study; these follow-up interviews were conducted in person, through telephone conversations, and via e-mails, and they continue to the time of this writing. It is fair to say that if my focus was more on the believing members of this emerging church, Ralph's primary focus was on what was happening with the homeless. When a serious schism at BnF began to brew, I openly retained cordial relationships with friends I had made on both sides of the divide. Although I made every effort to assume the stance of a neutral researcher, I knew that I had been captivated by what I initially observed at BnF and by VanCronkhite's charisma and vision. I was personally troubled by its unraveling, and without Ralph it would have been tempting to abandon the project. Ralph had never accepted the validity of David VanCronkhite's vision with respect to its concern for the poor, but he was intrigued by the possibility of studying a faith-based program that claimed it could rehabilitate inner-city crack addicts. By the time of the schism it became clear that is was impossible to carry out the original research design of a longitudinal tracking of addicts as they went through BnF's Program. The Program itself soon collapsed.

The differences in involvement and perspective between Ralph and me undoubtedly strengthened our project. Our complementary disciplines, mine as a sociologist and Ralph's as a psychologist, served further to sharpen our observations and assessments. The common ground we shared as social scientists and ethnographers enabled us to work as a team using the research tools of the trade. As a fully involved participant observer I found myself doing much emotional work to balance affective care and concern with a detached analytic stance. As the BnF story unfolded, I shared in the pain of community members on both sides of the schism who had come to regard me as family. Although I stood with Ralph as a researcher who sought the facts that would advance the insights of social science, it was not always easy or perhaps even desirable to hide behind this façade. We were surrounded by research subjects—BnF members, the homeless men and women who were beneficiaries of the ministry, board members—who openly shared their hopes and dreams with us. At times developments left me disappointed, sad, or even angry, responses that could be shared with Ralph and put into perspective.

Ralph insisted that we had a story that needed to be told, despite its being for both of us a sad ending to a promising experiment. It is Ralph who suggested that we use a technique used by Thomas Burton (2004) in his report on Glen Summerford, an Appalachian serpent handler convicted for the attempted murder of his wife, to present our data. Burton allowed persons within and outside the serpent handling tradition, as well as Glen and his wife, to tell their own stories. He provided no overarching meta-narrative within which the numerous narratives told could be absorbed. In this sense, Burton and we accept what for many is a post-modern claim, that no narrative is more privileged or more foundational than any other. Narratives are to be explored, bounced off one another, and left to tell a never ending and impossible to complete single grand narrative. This strategy enabled us to sort out personal emotional reactions from the accounts that we secured from the different voices that we used to tell the BnF story. It also freed us from the burden of some kind of final assessment or judgment. While we do not judge BnF from the stance of any grand narrative, we do present and evaluate specific claims made by BnF with empirical observations found in the data.

I must confess that this book was the most difficult work I have ever written, having to deal with my own disappointment, sadness, and even grief while presenting and processing the various interviews. Ralph confesses to less emotional involvement. He remains committed to a refusal to accept one grand narrative that reveals a singular truth about BnF. Yet, like me, he is saddened by some claims that are clearly falsifiable with respect to BnF's promise to transform the lives of the homeless, especially inner-city African Americans addicted to crack cocaine. Despite the demise of the community as we knew it, lives have been transformed at BnF. Through stories of personal renewal and revival, many of which have been presented in the body of this text, we too have experienced the transforming power of godly love.

Appendix B

Methodological Appendix, with Survey
Instrument (B-1) and Scale Construction (B-2)

Methodological Narrative

Although the journey toward a study of BnF began nearly five years earlier (see appendix A), the formal project can be dated back a letter of intent sent to the Institute for Research on Unlimited Love (IRUL) in response to a request for proposals (RFP) in 2002. In it we listed our research aims, which demonstrated the relevance of the proposed project in accordance with the IRUL guidelines found in the RFP. The research goals included the following:

1. To explore how spiritual moments (i.e., Spirit baptism and ongoing infilling of the Spirit) affect loving motivation and behavior.
2. To examine the complex sociological and social-psychological conditions that foster other-regarding virtues and behavior for BnF volunteers.
3. To assess how the positive emotions generated by P/C religious experiences affect radical commitment to social action.
4. To assess how the "other-regarding virtues" (i.e., caregiving love) expressed by the volunteers were learned and promoted by those being served through BnF.
5. To explore "the motivations behind other-regarding virtues" found in the volunteers at BnF.

In this research project, entitled "Charisma and Empowerment: Assessing the Effects of the Gifts of the Spirit on Unlimited Love," we proposed to use a triangulated design (Denzin 1989a, 1989b) that employed the tools of sociology and psychology. The focus of the study was on the social context and dynamic process of godly love, specifically on experiences of the love of God that energize other-regarding acts of human love. We proposed a triangulation of methodologies (including observation, interviews, surveys, and psychological assessments) and observers (sociologist and psychologist) to carry out our general goals. At the heart of the project was an ethnographic study of Blood-n-Fire with narratives to describe the social context in which godly love was experienced and the spiritual gifts (charismata) were exercised, qualitative data that would be used to generate quantitative research instruments.

The first year of the proposed two-year longitudinal study was designed to be largely ethnographic, using the qualitative data collected through observation and open-ended interviews to create instruments to assess godly love within the extended BnF community during the second year of the project. A particular point of focus for the second year was BnF's Training Program where we proposed to use psychological test scales and questionnaires to assess the efficacy of godly love for rehabilitating homeless addicts. While the first year of the project was to be directed largely to qualitative data collection from the Atlanta BnF family and ministry, we planned for the second year to collect quantitative data from the International BnFs together with a longitudinal quantitative assessment of homeless addicts as they moved through the nine-month program.

Ideal Methods and Real Situations

As seasoned field researchers we were aware of how the reality of the research site often forces modification of textbook methodologies. We were less prepared for the finding that our initial site visit offered a version of the Training Program that never in fact operated as described in the manuals. (One leader would later confess that she was reluctant to see us begin the evaluation project; she feared that we would soon discover the chinks in the much-touted program.) Six months into our study, David VanCronkhite took an unexpected "sabbatical," in reality a five-month-long mental health leave to recover from clinically diagnosed depression. We observed the development of a more structured Training Program in his absence that temporarily sustained our plan to carry out a longitudinal study of homeless drug addicts. This hope was finally dashed when VanCronkhite regained absolute control of both the BnF church and the family business. The schism and its aftermath, resulting in a dramatic restructuring and then dismantling of the drug program, would finally destroy any hope we had of executing a quasi-experimental study of the BnF ministry to homeless addicts.

While the effects of godly love generated by experiences of the divine continued to be our focus as 2003 gave way to 2004, the dissention within the community forced other important changes in the research design. We dropped our plans to visit other BnF sites to observe the unfolding changes in Atlanta, as we continued to observe how godly love would fare in the aftermath of the schism. The BnF board of directors now became important players in the unfolding schism in Atlanta, as did the leaders of the dozen or so BnFs in other locations who supported David Van-Cronkhite's return to power. By this time we had gradually become aware that BnF International was not in fact the network presented during our initial site visit. Although the ministries in most cases appeared impressive (though limited), extensive quantitative analysis of surveys to compare and contrast the BnFs was not feasible in ministries that had but a handful of volunteers at best.

Margaret spent much of 2003 conducting, transcribing, and analyzing interviews—supplemental interviews with fifty-two family members already in our study and first interviews with board members and with the International BnF leaders. In addition to formal interviews that were tape recorded and transcribed, an average of five hours per week was spent with community members in telephone conversations and e-mails exchanges as we tracked varying twists and turns of the schism. The ever-changing BnF Web site was also a marker for us of important changes in the functioning of the church and the family business. Ralph and his graduate students continued to tape interviews with men in the new Training Program and homeless residents of the Sanctuary. They also continued to hang out with the homeless to engage in informal dialogue with them during site visits to BnF.

By the end of 2004 when the study was scheduled for completion, David declared that the old BnF was dead and a new one was being birthed. We knew our study needed to continue for an undetermined time after the deadline until we could discern a decisive outcome of the struggle. Of particular interest was the emergence of a "new" BnF and the resolution of the dispute over the ownership of the warehouse properties. As it turned out, we monitored developments for three more years through occasional site visits, phone calls, and e-mails with family members who remained, as well as others who had left, and we also monitored the BnF Web site.

Margaret participated in a total of eighteen site visits from 2003 to 2007, most lasting from three to five days. During the first two years of the study Ralph or Chris or both met with Margaret whenever possible. During at least four of the site visits, Ralph and Margaret met jointly to talk with David and other BnF family members. Ralph and Chris, sometimes accompanied by other graduate students, also visited BnF on several occasions when Margaret was not there. By having both joint and independent visits to BnF we were able to have a broader base than would have been possible if we relied only on joint visits.

In a concluding section of our original proposal we wrote about our research strategy, noting how BnF was a vital community that had changed considerably during the five years that Margaret had informally monitored it. We called for "a flexible research protocol to monitor such change . . . one that could balance the study of a creative organization with the structure of surveys amenable to statistical testing." Little did we know that a seismic change would destroy BnF as we first encountered it. Without the flexibility inherent in field research, however, we would never have been able to pursue the unforeseen developments or to obtain the data we eventually gathered during this unique study of godly love.

A Survey Assessment of Godly Love

Although the proposed surveys for assessing the Training Program and Blood-n-Fire Internationals were aborted, we did conduct two surveys that have been woven into our narrative. The questionnaire (appendix B-1) was developed after ten months of participant observation and open-ended interviews with family members and their homeless clients. The surveys, conducted in January 2004, were administered by Margaret to the family members after one of the sessions of the annual family gathering, netting a sample of 88 completed surveys. Another 17 were collected from dissidents who elected not to attend the gathering for a total of 105 family respondents. Ralph and his graduate students administered the same survey to 117 homeless residents of the shelter. Results were used in the text to provide additional statistical data to describe BnF as well as for a statistical assessment of our thesis about godly love.

A copy of the survey instruments follows in appendix B-1; details on the composition of the scales used in statistical analyses can be found in appendix B-2. Significant statistical findings are presented in appendix C.

Appendix B-1
Survey Instrument

Blood-n-Fire Questionnaire

General Information and Instructions

As most of you know, I have been involved in a sociological research project at BnF for over a year in a study of "unlimited" love. Many of you have already talked at length with me and shared your stories, and I thank you for participating in the interview phase of the study. In order to collect comparable information from all BnF members, I have developed this questionnaire (based on these interviews and other general observations). I am asking each of you (even those whom I have interviewed) to respond to these questions to the best of your ability. Your individual responses will be held in strictest confidence, with only a collective report (in which you will not be identified) being presented to BnF leaders.

If you have any questions about what I am doing, feel free to contact me or one of the BnF leaders. I very much appreciate your willingness to participate in this important project.

Margaret M. Poloma, PhD

General Background Information

1. I am a member of:
   ____ BnF—Atlanta
   ____ BnF—Other _____ (please specify)
   ____ I do not consider myself a member of BnF

2. Number of years with BnF: _____

3. Are you involved with the BnF "Compassion Ministry" (shelter, public meals, Training Program)?

_____ Yes, full time with BnF

_____ Yes, Sanctuary resident

_____ Yes, client in the Training Program

_____ Yes, approximately half to three-quarters time

_____ Yes, less than one quarter of my time is spent with BnF

_____ No, at present I am not involved with BnF ministries

4. Which best describes where you live?

___ in the Sanctuary

___ in the Warehouse

___ very near to BnF

___ more than fifteen minutes away from BnF

___ outside Atlanta

5. Age: _____

6. Sex:

(1) _____ Male

(2) _____ Female

7. Race or Ethnicity:

(1) ___ Black

(2) ___ White

(3) ___ Biracial

(4) ___ Hispanic

(5) Other _____ (please specify)

8. Which best describes the level of education you have completed?

(1) ____ less than high school

(2) ____ high school graduate

(3) ____ vocational training

(4) ____ some college

(5) ____ college graduate

(6) ___ post college

9. What is your current marital status?
   (1) ___ single
   (2) ___ engaged
   (3) ___ divorced/separated
   (4) ___ married
   (5) ___ widowed

10. Which of the following best describes your religious background
    (before the age of eighteen)?
    (1) ___ Pentecostal-Charismatic
    (2) ___ Evangelical Protestant
    (3) ___ Baptist
    (4) ___ African American Protestant
    (5) ___ Mainstream Protestant (e.g., Methodist, Lutheran,
        Episcopalian, etc.)
    (6) ___ Catholic
    (7) ___ None
    (8) ___ Other _____ (please specify)

11. How much contact did you have with the poor before coming to BnF?
    (1) ___ no real contact
    (2) ___ some limited contact
    (3) ___ moderate contact
    (4) ___ considerable contact
    (5) ___ I grew up poor

12. How much contact did you have with addicts before coming to BnF?
    (1) ___ no real contact
    (2) ___ some limited contact
    (3) ___ moderate contact
    (4) ___ considerable contact
    (5) ___ I was/am an addict

13. How much contact did you have with ex-convicts before coming to BnF?
    (1)___ no real contact
    (2)___ some limited contact
    (3)___ moderate contact
    (4)___ considerable contact
    (5)___ I am an ex-convict

14. How much contact did you have with street people before coming to BnF?
  (1)____ no real contact
  (2)____ some limited contact
  (3)____ moderate contact
  (4)____ considerable contact
  (5)____ I am/was a street person

15. How much contact did you have with blacks before coming to BnF?
  (1)____ no real contact
  (2)____ some limited contact
  (3)____ moderate contact
  (4)____ considerable contact
  (5)____ I am black

16. How much contact did you have with whites before coming to BnF?
  (1) ____ no real contact
  (2) ____ some limited contact
  (3) ____ moderate contact
  (4) ____ considerable contact
  (5) ____ I am white

17. In a typical month, approximately what percentage of your personal finances come from each of the following sources?
  (1) paid employment outside BnF ____%
  (2) BnF's "family business" ____%
  (3) pledged support from family, friends, etc. ____%
  (4) personal assets and savings ____%
  (5) prayed in by faith ____%
  (6) other (specify) _____ ____%

The following three questions have to do with speaking or praying in tongues.

18. How often do you speak (pray) in tongues?
  (1) ____ I do not pray in tongues
  (2) ____ I used to pray in tongues but no longer do so
  (3) ____ I sometimes pray in tongues
  (4) ____ I pray in tongues at least weekly
  (5) ____ I pray in tongues at least daily
  (6) ____ I try to pray in tongues as often as I possibly can

19. Which of the following responses best describes your experience with praying in tongues?

    (1) ____ I spoke in tongues *before* coming to BnF,
        but it was *not* particularly meaningful

    (2) ____ I began to speak in tongues *after* coming to BnF,
        but it is *not* particularly meaningful

    (3) ____ I first spoke in tongues *before* coming to BnF,
        and it is *very* meaningful

    (4) ____ I first spoke in tongues *after* coming to BnF,
        and it is *very* meaningful

    (5) ____ I do not pray in tongues

20. How do you use the gift of tongues? (check as many as apply)

    ____ to worship God

    ____ to intercede for others

    ____ to sing praises to God

    ____ to edify, encourage, or build up myself

    ____ as spiritual warfare against demonic spirits

    ____ to hear God speak to me

    ____ to thank God for blessing

    ____ to call on God's protection

    ____ to grow closer to God

    ____ to experience the peace and joy of God

    ____ other _____ (please specify)

    ____ I do not speak in tongues on a regular basis

We are interested in how often you have other experiences of God. *Please circle* the number (1 through 5) that best corresponds to your experience of each item. The answers range from 1=never; 2=occasionally; 3=moderately; 4=often; 5=very often.

    1 = never
    2 = sometimes
    3 = moderately
    4 = often
    5 = very often

21. Prophetic words for another person
22. Prophecies from another person
23. A divine call to perform some specific act

24. God supernaturally providing finances
25. Divine revelation into future events
26. Divine healing of physical illness
27. God healing another person through your prayer
28. Personal inner or emotional healing
29. An experience of God in a way that escapes words of testimony
30. God's special protection from evil
31. Everything seeming to disappear except consciousness of God.
32. Your own self merging with God
33. An experience with God in which you lost awareness of time and things around you
34. An experience of God that no words could possibly express.

Using the same five-point scale with 1=never and 5=very often, describe how do you hear God speaking to you? Please circle the answer of your choice.

1 = never
2 = sometimes
3 = moderately
4 = often
5 = very often

35. During personal prayer
36. During corporate worship
37. Through journaling
38. In visions and dreams
39. Through leaders in authority
40. Through reading the Bible
41. Through family and friends
42. In ordinary daily living
43. Through nature
44. Through ministry with the poor
45. Through thoughts in my head
46. Other (please specify) _____

Continuing to use this same scale, how would you describe some ways you may experience God's love?

47. Through a deep sense of peace
48. Through bodily or physical sensation

49. Through miraculous provision for my needs
50. In visions and dreams
51. Through leaders in authority
52. Through reading the Bible
53. Through family and friends
54. In ordinary daily living
55. Through nature, art, and/or music
56. Through ministry with the poor
57. Through thoughts in my head
58. Other (please specify) _____

59. How would you *best* describe the coming Kingdom of God?
    (check no more than three)
    _____ as a perfect world
    _____ as walking in the supernatural gifts of the Spirit
    _____ as righteousness, peace, and joy
    _____ as personally growing closer to God
    _____ as living out one's personal destiny
    _____ as justice for the poor

The following statements represent some beliefs and opinions you may have. Please circle the number that best corresponds with how strongly you feel about the statement. The answers range from 1=strongly agree to 5=strongly disagree. Please circle the number (1 through 5) that best corresponds to what you think about the statement.

   1 = strongly agree
   2 = agree
   3 = neutral—no opinion
   4 = disagree
   5 = strongly disagree

PART 1.

60. It is important for me to be walking in the supernatural.
61. I have never felt Jesus withdraw his love from me.
62. I feel that some things are not Jesus's concern at all.
63. All of life exists by means of Jesus's love
64. Sometimes I feel that Jesus has abandoned me.
65. Jesus never withdraws his love from anybody in this world.

66. Jesus condemns those he does not love.
67. Love of Jesus cannot keep us from loving others.
68. I do not know what true love is because I have never experienced Jesus's love in my own life.
69. Jesus does not necessarily always love everyone.
70. When I do not feel loving towards others, it is because I feel that Jesus does not love them.
71. I have felt Jesus's love as the greatest power in the universe.
72. Jesus loves me only when I love other people.

PART 2. CONTINUE USING THE SAME RESPONSE SCALE.

73. Developing relationships with the poor is required of all Christians.
74. Political action is not a God-ordained way to bring justice for the poor.
75. It is *not* necessary for all Christians to be personally involved with the poor.
76. The only way the poor and homeless can come to know the love of God is through loving relationships.
77. Most Christians can fulfill the biblical mandate to care for the poor by giving financial support.
78. I know that I must have relationship with the poor in order to live out my calling as a Christian.
79. In general the poor and the homeless are reaping what they have sowed. I really don't understand how anyone can be homeless.
80. The poor and homeless do not deserve help if they refuse try to help themselves.
81. I feel sad when I am uncaring toward someone in need.
82. I am learning to love the poor simply as they are without any expectations on my part.
83. I cannot truly love a person who does not show some gratitude.
84. Sometimes I find myself feeling deep distress over the unmet needs of the poor.
85. Serving the poor and homeless gives me great joy.
86. I usually find it easy to forgive the poor when they hurt or offend me.
87. I feel I need the poor as much as or more than they need me.
88. I have tried my best to respond to the needs of the poor.
89. There are times that I have given away things I needed to help someone in need.
90. God expects us to take a balanced approach that includes taking care of my needs before giving to the poor.
91. I am willing to put myself in danger if it means helping someone in need.

92. Whether at BnF or elsewhere, I will always try to have personal relationships with the poor.

We would like to conclude by asking about your level of satisfaction or dissatisfaction with some things in your life. With 1 being very dissatisfied and 7 being very satisfied, select a number that best indicates how satisfied you are with each of the following. Circle your answer.

	Dissatisfied					Satisfied	
Relations with your biological family	1	2	3	4	5	6	7
Your sense of personal well-being	1	2	3	4	5	6	7
Your relationship with God	1	2	3	4	5	6	7
Your relationships with the poor	1	2	3	4	5	6	7
Your prayer life	1	2	3	4	5	6	7
Corporate worship	1	2	3	4	5	6	7
Your financial situation	1	2	3	4	5	6	7
Relationships within BnF	1	2	3	4	5	6	7
Friends outside the BnF family	1	2	3	4	5	6	7
Your work or employment	1	2	3	4	5	6	7
Your ministry with BnF	1	2	3	4	5	6	7
Your physical health	1	2	3	4	5	6	7
Your present marital status	1	2	3	4	5	6	7
Your sense of personal destiny	1	2	3	4	5	6	7
The place where you live	1	2	3	4	5	6	7
The people with whom you live	1	2	3	4	5	6	7
Relationships with your "Twelve"	1	2	3	4	5	6	7

If there is anything else you might wish to add, please feel free to do so in the space below.

(Optional) We would appreciate it if you would print your name below. It would enable us to match up the interviews with this survey information to help interpret the responses. All information obtained through this survey will be presented only in statistical format that uses all respondents. The identity of individual respondents will never be revealed without written consent.

Appendix B-2
Scale Construction

Altruism Scale (Cronbach's Alpha = .78)

- I have tried my best to respond to the needs of others
- I am willing to put myself in danger to help someone in need
- I have given away things I needed to help the poor
- I try to have relationships that include the poor

Charismatic Experience Scale (Cronbach's Alpha = .84)

- Divine healing from a physical illness
- Given a private prophecy
- Received a personal revelation from another person
- Heard a divine call to perform some specific act

Mysticism Scale (Cronbach's Alpha = .78)

- An experience of God in which you lost awareness of time and things
- Everything seemed to disappear but the consciousness of God
- Your own self merging with God
- An experience of God that no words could express

Conditional Divine Love (Cronbach's Alpha = .78)

- Sometimes I feel that Jesus has abandoned me
- Jesus condemns those he does not love
- I do not know what true love is because I have never experiences Jesus's love
- Jesus loves me only when I love other people

Judgmental Perception (Cronbach's Alpha = .74)

- The poor and homeless do not deserve help if they refuse to try to help themselves
- I really don't understand how anyone can be homeless
- In general the poor and the homeless are reaping what they have sowed
- I cannot truly love a person who does not show some gratitude

Empathy (Cronbach's Alpha = .68)

- Sometimes I find myself feeling deep distress over the unmet needs of the poor
- Serving the poor gives me great joy
- I feel I need the poor as much as or more than they need me
- I feel sad when I am uncaring toward someone in need

Appendix C

Statistical Appendix, with Bivariate Matrix (C-1) and Multivariate Analysis (C-2)

The correlation matrix following in C-1 uses select variables and scales constructed from item responses in the survey to assess a core question found in the research proposal, namely, do "spiritual moments (i.e., Spirit baptism and ongoing infilling of the Spirit) affect loving motivation and behavior." In addition to demographic items, we used responses to questions about the charismata and mystical experiences, perception of God, satisfaction with relationship with God, empathic motivation, and reported care-love behavior, particularly for the poor. The numbers presented in the correlation matrix are decimals; the higher the number, the stronger the correlation between the two variables; "ns" indicates that the relationship was not statistically significant (probability level was greater than .001).

We wish to note a few important findings to assist the reader in exploring the wealth of information found in the correlation matrix. In following the first row ("Sanctuary/BnF") horizontally across the table, the differences reported in chapter 6 between the homeless and family members are documented. The homeless, when compared with family members, tend to be African American (r=-.56), older (r=-.25), male (r=-.19), and less educated (r=.32). They are less likely to value walking in the supernatural (r=-.28) and to report being satisfied with their relationship to God (r=-.33); they are less likely to pray in tongues (r=.10), but more likely to experience divine healing (r=-18) and to score higher on a general mysticism scale (r=-.31). They are also more likely to perceive God as a conditional lover (r=-28) and to be harsher in their judgment of homeless addicts (r=-33). Of greatest importance to our assessment of the outcome measures of empathic motivation and altruistic behavior in appendix C-2, there are no bivariate statistical differences between the two groups in empathy and altruism scores.

With the data presented in C-1, other questions can be explored. For example, the charismata and the mysticism scales demonstrate a strong bivariate relationship (r=.61). Glossolalia or tongues is related to the charismata (r=.27) but not to mysticism. The charismata scale also demonstrates a strong relationship to personal experiences of healing (r=.69) and being used in the divine healing of others (r=.68). Mysticism is also related to divine healing, but the correlations are more moderate (r=.45 and r=.48). Important to our central question about the relationship between spiritual experiences and empathy and altruism, with the noteworthy exception of tongues, all of our spirituality measures have significant bivariate relationships with the two outcome measures. In one sense these findings raise as many questions as they answer. The variables seem to be intertwined into a finely woven strand that makes it difficult to determine whether it is valuing the supernatural, being satisfied with one's relationship to God, experiencing the charismata and healing, or general mysticism that actually affects the differences in empathy and altruism scores.

We will attempt to unravel the threads through a statistical procedure known as multivariate analysis, which explores the interrelationship of select variables from the bivariate analysis just presented. The results of these statistical equations are found in appendix C-2.

Appendix C-1 Bivariate Matrix

	1	2	3	4	5	6	7	8	9	10	11	12	13	14	15	16
1 Sanct./BnF	1	-56	-25	-19	32	28	-17	-28	-33	48	ns	-18	-18	-31	ns	ns
2 Race		1	15	-16	-30	-29	ns	ns	ns	-33	ns	ns	ns	24	ns	ns
3 Age			1	ns	15	ns	19	ns	ns	ns	ns	ns	ns	16	16	ns
4 Sex				1	19	ns	ns	ns	ns	ns	ns	ns	ns	ns	ns	ns
5 Educ.					1	15	ns	-25	-22	20	ns	ns	ns	ns	ns	ns
6 Walk Super.						1	ns	ns	ns	43	23	ns	ns	ns	24	32
7 Rel. God							1	ns	ns	ns	34	35	29	36	18	29
8 Con. Love								1	46	-24	-21	-15	ns	ns	-22	-18
9 Judg. Per.									1	ns	ns	ns	ns	ns	ns	ns
10 Tongues										1	27	ns	16	61	ns	41
11 Charismata											1	69	68	45	36	29
12 Heal Self												1	55	61	25	19
13 Heal Others													1	48	17	40
14 Mysticism														1	28	73
15 Empathy															1	73
16 Altruism																1

*Coefficients are reported only for statistically significant relationships; ns=not significant.

1 Sanctuary/BnF—dummy coded: Sanctuary=0; BnF family=1

2 Race: white=0; black=1

3 Age: chronological numbering.

4 Sex: male=0; female=1

5 Education: less than high school through post-college.

6 "It is important for me to be walking in the supernatural": strongly disagree=1 through strongly agree=5

7 "How satisfied are you with your relationship with God?": very dissatisfied=1 through very satisfied=7

8 "Conditional divine love" (see B-2): high score indicates conditional (rather than unconditional) love

9 "Judgmental perception" scale (see table 1): high score, more judgmental

10 "How often do you pray/speak in tongues?" ("never"=1 through "very often"=5)

11 Charismata scale (see table 1)

12 "How often have you experienced a divine healing of a physical illness?" ("never"=1 through "very often"=5)

13 "How often have you experienced God healing another through your prayer?" ("never"=1 through "very often"=5)

14 Mysticism scale (see table 1)

15 Empathy scale (see table 1)

Appendix C-2

Multivariate Analysis

Effects of Select Variables on Empathic Emotions

Variables	B	Std Error	Beta β	t	Sig.
Walking in the supernatural	.472	.228	.162	2.073	.040
Satisfaction with divine relationship	.096	.165	.048	.583	.562
God as conditional Lover	-.131	.063	-.163	-2.094	.038
Charismata scale	.112	.044	.257	2.520	.013
Mysticism scale	.057	.067	.085	.844	.400
Adjusted R Square = .176					.000

Given the recognized importance of empathic emotions in the study of altruism (Batson 1998), we first tested for the potential impact of select spirituality measures on the empathy scale. The overall equation was statistically significant, explaining nearly 18 percent of the variance in empathy scores. Using a significance level of .05 for the five variables included in the model, only three were statistically significant and thus help to explain differences in empathy scores. Those scoring higher in empathic motivation were more likely to experience the spiritual gifts with regularity (beta=.26), were less likely to see God's love as being conditional (beta=-.16), and were more likely to report that walking in the supernatural was important to them (beta=.16). This finding is important as we test for the effects of select variables on altruistic behavior; spirituality measures appear to *directly* affect differences in empathy scores and may thus *indirectly* affect altruism (through empathic motivation). We explore these relationships further in the following table that tests for the effects of godly love on reported altruistic behavior.

Effects of Select Variables on the Altruism Scale

Variables	B	Std Error	Beta β	t	Sig.
Walking in the supernatural	.558	.211	.159	2.646	.009
Satisfaction with divine relationship	.003	.155	.001	.021	.983
God as conditional lover	- .072	.060	-.072	-1.198	.233
Mysticism scale	.196	.061	.246	3.220	.002
Charismata scale	.051	.041	.098	1.254	.212
Empathy	.622	.077	.523	8.106	.000
Adjusted R Square = .545					.000

This equation is statistically significant, explaining almost 55 percent of the variance in reported altruistic behavior. As expected, empathic emotions is the leading predictor; it produced a partial correlation of .53 (beta). With a beta of .25, the general mysticism scale is the second-leading predictor and walking in the supernatural comes next with a beta of .16. The remaining variables are not statistically significant. Based on these two equations, spiritual experiences are clearly a factor in empathic emotions (the leading predictor of altruism) as well as for empathy itself.

We did test the above equation, first by omitting the mysticism scale and then by deleting the charismata scale to see if we could tease out if one of these two spiritual experience measures is better than the other for explaining altruistic behavior for this BnF sample. Given the strong bivariate correlation between mysticism and the charismata scales, we suspected a problem with "multicollinearity," where the two variables tapped the same underlying phenomena. In such cases, the effects of the one measure are suppressed by the other when both are used in the same equation. This seemed to be the case for the BnF study. When mysticism was used (but not the charismata scale), the explained variance (adjusted R square) remained at .54. When the charismata scale (but not the mysticism scale) was used in the above model, the adjusted R square dropped, but only slightly to .52. It would appear that despite the differences in the kinds of questions included in the two scales, they are both tapping an important component of godly love and provide support for our guiding hypothesis. Interaction between God and a pray-er empowers altruism toward the poor.

References

Albrecht, Daniel. 1999. *Rites in the Spirit: A Ritual Approach to Pentecostal/Charismatic Spirituality.* Sheffield: Sheffield Academic.

Anderson, Ray S. 2006. *An Emergent Theology for Emerging Churches.* Downers Grove, IL: InterVarsity.

Anderson, Walter Truett. 1990. *Reality Isn't What It Used to Be.* San Francisco: Harper.

Armstrong, Karen. 2005. *A Short History of Myth.* Edinburgh: Canongate.

Bartkowski, John P. and Helen A. Regis. 2003. *Charitable Choices: Religion, Race, and Poverty in the Post-welfare Era.* New York: New York University Press.

Batson, Daniel C. 1998. "Altruism and Prosocial Behavior." In *The Handbook of Social Psychology,* 282–308, edited by D. T. Gilbert, S. T. Fiske, and G. Lindzey. Boston: McGraw-Hill.

Blau, Joel. 1992. *The Visible Poor: Homelessness in the United States.* New York: Oxford University Press.

Bogart, Jon. 1997. "Blood'N Fire: Expanding the Kingdom in Atlanta's Inner City." *Voice of the Vineyard* (fall): 20–25.

Bowker, J. 1971. *The Sense of God.* London: Oxford University Press.

Brookes, Adrian. 2008. "One Woman vs. the Dragon." *Charisma* (March): 33–38.

Burton, Thomas. 2004. *The Serpent and the Spirit: Glenn Summerford's Story.* Knoxville: University of Tennessee Press.

Cahoone, L., ed. 2003. *From Modernism to Postmodernism.* 2nd ed. Malden, MA: Blackwell.

Cartledge, Mark J. 2006. *Speaking in Tongues: Multidisciplinary Perspectives.* Waynesboro, GA: Paternoster.

Claiborne, Shane. 2006. *The Irresistible Revolution: Living as an Ordinary Radical.* Grand Rapids, MI: Zondervan.

Clough, William R. 2006. "To Be Loved and to Love." *Journal of Psychology and Theology* 34(1): 23–31.

Collins, Randall. 1975. *Conflict Sociology: Toward an Explanatory Science.* New York: Academic.

———. 2004. *Interaction Ritual Chains.* Princeton, NJ: Princeton University Press.

Csordas, Thomas. 1997. *Language, Charisma, and Creativity: The Ritual Life of a Religious Movement*. Berkeley and Los Angeles: University of California Press.

d'Aquili, Eugene and Andrew B. Newberg. 1999. *The Mystical Mind*. Minneapolis: Fortress.

Daigle, Richard. 2002. "Saving Souls—12 X 12." *Atlanta Journal-Constitution* 30 (November): B1–B2.

———. 2003. "Escape from the Suburbs." *Charisma* (May): 68–75.

Denzin, Norman K. 1989a. *The Research Act*. 3rd ed. Englewood Cliffs, NJ: Prentice Hall.

———. 1989b. *Interpretive Interactionism*. Newbury Park, CA: Sage.

Di Sabatino, David. 1999. *The Jesus People Movement*. Westport, CT: Greenwood.

Feuerstein, Georg. 1990. *Holy Madness: The Shock Tactics and Radical Teachings of Crazy-wise Adepts, Holy Fools, and Rascal Gurus*. New York: Viking.

Galanter, Marc. 1999. *Cults: Faith, Healing, and Coercion*. 2nd ed. New York: Oxford University Press.

Gibbs, Eddie and Ryan K. Bolger. 2005. *Emerging Churches: Creating Christian Community in Postmodern Culture*. Grand Rapids, MI: Baker Academic.

Goffman, Erving. 1961. *Asylums: Essays on the Social Situation of Mental Patients and Other Inmates*. Garden City, NY: Doubleday Anchor.

Hilborn, David. 2006. "Glossolalia as Communication: A Linguistic-pragmatic Perspective." In *Speaking in Tongues: Multidisciplinary Perspectives*, 111–45, edited by M. J. Cartledge. Waynesboro, GA: Paternoster.

Hood, Ralph. W., Jr. 2001. *Dimensions of Mystical Experience: Empirical Studies and Psychological Links*. New York: Rodopi.

———. 2007. "Conceptual Paper: Methodological Atheism, Methodological Agnosticism, and Religious Experience." *Spirituality and Health International*. Published online in Wiley InterScience (http://www.interscience.wiley.com).

Hood, Ralph W., Jr., Bernard Spilka, Bruce Hunsberger, and Richard Gorsuch. 1996. *The Psychology of Religion: An Empirical Approach*. 2nd ed. New York: Guilford.

Jackson, Bill. 1999. *The Quest for the Radical Middle: A History of the Vineyard*. Cape Town: Vineyard International.

Jacobs, J. L. 1989. *Divine Disenchantment*. Bloomington: Indiana University Press.

Jenkins, Kathleen E. 2005. *Awesome Families: The Promise of Healing Relationships in the International Churches of Christ*. New Brunswick, NJ: Rutgers University Press.

Johnson, Rolf M. 2001. *Three Faces of Love*. DeKalb: Northern Illinois University Press.

Johnston, Barry V. 2006. "Pitirim A. Sorokin on Social Order, Chance, and the Reconstruction of Society: An Integral Foundation." In *Integralism, Altruism, and Reconstruction: Essays in Honor of Pitirim A. Sorokin*, 145–55, edited by E. Del Pozo Avino. Valencia: Publicacions de la Universitat de Valencia.

Kanter, Rosabeth Moss. 1972. *Commitment and Community: Communes and Utopias in Sociological Perspective*. Cambridge, MA: Harvard University Press.

Kimball, Dan. 2003. *The Emerging Church: Vintage Christianity for New Generations*. Grand Rapids, MI: Zondervan.

Land, Steven J. 1993. *Pentecostal Spirituality: A Passion for the Kingdom*. Sheffield: Sheffield Academic.

Lee, Shayne. 2005. *T. D. Jakes: America's New Preacher*. New York: New York University Press.

Livermore, Dave. 2007. "Emerge or Submerge: Is 'Cultural Relevance' an Effective and Theologically Sound Wineskin for the Emergent Church or Is it Moving Christianity Toward Oblivion?" *The Pneuma Review* 10(1): 31–55.

Lupton, Robert D. 2005. *Renewing the City: Reflections on Community Development and Urban Renewal*. Downers Grove, IL: InterVarsity.

May, Rollo. 1991. *The Cry for Myth*. New York: Dell.

McLaren, Brian D. 1998. *Reinventing Your Church*. Grand Rapids, MI: Zondervan.

———. 2004. *A Generous Orthodoxy*. Grand Rapids, MI: Zondervan.

Miller, Donald E. 1997. *Reinventing American Protestantism: Christianity in the New Millennium*. Berkeley and Los Angeles: University of California Press.

Mills, Watson E. 1986. *Speaking in Tongues: A Guide to Research*. Grand Rapids, MI: Eerdmans.

Pargament, Ken. 2004. "An Innovative Model: Attracting Excellence to an Emerging Field." In *The Spiritual Transformation Scientific Research Program of the Metanexus Institute on Religion and Science*, 8. Philadelphia: Metanexus Institute.

Pinnock, Clark H. 1996. *Flame of Love: A Theology of the Holy Spirit*. Downers Grove, IL: InterVarsity.

———. 2001. *Experiencing the Blessing*. In *Testimonies from Toronto*, 4–7, edited by J. A. Arnott. Ventura, CA: Gospel Light.

Poloma, Margaret M. 1982. *The Charismatic Movement: Is There a New Pentecost?* Boston: Twayne.

———. 1989. *The Assemblies of God at the Crossroads: Charisma and Institutional Dilemmas*. Knoxville: University of Tennessee Press.

———. 2003. *Main Street Mystics: The "Toronto Blessing" and Reviving Pentecostalism*. Walnut Creek, CA: Alta Mira.

———. 2004. "Prayer and the Elderly: Exploring a 'Gerontological Mystery.'" In *Religious Influences on Health and Well-being in the Elderly*, 104–13, edited by K. W. Schaie, Neal Krause, and Alan Booth. New York: Springer.

———. 2005. "Charisma and Structure in the Assemblies of God: Revisiting O'Dea's Five Dilemmas." In *Church, Identity, and Change*, 45–96, edited by D. R. Roozen and J. R. Nieman. Grand Rapids, MI: Eerdmans.

———. 2006. "Old Wine, New Wineskins: The Rise of Healing Rooms in Revival Pentecostalism." *The Pneuma Review* 28(1): 59–71.

Poloma, Margaret M. and George H. Gallup Jr. 1991. *Varieties of Prayer: A Survey Report*. Philadelphia: Trinity Press International.

Poloma, Margaret M. and Lynette F. Hoelter. 1998. "The 'Toronto Blessing': A Holistic Model of Healing." *Journal for the Scientific Study of Religion* 37:258–73.

Poloma, Margaret M. and Brian F. Pendleton. 1991. "The Effects of Prayer and Prayer Experiences on Measures of General Well-Being." *Journal of Psychology and Theology* 19:71–83.

Popora, Douglas V. 2006. "Methodological Atheism, Methodological Agnosticism, and Religious Experience." *Journal for the Theory of Social Behavior* 36(1): 57.

Post, Stephen. 2002. "Introduction: Pitirim Sorokin as a Pioneer in the Scientific Study of Unlimited Love." In *The Way and Power of Love*, xv–xxviii, Pitirim A. Sorokin. Philadelphia: Templeton Foundation Press.

———. 2004. Quoted in *The Spiritual Transformation Scientific Research Program of the Metanexus Institute on Religion and Science*. Philadelphia: Metanexus Institute.

Post, Stephen G, Lynn G. Underwood, Jeffrey P. Schloss, and William B. Hurlbut, eds. 2002. *Altruism and Altruistic Love: Science, Philosophy, and Religion in Dialogue*. New York: Oxford University Press.

Pullinger, Jackie. 1980. *Chasing the Dragon*. Ann Arbor, MI: Servant.

Rank, Mark Robert. 2005. *One Nation Underprivileged: Why American Poverty Affects Us All*. New York: Oxford University Press.

Ritzer, George. 1992. *Sociological Theory*. New York: McGraw-Hill.

Robeck, Cecil M., Jr. 2006. *Azusa Street Mission and Revival: The Birth of the Global Pentecostal Movement*. Nashville: Thomas Nelson.

Rozak, T. 1968. *The Making of a Counterculture*. New York: Doubleday.

Sheppard, Gerald T. 2001. "Prophecy from Ancient Israel to Pentecostals at the End of the Modern Age." *The Spirit and the Church* 3(1): 47–70.

Smith, Christian. 1998. *American Evangelicalism: Embattled and Thriving*. Chicago: University of Chicago Press.

———. 2007. "Why Christianity Works: An Emotions-focused Phenomenological Account." *Sociology of Religion* 68(2): 165–78.

Snow, David A. and Leon Anderson. 1993. *Down on Their Luck: A Study of Homeless Street People*. Berkeley and Los Angeles: University of California Press.

Sorokin, Pitirim A. 1954/2002. *The Ways and Power of Love: Types, Factors, and Techniques of Moral Transformation*. Philadelphia: Templeton Foundation Press.

Spittler, Russell P. 2002. "Glossolalia." In *International Dictionary of Pentecostal and Charismatic Movements*, 670–71, edited by S. M. Burgess. Grand Rapids, MI: Zondervan.

Storr, Anthony. 1996. *Feet of Clay*. New York: Free Press.

Swidler, Ann. 2001. *Talk of Love: How Culture Matters*. Chicago: University of Chicago Press.

Teasdale, Wayne. 1999. *The Mystic Heart*. Novato, CA: New World Library.

Thumma, Scott. 2006. "The Shape of Things to Come: Mega Churches, Emerging Churches, and Other New Religious Structures Supporting an Individualized Spiritual Identity." In *Faith in America: Changes, Challenges, New Directions*, 185–206, edited by Charles Lippy. Westport, CT: Praeger.

Trice, Harrison M. and Janice M. Beyer. 1993. *The Cultures of Work Organizations*. Englewood Cliffs, NJ: Prentice Hall.

Turner, Victor. 1969. *The Ritual Process: Structure and Anti-Structure*. Ithaca, NY: Cornell University Press.

Unruh, Heidi Rolland and Ronald J. Sider. 2005. *Saving Souls, Serving Society: Understanding the Faith Factor in Church-based Social Ministry*. New York: Oxford University Press.

VanCronkhite, David. 2000. *A Supernatural People with a Supernatural Language: Speaking in Tongues*. Blood-n-Fire Ministries. PO Box 38194. Atlanta, GA 30034.

———. 2002. *"I Want a Story": A Collection of Letters from the First Ten Years of Blood N Fire*. Blood-n-Fire Ministries. PO Box 38194. Atlanta, GA 30034.

———. 2003. *Blood-n-Fire Twelve: Intense Commitment to Relational Community*. Blood-n-Fire Ministries. PO Box 38194. Atlanta, GA 30034.

Wacker, Grant. 2001. *Heaven Below: Early Pentecostals and American Culture*. Cambridge, MA: Harvard University Press.

Wagner, C. Peter. 2002. "Wimber, John." In The *New International Dictionary of Pentecostal and Charismatic Movements*, 1199–1200, edited by S. M. Burgess. Grand Rapids, MI: Zondervan.

Wagner, David. 2000. *What's Love Got to Do with It? A Critical Look at American Charity*. New York: New York Press.

Williams, Don. 2005. "Theological Perspective and Reflection on the Vineyard Christian Fellowship." In *Church, Identity, and Change*, 163–87, edited by D. A. Roozen and J. B. Nieman. Grand Rapids, MI: Eerdmans.

Wuthnow, Robert. 2004. *Saving America? Faith-based Services and the Future of Civil Society*. Princeton, NJ: Princeton University Press.

Index

Addicts, 141–42. *See also* Training Program

Adequacy, 9, 61–63. *See also* Dimensions of love

Altruism, 64; as care love, 116; as godly love, 94; multivariate statistical analysis, 243–44

American dream, 24–25, 212–13; conflict with Kingdom of God, 49

American Pentecostalism, 14. *See also* Neo-Pentecostalism

Anderson, Ray, 208

Angels, visions of, 99

Appreciation-love, 90–92; for homeless, 143–45. *See also* Love

Arts in worship. *See* Creative combustion

Association of Vineyard Churches (AVC), 13, 19

Atlanta Vineyard Fellowship, 20, 28

Automatic writing, 103. *See also* Signs and wonders

Azusa Street Revival, 5

Bapticostal, 142

Bartkowski, John (and Helen Regis), 204

Batson, Daniel, 243

Bigelow, Rose, 72–73, 191–92, 210

Blood-n-Fire (BnF): beginning of schism, 172, 180; covenant vs. contract, 204–8; culture of love, 147; differences between members and homeless, 120–22; emerging church, 4, 42; establishment of, 2, 14, 20–21; funeral for, 197; member demographics, 67–68; origin of name, 20; phases, 31; vision, 14; withdrawal from AVC, 13, 20

Blood-n-Fire 2 (BnF2) birth of, 197, 200; changes between BnF1 and BnF2, 200–202

Blood-n-Fire International, 46, 70, 172–73, 181–82, 185, 213–14

Board of Directors, 151–52, 160–61, 207

Booth, William and Catherine/anointing, 22, 42

Born-again, 69

Burton, Thomas, 221

Café Ruach, 155–57, 162

Call to the poor, 24–25, 79–80

Capitol Corridor, 155, 159

Capitol Homes, 21, 123, 159

Care-love, 90–91; altruism in, 116; and charismata, 115–16; for homeless, 143–45. *See also* Love

Cash Cow, 36–37, 44

Cathy, Dan, 56, 152

Charismata 69–70. *See also* Signs and wonders

Charismatic communities, 49

Charismatic movement, 48, 206

Church family, 42–48

City presence, 38–39, 155–56

Claiborne, Shane, 1

Codependency, 136

Collaborators, 211–14

Collins, Randall, 11–12, 40–41, 64–65, 94, 146–47, 212

Communitas, 114–15

Compassion Center, 169, 173–74, 180, 182, 185, 189

Compassion for the poor, 23–24

Conversion, 45, 70, 85

Covenant vs. contract, 204–8

Crabbs, Duane, 27

Crazy wisdom, 172

Creative combustion, 33–34, 210

Crist, Johnny, 20–21, 193–95

Days Inn of America, 193

Demonic, 99, 102

Diamonds on the Lake, 26, 40

Dimension Ministries, 24

Dimensions of love, 8, 61–63, 118–19, 143–45. *See also* Adequacy; Duration; Extensity; Intensity; Purity

Discursive prayer, 107

Dissatisfaction of homeless, 127, 129

Divine communication, 19, 41; BnF member survey, 108–9; as personal empowerment, 110

Divine covenant, 206

Divine destiny, 127, 129

Divine inheritance, 185

Divine presence, 73

Divine proclamations, 26

Divine visitation, 78–79

Dreams: interpretation, 70; as prophecy, 107. *See also* Signs and wonders

Drug rehabilitation. *See* Training Program

Duration, 9, 62. *See also* Dimensions of love

Edgewood, 39, 155–56

Emerging church, 1–3, 30–31, 49, 209; BnF as, 4–5, 42, 150–51; compared to new paradigm churches, 13–14, 36, 149

Emotion contest, 183

Emotional energy (EE), 11, 64–65, 183; in appreciation love, 93; and charismatic leaders, 199; conflict, 147; as glossolalia, 98–99; in myth-making, 17; negative, 146–47; in David VanCronkhite, 28

Evangelical, 12, 49

Evolutionary biology, 64

Extensity, 9, 62, 118. *See also* Dimensions of love

Extravagant giving, 34, 88–89, 139, 158

Faith-permeated organization, 60

Familial clients, 137. *See also* Sanctuary

Familial love, 44

Familial relationships with homeless, 131, 137

Family as relational community, 35, 42–45, 85–88; as intentional community, 48–49

Family business, 42, 50–52, 59–60

FCS Urban Ministries, 28, 195

Feeding program. *See* Sobre La Mesa

Feurstein, Georg, 172

Fourth Ward, 39, 155

Fox, George, 4

Francis of Assisi, 4

Franklin, Chris (and Linda), 44, 77–79, 107, 112, 158, 162–64, 173–76, 183, 186, 189, 191

Gibbs, Eddie (and Ryan Bolger), 3, 13, 30–31, 40, 154

Gifts of the Spirit, 14; and liminality, 113. *See also* Signs and wonders

Glossolalia, 69–70, 97–101, 103, 115; as emotion energy, 109–11. *See also* Signs and wonders
Godly love, 2, 4–6, 213; assessments of, 61–63, 145–45; in charismata, 94; in cultural context, 212–13; for homeless, 143–45; in mythmaking, 18; social scientific theory and, 6; survey methodology, 226–35
Goffman, Erving, 118–20
Goll, Jim, 166
Grady Memorial Hospital, 112, 155
Graham, Billy, 23
Group of Twelve, 37–38

Harley Davidson motorcycle, 51
Harvest House, 59
Healing, 109–13; BnF member survey, 109; emotional and inner healing, 102; healing rooms, 112; of homeless, 142; physical healing 111; as spiritual transformation, 70. *See also* Signs and wonders
Hill, Ned and Susan, 70–71, 158
Hollywood, 95
Holy madness, 172
Homeless shelter. *See* Sanctuary
Houston, Jean, 92

Ideal types, 125
Ideology, 148–49, 160, 165–66, 169–71
If I have Withheld conference 23, 42
Impartation, 23, 71
Inadequate love, 61
Instrumental clients, 123, 125–31. *See also* Sanctuary
Integrated Health Systems, Inc., 20
Intensity, 8, 118. *See also* Dimensions of Love
Intentional community, 48–49
Interaction ritual, 2, 12, 40, 206

Interaction ritual theory (IR), 10–12, 40–42, 146–47, 212
Islam, 45

Jacobs, Cindy, 26
Jehu Customs, 162
Jenkins, Kathleen, 46
Jesus People Movement, 28
Johnson, Rolf, 89–93
Jones, Jane, 111
Justice, 39; as part of appreciation love, 92

Kanter, Rosabeth Moss, 48–49
Keating, John, 165
Kimball, Dan, 150, 208
Kingdom of God, 2, 13, 20, 51, 115, 121–22, 198, 204; central values, 30–32; conflict with American Dream, 49
Kula, David and Val, 26, 166,181; conflict with David VanCronkhite 166–69, 181

Legitimacy of spiritual authority, 196
Liminality, 113–15
Logos, 19, 182
Long-term feedbacks, 199
Love, 89–90: appreciation love, 91–92; care-love, 90; central meanings of 90–93; of God and neighbor, 84; from homeless perspective, 140–42; in relational church, 91; unconditional love, 215; union-love; 92–93. *See also* Dimensions of love; Godly love
Love energy, 8. *See also* Dimensions of Love
Lupton, Bob (Robert), 28, 195–96

Main Street Mystics, 65
March for Jesus, 22

Matrix Construction, 162
Matrix, The, 96, 101
McLaren, Brian, 4, 13, 150
Meal program. *See* Sobre la Mesa
Mega-churches, 33
Methodological agnosticism, 8, 41
Methodological atheism, 7–8, 11
Methodology, 223–26
Military language, 22; change from
    military to family metaphor, 150
Miller, Donald, 12
Ministry to the poor, development of, 21
Mother Teresa, 4, 92
Music in worship. *See* Creative
    combustion
Mutual focus, 17–18; for community,
    40
Mysticism, 69; glossolalia and charis-
    mata as, 115
Myth, mythmaking, 17–19, 40; post-
    modern critique of, 18
Mythos, 19

Negative emotional energy, 146–147.
    See also Emotional energy (EE)
Negative emotions, 102
Neo-monastic, 2, 14
Neo-Pentecostal, 94–95, 212, 217
New Beginnings, 58. *See also* Training
    Program
New paradigm church, 12; compared
    to emerging churches, 13

Occult, 72–73, 102
One Way Companies, 154–55
Ortega, Jose Bettancourt, 217–18

Papa Jack. *See* Taylor, Jack
Pargament, Kenneth, 69
Pearson, LeAnn, 158, 164, 173, 186,
    189, 191

Pentecostal movement, 5, 217. *See also*
    Neo-Pentecostal
Pentecostal worldview, 3, 5, 60
Pinnock, Clark, 95
Pneumatological theology, 5
Portal, 57. *See also* Training Program
Post, Stephen, 64, 66
Post-modern Christians, 12
Post-modernism in emerging
    churches, 3; critique of myth, 18
Power evangelism, 33
Prayer, 212; as interaction ritual, 41;
    intercession 208; intuitive, 107; pro-
    phetic, 106–8; in BnF, 207–8
Prayer language. *See* Glossolalia
Praying in the spirit. *See* Glossolalia
Prophecy, 19, 70, 103–5, 184–85; de-
    fined, 105–8
Pullinger, Jackie, 23–24, 71, 219
Purity, 9, 62. *See also* Dimensions of
    love

Rational choice theories, 64
Relational church, 14, 213; love in, 91
Relational clients, 124, 131–37. *See
    also* Sanctuary
Relational community, 36–38, 42–45
Relational covenant, 204
Relationship-building, 87
Relationships with the poor, 34, 79–80
Restoration, 58. *See also* Training
    Program
Revelation, 106–7
Rhema, 182
Richardson, John and Beckett, 190
Ritual interaction chains, 10
Ruff, Steve, 187–89

Salvation Army, 20–22
Sanctuary, 15, 51–54, 203, 207; closure
    of, 202, 207; familial clients, 137;

instrumental clients, 123, 125–31; relational clients, 124, 131–37

Sects, 49

Seymour, William Joseph, 5

Signs and wonders: in Pentecostalism, 5; in power evangelism, 33. *See also* Glossolalia; Healing; Prophecy; Visions

Silver, Christopher F., 176–79

Simpson and Ashby, 39, 155

Smith, Christian, 7

Smith, Zach, 209–10

Sobre La Mesa, 54–56; end of food program, 201

Social construction of human experience of God, 8

Sorokin, Pitirim, 8–9, 61–63, 118–20, 143, 206, 211

South Street Mission, 27

Speaking in tongues. *See* Glossolalia

Spirit baptism, 69

Spirit beings, 105

Spiritual army, 22

Spiritual direction, 99

Spiritual empowerment, 69, 99

Spiritual family, 35, 43–44, 46–47

Spiritual journey. *See* Spiritual transformation

Spiritual mediocrity, 186

Spiritual transformation, 36, 69; of David Van Cronkhite, 23–24, 41

Spiritual warfare, 2, 101–3, 110

Stagg, Eric and Debbie, 159–60, 214

Street ministry, 27–28; transition away from, 50; return to, 206

Storr, Anthony, 205

Swidler, Ann, 146–49, 160

Taking Atlanta, 39–40, 150

Taylor, Jack, 24, 26, 46, 161, 163–64, 186

Temple, Gray, 217–18

Tension between traditional and ideological, 169–71

Thumma, Scott, 13

Tongues. *See* Glossolalia

Toronto Airport Christian Fellowship, 24

Toronto blessing, 95

Total institution, 119–20

Tradition, 169–71

Training Program, 15, 51, 189; phases, 57–58

Transforming lives of homeless, 154, 205

Transitional 58. *See also* Training Program

Turner, Victor, 113–14

Twelve, 35, 42, 47; erotic intimacy in, 38

Underlife, 120

Union love, 92–93; for homeless, 143–45. *See also* Love

Unruh, Heidi (and Ronald Sider), 59–60

Valparaiso, 166

VanCronkhite, David: background, 20; charismatic leader, 204–6; clergy support for, 193; conflict with David Kula, 166–69; depression, 164–65, 170; dissension with board of directors, 152, 160–64; dissolve the ministry, 202–3; erratic behavior, 173–74; exile, 140, 173; ideology, 147–49; prophecy, 26, 19, 185, 214; regain control of BnF, 196–97; repentance, 185; return from exile, 164–65, 185, 189; spiritual accountability, 196; spiritual transformation, 23–24, 41; visionary, 19–20, 212

VanCronkhite, Janice, 20; prophetic painting, 210. *See also* Diamonds on the Lake
VanCronkhite, Kathryn, 71–72, 180–81
VanCronkhite, Katina, 111, 165
Victory Fellowship, 16
Vineyard Church, 13, 20; statement of faith, 31
Vision, 199–202, 204, 211–12; as appreciation love, 144; as godly love, 147; as prophecy, 107
Visions, 99. *See also* Signs and wonders

Wagner, David, 117
Walking in the supernatural, 86; in glossolalia, 97; BnF members compared to Sanctuary residents, 96, 105; homeless experiences, 117
Warehouse, 15; acquisition, 28–30; as a mythic symbol, 30, 165; dismantling of, 202–3
Watson, Cissy, 150, 157, 166, 187
Wedding, 180–81
Wesley, John, 4
West End, 39, 156
White, Edward, 193
Wimber, John, 13, 19–20, 23, 34, 149–50, 153
Words of knowledge, 99. *See also* Signs and wonders

Xenolalia, 97

About the Authors

MARGARET M. POLOMA is Professor Emerita in the Department of Sociology at the University of Akron and previously taught there from 1970 to 1995. She is the author or editor of numerous books, including, most recently, *Main Street Mystics: The "Toronto Blessing" and Reviving Pentecostalism* (2003) and *The Politics of Protestant Preachers* (1997).

RALPH W. HOOD JR. is Professor of Psychology at the University of Tennessee, Chattanooga. He is the coauthor of *The Psychology of Religious Fundamentalism* (2005) and the editor of *Handling Serpents: Pastor Jimmy* (2005). He is a former editor of *The Journal for the Scientific Study of Religion*.